SING

A

SONG

OF

SOCIAL

SIGNIFICANCE

SING

A

SONG

OF

SOCIAL

SIGNIFICANCE

R.
SERGE
DENISOFF

Bowling Green University Popular Press

Library of Congress Catalogue Card Number: 78-186631
ISBN: 0-87972-036-0

Printed in the United States of America.

FOR

ALLEGRA

Acknowledgments

All authors incur many debts by the time a book leaves the printers and winds up in your hands. In this case it is doubly true. As noted in the text Mark Levine and Richard Reuss co-authored some of the sections included herein. Their help in other areas of this endeavor was equally invaluable. I wish also to acknowledge the aid and assistance of many others such as Thomas Duggan, Andrew P. Phillips, Tom Bottomore and Archie Green particularly since he literally "turned me on" to protest songs nearly a decade ago. I also wish to publicly thank Ray B. Browne for his help during the birth of this book.

No acknowledgment listing would be complete without some note of thanks to my wife Carol for her helpful suggestions and constant encouragement to finish this work.

CONTENTS

INTRODUCTION

Despite the increasing use of music as a tool for social and political commentary, we know relatively little about the protest song. In discussing this phenomenon it is quite easy to fall into Platonic cliches about the power of music to corrupt the young and unaware. Indeed, many have done so. Journalists in pursuit of a quick Sunday supplement piece to ministers in search of a sermon topic have decried the content of popular music. Other well-known and not so popular spokesmen have pointed to the power of song to "hypnotize" and "brainwash" American adolescents. Vice-President Spiro Agnew recently accused rock music groups such as the Beatles, the Byrds and the Jefferson Airplane of creating songs which "threaten to sap our national strength unless we move hard and fast to bring it under control." Other public figures such as Rev. Billy James Hargis, Art Linkletter, and the late Congressman James Utt have all made similar comments.

On the opposite side of the opinion spectrum countless parents and some social scientists have come to view popular music as insatiable background noise with little if any social significance. Parents look longingly in many cases to the day their teenagers will outgrow "loud" rock music and begin to appreciate the finer genres and styles of Frank Sinatra or even Lawrence Welk. Both stances have their intellectual appeal. The notion that song has political power is as old as Plato. The idea that music is frivolous can similarly be traced back to the ancients. Somewhere between these positions lies the most fruitful area of investigation.

Music is unquestionably a form of communication, but what

is it saying and to whom? High school kids Bugaloo and Fug to the civil rights anthem "We Shall Overcome" while Southern sharecroppers sing the song to reaffirm their courage to go down and face *the man*. Merle Haggard's "Okie from Muskogee" receives a thunderous ovation from an audience of Southern supporters of Governor George Wallace. Meanwhile Arlo Guthrie's rendition of the same song generates an equally positive response from the very people Haggard was condemning. From these illustrations, it becomes readily apparent that the mere hearing of protest song x will not turn the listener into being a supporter of x ideology or group. If this were the case the average listener to Top Forty radio would be a Green Beret supporter of pacifist causes who takes drugs and beats up long-haired youths for opposing the Vietnam War. Such a bizarre and schizoid collection of attitudes has rarely been encountered by either social scientists or psychiatrists.

If the power and quality of song were social determinants of political power then the Blackman would have overcome decades ago; and the Industrial Workers of the World, not the CIO, would have unionized factory workers and the "Masters of War" would not have led a nation into a foreign jungle entanglement. Without further belaboring this point it should be by now blatantly clear that the "brainwashing" thesis is not a persuasive one. Nonetheless, song is a definite form of propaganda. All songs propagate a message, both intellectually and sensually. Television jingles and love songs are propaganda songs as much as any march or lyric of social commentary. Although the effectiveness of jingles is most questionable, the impact of songs addressed to romantic love is no doubt much greater. Most people identify a song with a romantic relationship. Couples have "their song" albeit a 20 year old standard or last week's Top Forty favorite. Love, alas, is not a primarily intellectual relationship. Only national and patriotic anthems and religious hymns, both being grounded in tradition, provide parallels to the emotionalism of "love songs." Protest songs basically stress the lyric or intellectual aspect of song by attempting to convince the listener that something is wrong and in need of alteration. A good musical structure can either be beneficial to the message or it can be distracting. An effective protest song ideally should be both lyrically and musically convincing, as with a hymn. As will be seen, the power of a hymn with altered lyrics was quickly discovered by European and American protesters who adapted the "word of God" to speak for man. Much, we might add, to the consternation of religious traditionalists and fundamentalists.

Similar to the hymn was the folk song, which exhibited, it was believed, a simplistic musical structure with a stress on the lyrics. For radical intellectuals of the 1930's, 1940's and 1950's this genre was to be a Marxist "cry for justice." "Working class intellectuals" as well as a small assortment of bona fide folk wrote and sang songs indicting the capitalist civil society for brutalization, racism, war-mongering and other crimes against humanity. They were "voices crying in the wilderness." The social concerns of Marxists remain unsolved when the folk-styled song of persuasion gained public acceptance. In the process the harsh lyrics became softer and smoother tempered by additional guitars, drums, and even symphonic string sections. "Folk-pop" and "folk-rock," both hybrids, incorporated intellectually stimulating ideas with emotionally appealing musical arrangements. This mix did not always work nor did it appeal to those dedicated to the creation of political consciousness and the advent of social change.

Folk-rock, unlike the folk ditties of the days of the Almanac Singers and People's Songs Inc., was in the mainstream of American popular culture, a highly unique position for a mix of genres previously treated as *declasse*. The incorporation of primarily intellectualized musical formats into the world of teenage love rites, "Purple People Eaters," Alvin's chipmunks, and adolescent funeral songs encouraged both journalistic and scholarly concern with popular music. Popular music, reported *Life* after the popularization of "Mr. Tambourine Man," "Laugh at Me," and "Eve of Destruction," was saying something. The Beatles' classic *Sgt. Pepper's Lonely Hearts Club Band* only reaffirmed the new status of popular music as an intellectual commodity. This is not necessarily to concur with the "high-culture" characterization afforded popular music by some critics but rather to suggest that both a structural and ideological transformation of popular music occurred in the mid-1960's. By the 1970's so-called "protest songs" by soul singers, underground groups, and country singers were commonplace. Yet we can easily ask "Do protest songs actually protest anymore?" Are they, as some would claim, basically a form of intellectual masturbation or the cries of a generation?

This book attempts to answer some of these questions and raise many others. Our attention will be directed primarily to the dilemma of what properly constitutes a protest song in a given time and historical place. Equally, who are the singers of songs of persuasion? Here we will be directly concerned with the social milieu of musical statements of dissent. Having outlined the properties of political propaganda songs we will be concerned with their use by religious movements, segments of the new and old Left, especially emphasizing the American Communist movement and its variant Stalinist and Trotskyist groups. This book will take a look at the current political statements on the Top Forty, stressing the impact of these songs on their listeners. Finally, we will examine what Karl Mannheim termed "the confusion of tongues" in popular music. That is, how do the various constituencies of rock music, and indeed, other forms respond to it. And, what role does music play in this period of political polarization and turmoil.

Two of the more controversial aspects in treating "folksongs of protest," particularly in the urban milieu, are the taxonomical and typological questions. These two questions will be treated sociologically here; and hopefully several suggestions in the realm of conceptualizing and classifying so-called protest material will be intimated.

The songs under consideration are propaganda songs performed and composed in the folk idiom or songs performed using the instrumentation and presentation techniques traditionally associated with nonprofessional rural singers of songs—traditional ballad singers. Until the so-called "folk revival" of the late fifties these songs were in the urban scene primarily associated with urban social movements or were corollaries to them. People's Songs (and later People's Artists) and the American Folksay group are just a few examples of the phenomenon. This is not to suggest that all propaganda songs are composed for this purpose, but rather that, whatever their original purpose, these songs were taken by social movements to serve specific functions (for example, Margaret Larkin's introduction of the songs of Ella May Wiggins into the city, where they were used as an identification mechanism by radicals who wanted to associate themselves with the Gastonia textile strike).[1] This work will, therefore, concentrate on areas other than the entertainment aspect of propaganda songs or songs of persuasion.[2] Persuasion refers to the purposes of opinion and behavior formation that the songs were put to rather than to the

1

intent of the composer.

In analyzing this material the functional model will be employed—that is, the role or province of the song in the group, movement, community, and society in which it is enacted. In the functional model the major emphasis is not placed on the motivation or intent of the composer, but rather on the content and usage of the musical and lyrical material. The Wobbly (Industrial Workers of the World) parodies of religious songs, the Irish eulogy to Kevin Barry, and the Wiggins-Larkin occurrence have all transcended the original purposes of their respective composers. The usage of the song, therefore, becomes the prime requisite of analysis.

Usage refers, here, to a dynamic schema (as opposed to a static model); that is, the function of the song must be seen in its historical and social setting. "Viva La Quince Brigada" in the late thirties performed a cohesive function among the members of the Abraham Lincoln Battalion and encouraged external support among various groups and organizations for the Loyalist cause. Conversely, the performance of this Spanish Civil War song today primarily serves the entertainment function, in addition to providing a nostalgic and sentimental appeal to Leftists. Similarly, the contemporary singing of "Solidarity Forever," originally a picket line standard, by unionists at a Miami convention hotel contemporarily has become little more than a historic ritual. Songs of persuasion can only be perceived functionally when they are performing the requirements of invoking some form of reaction or interaction.

A propaganda song in the folk idiom may be conceived of as a song designed to communicate social, political, economic, ideological concepts, or a total ideology, to the listener and one which employs those attributes generally identified with a folksong. Songs of persuasion can be perceived as functioning to achieve six primary goals:

1. The song attempts to solicit and arouse outside support and sympathy for a social or political movement.

2. The song reinforces the value structure of individuals who are active supporters of the social movement or ideology.

3. The song creates and promotes cohesion, solidarity, and high morale in an organization or movement supporting its world view.

4. The song is an attempt to recruit individuals for a specific social movement.

5. The song invokes solutions to real or imagined social phenomena in terms of action to achieve a desired goal.

6. The song points to some problem or discontent in the society, usually in emotional terms.

In order to meet these functions, songs of persuasion fulfill certain structural prerequisites generally cited in the literature of "folksongs of protest." "Structural prerequisite" connotes the elements necessary for the song to function in the manner of making possible communication and opinion formation. The first prerequisite most commonly noted by students of this topic, such as Greenway, Fowke and Glazer, Green, and the Marxian school, is that the song of persuasion points to some perceived "problem-situation" in the social system.[3] These problem-situations, usually referred to as discontents, run the spectrum of human grievances over low wages, through the entire economic structure of a society, to the internecine ideological warfare of Lyons' "red decade." Second, as Greenway and others state, the song must have ease of communication, that is, be familiar to and have a simplistic musical scale facilitating audience attention and participation.[4] For example, during the Almanac Singers' tour of Detroit in 1942 the group could rarely achieve the goal of motivating auto-workers to sing except to "Solidarity Forever," with which most of the membership of the embryonic UAW was familiar.

The function of a propaganda song in the folk idiom is to communicate a specific "sense of reality" or view of the world. One political scientist characterizes this function in the following terms: ". . . the songs of labor movements, of temperance workers, of prisoners, of the exiled, and of oppressed peoples everywhere have helped to recruit supporters, to arouse sympathy, to counteract the feelings of despair, to encourage or inspire with hope for a new and happier future."[5]

Qualter's description indicates functions included in the definitional criteria presented, those of arousing outside support or external empathy, countering the feelings of despair and regenerating existing beliefs, and the promotion of group cohesion. One leader in the labor movement supports this view and adds that songs of persuasion ". . . have expressed not only the dreams of an aspiring labor movement, but also been purposely used as a rally cry to maintain discipline, morale, and high spirits in great movements of struggle."[6] Hillman thus dichotomizes the cohesive function into morale and maintaining the members' commitment in the face of adversity.

One of the major functions of the song of persuasion is to create solidarity or a "we" feeling in a group or movement to which the song is verbally directed. Songs indicating the unity of the group and the relationship of the individual to the group are performed at rallies and on picket lines. Songs of this nature stress "side by side we battle onward/ victory will come." In the civil rights fight, as Martin Luther King commented, the songs of the protest movement ("We Shall Overcome," "Oh Freedom," and others) emphasize the strength-in-unity pattern of the movement and that in individualistic terms the participant is not isolated but a segment of a group. The need for solidarity is essential, especially for an organization espousing views deemed by other sectors of the society to be subversive or radical, if that organization is to survive. The phrase "divide and conquer" is not confined to armed conflict, but equally applies to the destruction of a social movement. In the years of labor strife the attempts of management to create company unions and other such ploys were designed to accomplish one dominant goal, the destruction of unity among the ranks of the labor movement. Until the decline of Left Wing organizations, songs such as "Which Side Are You On" measured this concept of being either in or against a given movement. Barrie Stavis, one biographer of Joe Hill, suggests that the Wobblies' songs served this function: "They were a potent weapon for union organization, holding the men together, giving them a unity in the face of great odds in a hostile world."[7]

The function of the propaganda song is also to reinforce the a priori belief system of the listener. Persons in the milieu of the "politics of isolation" accepted the tenets of a specific ideology and attended gatherings and "hoots" which supported their system of reality. In the early years of the citybilly phenomenon, for example, many persons who purchased the recordings of politically oriented folk entrepreneurs, appear in general to be in sympathy with the sociopolitical sentiments expressed in the songs included in the record albums.[8] This process is not dissimilar to that of the conservative voter who listens only to the oratorio of the candidate of his party, while refusing to pay attention to the views of the opposition party on the grounds "they are nothing but socialists." This interaction can be presently observed in terms of the segmentation of so-called folk music publics, which follow specific artists as reflective of their interests and societal subcultures.

Another function of the song of persuasion is to recruit and attract new members. *Fortune* magazine, in reporting the formation of People's Songs Inc., indicated that these "ditties" were effective in the same manner as industry supported and sponsored public relations.[9] Empirically, as Korson suggests, this position is difficult to demonstrate, since the song frequently was the only weapon at the disposal of labor pickets. The rationale behind the song of persuasion as a means of attracting supporters or adherents in and for any movement is contingent on a number of factors, few of which were influenced by the performance of propaganda songs.

The manner by which a song of persuasion fulfills the functions based on the prerequisites cited provides a guideline by which to identify and categorize songs of persuasion. These functions are achieved by two types of propaganda songs, the magnetic and the rhetorical.

The magnetic song of persuasion is defined as a song written by a folk entrepreneur (distinguished from the genuine folksinger) or composer which appeals to the listener for the purposes of attracting the nonparticipant listener to a movement or ideology. Within the ranks of adherents, it creates cohesion and morale in the movement which a priori supports the goals expressed in the songs.[10] Two essential factors are included within this definition: first, the song functions to persuade individuals, both emotionally and intellectually, into supporting and possibly joining the movement or the goals implied by the material and of the organization utilizing the song; second, the song's construction is such as to create social cohesion or a feeling of solidarity among the membership of a social movement or specific world view. This is frequently accomplished by the utilization of popular or familiar tunes to which new lyrics are adapted. This places emphasis on a commonality of experience and speeds communication in terms of a perceived social discontent. The usage of hymns and popularly known tunes such as "My Bonnie Lies Over the Ocean" and "Marching Through Georgia" by various social movements is indicative. This classification dichotomizes Merton and Lazarsfeld's concept of "reciprocal reinforcement," that is, the involvement of the individual in a movement or ideology beyond the intellectual level (canalization) and his feeling of belonging to others in the group who have similar ideological orientations (supplementation).[11]

The second type of propaganda composition is the rhetorical song, which may be defined as one written by a folk entrepreneur to identify and describe some social condition, but one which offers no explicit ideological or organizational solutions, such as affiliation with an action or movement. Instead, the song poses a question or a dissent from the institutions of the society, for example, railroad rates or taxes. The rhetorical song may point to an event which is specific or endemic to a geographical or historical space in time and requires little commitment on the part of the listener or, indeed, the composer. Contemporary propaganda songs such as "Eve of Destruction" exhibit this theme. This type of material can also be a parody such as those frequently utilized by the IWW to ridicule social institutions like the "Starvation Army." The rhetorical song fits most of the definitional criteria of a protest song rather than of a propaganda song as it is presently used in the literature. In this typology based on function, a protest song is conceptualized as a type of opinion formation in a social context; that is, the reinforcement of an existent ideological or attitudinal frame of reference. These songs can be equally useful in promoting unity within a movement and higher morale among the followers, given the presence of the functional prerequisites, but can have little influence on nonadherents and may negatively affect nonparticipants. The Almanac Singers' rendition of the "Ballad of October 16th" and its treatment of Roosevelt alienated large segments of the general public after Pearl Harbor. Numerous observers of this period cite the ballad as an index of the degree of vehemence expressed in opposition to FDR's foreign policy during the nonintervention phase of the American Left.[12]

Rhetorical songs can be divided into subcategories of the universal or the specific. A song such as "John Brown's Body" transcends time and sectional geographic boundaries and political movements. The lyric, originally written to commemorate the abolitionist cause, is equally functional in the contemporary civil rights movement. On the other hand, specific songs of persuasion deal with singular events or topics, such as strikes, rent controls, or a massacre. Most of these songs do not transcend the historical context of the lyric. Specific songs exemplified by "The Marion Massacre," "Plow Under," and "The Mill Mother's Lament" are today confined to dusty collections.

Magnetic songs of persuasion follow several structural patterns with numerous deviations, frequently contingent on the needs and the type of movement employing the songs.[13] One of the more common structures found in the propaganda song employing the folk idiom is the situation-remedy structure. This structure is a classic form of stating and describing a situation in negative terms, like the exploitive boss, the warmonger, and the brutal law-enforcement official. Stating a situation in negative terms, the performer customarily states the solution to the social condition in the final verses: organize a union, join a movement, sit-down, or sit-in. Numerous songs from various movements and individual performers exhibit this theme. Songs such as Maurice Sugar's "Sit-Down" and "Old Hank Ford" and Joe Hill's "There is Power in a Union" and "Should I Ever be a Soldier" are excellent overt examples of this type of structure.

A more specific illustration is Woody Guthrie's 1942 composition, "Lindbergh." In the opening stanzas, the song connects the trans-Atlantic hero with the Nazi movement in Germany (the negative reference group or testimonial). The song effectively builds a house of cards by adding one negative reference group, a model of what not to do, to another. The song indicts the America First Committee and then suggests that Herbert Hoover and Lindbergh view an alliance between the Committee and Germany as a means of regaining political power. The introduction of Hoover as a backer of the Firsters is a highly effective device. The memory of the public still linked Hoover with the Great Depression and "Hoovervilles," and therefore with bitter recollections the populace was liable to reject any position the former president took. The material proceeds to cite controversial figures who were generally unpopular, supporters of the Committee like Father Coughlin and the enigmatic John L. Lewis. Having enumerated the fallen heroes of America, the song reiterates the conspiracy theme, linking the leadership of the Firsters with the Japanese attack on Pearl Harbor. This song of persuasion, having stated its indictment, then employs the government, a legitimate institution, to support the statement. This technique of propaganda is termed "transfer," referring to the carrying over of an authoritative source—religion, tradition, government—to a statement in order to validate it as evidence. The situation having been cited, the Firsters are accused and colored with negative images in society—social degradation—through association with Nazism, Hoover, and the bombing of Pearl Harbor. Climactically, the remedy is provided for the audience:

> So I'm goin' to tell you people if Hitler's goin' to be beat
> Common workin' people has got to take the seat
> In Washington, in Washington . . . .

Several functional interpretations of this stanza, given the historical context, are possible. First, the working class is encouraged to participate in political affairs, attain elective governmental office, and assist in accelerating the war effort from a position of legitimate power. This is the overt denotation if the song is taken out of the context of its inception. The second possible perception of this line is that labor unions should strive to gain control in the halls of Congress, since the term "workers" has been used synonymously with the labor movement. Finally, a more controversial definition is that by "working class" the composition is referring to the American Left Wing. The most reliable interpretation of the song's connotation appears to be a synthesis of the above; that is, the material argues that the removal of isolationists from the seat of power is the ideal course of action. The number of possible explanations of this song underlines the broad appeal which can be generated by this type of material; that is, persons could identify with the action role prescribed on the basis of class, occupation, and ideology.

Another common structure is the "remedy in the movement" type of magnetic propaganda-song progression. This song framework recites the accomplishments and glories of a social movement in attempting to buttress the commitment of the existing membership and in recruiting proselytes. In this instance, the basic assumption of the composition is that the listener is conscious of the problem situation and the song then sets forth a solution or means of action to ameliorate the undesired situation. Many of this kind of song lend themselves to group singing, thus further involving the listener in the "reality" of the situation and increasing his identification with the social movement. This ethos is facilitated by the prerequisite of ease of communication. A myriad of composers, such as Hill, Chaplin, and Sugar, have produced songs familiar to their audiences as patriotic and religious tunes. "In the Sweet Bye and Bye" was transformed in parody into the "Preacher and the Slave," and "Billy Boy" has been utilized to protest war (specific and general), congressional investigating committees, and so on.[14] Furthermore the appeal to join is explicitly expressed in the song. Lines such as "No, you can't scare me, I'm sticking to the union," "hold the fort, for we are coming," and the most popular union song of the century, "Solidarity Forever" all stress this structural motif. "Solidarity" commences by elaborating the power of a labor union:

> When the union's inspiration through the worker's blood
>   shall run
> There can be no power greater anywhere beneath the sun
> Yet what force on earth is weaker than the feeble strength
>   of one,
> But the union makes us strong.[15]

The remainder of the song repeats the motif of strength in cohesion in the movement and its curative role in relation to problem-situations and social strains. Joe Hill, the so-called Wobbly bard, wrote a similar song to the religious hymn "There is Power in the Blood," entitled "Power in a Union."[16]

> There is power, there is power
> in a band of workingmen . . .

In sum, these songs suggest the remedy-in-the-movement theme and attempt to intellectually and emotionally involve persons in social action.

The structure and composition of the rhetorical song is primarily "emphasized negativism" to a societal situation, either as an individual or organizational consciousness of dysfunction. Whether the song is individualistic or collectively oriented is contingent on several dominant features—the significance the song has for its audience (that is, external or internal to the setting of a social movement) and whether the composition is a singular expression of discontent or a statement of organizational policy. The rhetorical quality of the material is therefore based upon structure and the frame of reference of the existentially projected audience.

Many of the rhetorical songs found in the *People's Song Book* contain individualistic statements of social dissatisfaction, such as "A Dollar Ain't a Dollar Anymore" and "Listen Mister Bilbo." For the followers of the postwar Left these songs connoted a shared grievance to be musically expressed at rallies and meetings. The working class costume of many folk enterpreneurs added to the significance of the material, accenting the statement of discontent as ideologically representative of a strata of the population. Conversely, to nonadherents the songs only specified a negative view of reality stated in a "folksy" manner. The former view functioned to solidify a definite sense of issue-oriented reality. For the latter, it pointed to dissension which could be interpreted as legitimate or invalid dependent upon the listener's value system. For neither group does the lyric stress association, and therefore it remains rhetorical.

The second element can be observed by the content analysis of a song in a particularistic context. Songs like those composed by contemporary folk enterpreneurs are consciously individualistic statements of vexation. Ochs's "Here's to the State of Mississippi," Paxton's "High Sheriff of Hazard," and Dylan's "Masters of War" are all first person "put downs" of existing conditions in the current social scene. This type of song is overtly evidenced by excerpts from an anonymous composition titled "The Disgruntled Pacifist." This piece states the dissent of peace work during the 1950's and 1960's:

> I've walked for peace and sung for peace,
> and been hit on the head . . .
> Now I'm living in a cave
> That's stocked up pretty well,

And all you damned warmongers.
You all can go to hell.[17]

The essence of this song is predominantly Schopenhauerean and nihilistic, explicitly appealing to few social movements, although segments of the popularly labeled New Left may concur with the sentiments expressed in the lyric since their world view appears to reject the traditional "peace movement" approach to questions of war and peace.

The rhetorical songs of the thirties and forties frequently reflected the policies of given sociopolitical organizations and contained exact meanings for participants of an organized collectivity. The Almanac Singers' album *Songs For John Doe* contained numerous ditties, such as "Plow Under," which appealed primarily to members of American Peace Mobilization and other political organizations, since a given policy statement was inherent in the contents of the songs. Similarly, the utilization of rhetorical songs, frequently of parody, during the ideological disputes of the thirties also served to extol organizational platforms. Segments of the American socialists musically noted and assailed the Molotov-Ribbentrop Pact as it applied to their arch-enemies the C.P.U.S.A. In equal measure the C.P.U.S.A. during the Popular Front era deliberately altered songs attacking the Socialist Party. These esoteric refrains, however, had little if any impact on those outside the arena of the sectarian discords of the thirties. Rhetorical songs symbolize a discontent in negative terms functioning to maintain previous attitudinal orientations of Hoffer's believers.[18]

Songs of persuasion generally are limited in effect by the exposure factor. In the thirties and forties the exposure was limited to an immediate gathering—a sit-down, a camp meeting, or hoot—attended by supporters rather than neutral or disinterested outsiders to whom the musical message might be addressed. In the thirties when many curious and undecided workers attended union meetings, for instance, the magnetic factor was valid in the sense that the music was being directed at nonparticipants and frequently was the high point of the meeting. Following World War II this was not the case, as membership rolls in the house of labor began to stabilize, recruitment activities declined, and the success of the CIO emerged. A corollary factor is that propaganda songs in this context were usually performed in situations where individuals supported the sentiments of the material.[19]

Propaganda songs in the main reflect the attitudes of a given movement and many only receive esoteric support from within the movement. Current Salvation Army hymns are particularistically relevant to members rather than outsiders. Comparatively, the songs of the IWW and the Communist Party during specific phases of their history reflected the value structure of the movement rather than appealing to an external public, despite their use.

The folk styled song of persuasion was especially susceptible to the problem of esoterica. The song was culture bound, familiar only in the folk community. After 1920 an ever increasing majority of the population lived in metropolitan areas. The folk song was *not* a favorite genre of most urban dwellers, far removed from the *Geminschaft* community. The use of folk material in urban areas contradicted the structural prerequisite of familiarity. This contradiction created a number of problems for the folk styled propaganda song prior to the revival of the 1950's.

The first limitation was access and exposure above and beyond the sphere of social movements. Persons not interested in folk music would have little reason to attend a performance given by Woody Guthrie, Leadbelly, the Almanac Singers or other rural styled singers. During the 1930's and 1940's the popularity of folk music was limited, as noted, to specific academic and political groups. "Folksinging" was tied to a picket line, a rally, or a camp meeting attended by supporters rather than by the neutral or "open-minded" outsiders to whom the musical message might be directed. Consequently the folk styled propaganda song functioned primarily to reaffirm existent belief systems. The Communists and their supporters, who accepted the tenets of a particular ideology, were the ones who attended benefits, revues, and "hoots" where songs of persuasion were sung. In the early years of the "citybilly" phenomenon, individuals who purchased the recordings of politically oriented folk entrepreneurs in general appear to have been in sympathy with the sociopolitical sentiments expressed in the albums. The reason for this is that exposure was limited to segments of labor and "progressive" movements. The *New York Times* reviewed an album recorded by the Almanac Singers only once. *Time* reviewed *Talking Union* and *Songs for*

John Doe, but in highly negative tones.[20] Only the subscribers of
the *Daily Worker, People's World,* and *New Masses* were generally
aware of the products of the Almanacs. This process is not dissimilar to the contemporary phenomenon of "drug freaks" who
prefer records that compliment their chemically induced state of
euphoria or the Southern red-neck buying a disc such as "Send
Them Niggers North," "Welfare Cadilac," (sic) or "The Fighting
Side of Me."

The folk styled song of persuasion as a weapon was directed
to the internal cohesion function of moral reaffirmation. Its
effectiveness as a recruiting device was limited by its esoteric
nature. As a rhetorical song, the folk song, being confined to
ideological supporters, again served the magnetic function. Thus
we can come to only one conclusion, despite the effect it seemed
to achieve, the song of persuasion was not as effective in the urban
milieu as other more familiar material.

The Folk Entrepreneurs

Despite the differences in style, environmental background,
and other factors, most singers performing in the folk idiom are
popularly defined as "folksingers." As Professor Charles Seeger
and others have suggested, further definitions are needed to deal
with this question.[21] Seeger proposed a formula by which singers
and styles of performance could be categorized and evaluated:
"*f* (folk); *hb* (hillbilly); *cb* (citybilly); *c* (concert)." Charles
Seeger and others have also suggested that a progression from *f* to
c frequently occurs. Indeed, in later decades *hb* and *cb* to *c* is a
more likely form of transfer.[22] One well-known folk singer
addressed this definitional question as follows:

> I must regretfully class myself as an outsider in relation
> to any folk song, since my own community . . . [which]
> . . . we might call the Urban Literate Southern California
> Sub-Group of the Early Atomic Period has not yet pro-
> duced a distinct body of folk music of its own. My innova-
> tions are therefore spurious, not being a part of any folk
> tradition.[23]

Other writers and performers such as Ewan MacColl, Oscar Brand, Ellen Stekert, Whitman and Kegan, and others have dealt with this topic. Ewan MacColl suggests that many urban performers fall into three categories: "The dirty commercial traveler syndrome," "the simple-honest-John," and "the personality effect." The first he associates with singers of bawdy songs; the second with singers who perform the songs for laughs, almost a comedy routine; the third with performances dependent upon the star structure of the performer and his gimmicks.[24] Brand and others have employed terms such as "ethnophiles" and "folkniks" as terms of classification.[25] Ellen Stekert has suggested four types of urban performers: the "traditional," the "imitators," the "utilizers" and the "urban utilizers."[26] This typology is primarily based on urban usage and the musical aesthetic adhered to. For example, urban utilizers are viewed as having their own aesthetics, that is, "a merger of vocal and instrumental . . . styles," as opposed to the imitators who have ". . . found meaning in the traditional songs and style of presentation of the authentic folk-singer . . ."[27] Whitman and Kagan present a similar typology based on the styles found in recordings. They suggest that five major categories emerge: traditional, interpretive, straight, art-pop, and parody.[28]

In addition to these typologies developed by individuals active in the urban folk song field, journalists have also attempted to categorize the various approaches to folk material. *Time* magazine, in the Fall of 1962, defined three categories: "The commercial category"—also labeled the "Impures or the Popularizers," "The Semi-pures, the Adapters, the Interpreters." "At the other extreme are the Pures, the Authentics, the Real Articles—living source material."[29] Similarly, Dean Wallace of the *San Francisco Chronicle* suggested four categories:[30]

Group I	The unsophisticated participant in a true oral tradition
Group II	Folklorists who sing
Group III	Musicians who use folk material
Group IV	The folksingers who partake in some measure of all the other three

The majority of their classification schemes are based primarily upon three criteria: the types of songs performed, musical style and the cultural heritage of the performers. The creators of these typologies are primarily concerned with the degree of "folkness" of a performer, generally in the commercial or recorded field. However, the commercial value of folk material was negligible prior to the late fifties. Even when definitional criteria have been made explicit, there is difficulty in classifying individual performers. As one writer put it:

> . . . the weakness in any such categorization will become apparent to any discerning person who attempts to place individual performers in their proper slots.[31]

This is particularly true of the period of the thirties and forties, where traditional folk singers and folklorists were an esoteric breed confined to the hills and valleys of rural America and to occasional visits to scholarly institutions of learning. Hardy scholars such as Lomax and Botkin ventured forth from academe, but they were exceptions. Given the limitations of categorization, we will suggest a criterion of "folk singers" based on the notion of acceptance or rejection of commonly held values and perceptions.

Since this work is not primarily concerned with traditional folk singers, with the exception of their performance of songs of persuasion in the urban areas, we need criteria other than the simplistic dichotomy of "folk or non-folk," "commercial or ethnic," or even a threefold classification of "Impure, Semi-pure, or Pure." We need first to ask: What is the role of the artist in the social structure? or, What is the singer's position in society? Is the artist an integral part of society or is he isolated from the mainstream of society? Secondly we need to inquire into the ideological aspect of the role of the urban "folk singer." Why does the individual play the role of a singer of folk styled songs? In attempting to answer these basic questions we can better define a folk entrepreneur.

The term "entrepreneur" is derived from the French word *entrepot*, meaning the right to exploit a specific market. The word "folk," when applied to an aggregate of people indicates:

> . . . a homogeneous unsophisticated group living in but

> isolated from a sophisticated society by such factors as
> topography, economics, race . . .[32]

By combining the concepts of "folk" and "entrepreneur" we may define the "folk entrepreneur" as an individual who composes and performs songs in the folk idiom in order to exploit a market outside of the original folk group. Aside from the psychological factors of public exposure and aesthetic variables of musical enjoyment, folk entrepreneurs employ folk material for reasons other than self-entertainment. As Wallace implies:

> . . . the songs have become subservient to a personal
> cause or goal—to get on a gravy train, to propagandize, to
> entertain, to draw personal attention, or any other such
> extrinsic reason.[33]

Folk entrepreneurs appear only in specific historical periods. Minstrels, for example, used the songs of the peasants to entertain feudal lords. However, they did not consciously mimic the "folk." Moreover, these troubadours often entertained simply to reap the material benefits supplied them by aristocracy. Folk entrepreneurs, on the other hand, may perform for sociopolitical reasons, as well as for economic rewards. Folk entrepreneurs, therefore, may be divided into two general categories: those who perform for economic rewards and those who entertain for sociopolitical reasons.

As Merton, Goodman, Lipset and others indicate, economic success is a dominant goal in American society.[34] Folk entrepreneurs accepting these values can therefore be regarded as being within the mainstream of society and integrated into their society. The "integrated" folk entrepreneur may thus be defined as an individual who performs and writes songs in the folk idiom as a means of achieving socially accepted aspirations, e.g., simply to make money or to support accepted social goals. Folk entrepreneurs in this category include the many commercial groups of the revival period (1957-1965) and, prior to the fifties, artists such as Burl Ives.

On the other hand, performers may use folk material as a medium to perpetuate social change or ideological ends outside the

value structure of the social system. Folk entrepreneurs may sub-
scribe to values which Selznick calls "impenetrable ideologies."
This set of beliefs tends to isolate these artists from the mainstream of society. These performers are persons who primarily
identify with social movements or organizations considered deviant
by the majority in a given nation. The Almanac Singers, the
membership of People's Songs Inc., and People's Artists all fit
into the isolated folk entrepreneur category. Their goals were not
those of the dominant society.

These classifications (as with most categories) are subject to
historical and attitudinal or value changes in a society or culture.
As we shall see, given folk entrepreneurs at one point in their
careers may be defined as isolated performers and at a later time
as integrated artists. The career of the late Josh White is illustrative. During the forties this Negro guitarist performed some songs
of bitter protest against racial discrimination in the United States,
pointing out the fact that this discrimination was tacitly supported
by a majority of Americans. As a result, his performances of
songs dealing with race during this decade were confined to audiences who supported this indignation. When he did venture to
express these views in musical form to the general public he frequently met with disapproval. However, because of changes in
American attitudes such songs evoked little adverse societal reaction in the sixties. Here the social attitudes of the performer
have not changed, but the values of the external society have
undergone change. Conversely, the value structure of society may
remain relatively static while the goals and aspirations of the folk
entrepreneur may be transformed. Singers such as Burl Ives, who
began with the Left-wing during the late 1930's and later changed
his views and became an integrated folk entrepreneur, exemplify
this type of change. In addition, both the society's and the performer's attitude or "world view" may change simultaneously.
Conditions in society may dictate the adoption of the integrated
role. The McCarthy period made the role of isolated folk entrepreneur most difficult and costly. The Second World War, as
another illustration, moved ideological isolates into a common
endeavor to defeat the Axis. When protest songs were popularized
in recent years integrated folk entrepreneurs performed them even
if they did not agree with the sentiments of the song.[35] The

dichotomization of the integrated and isolated folk entrepreneur is important in periods of conflict, such as in the McCarthy period when performers were required to stand up for their beliefs before Congressional investigating committees.

With the advent of the Weavers in the early 1950's the differentiation suggested here, however briefly, became blurred. The Weavers' ability to function in the commercial sphere, while retaining an esoteric value system, was sharply curtailed by the attacks of "patriotic groups" and Congressional investigators. Conversely, the Kingston Trio typified the "integrated" folk entrepreneur, being primarily concerned with making records and appearing at concerts. Bob Dylan, perhaps, during the early phase of his career was the closest to a compromise between the two roles. He was commercial yet he appeared to express sentiments not in keeping with popular public opinion.[36] Dylan's shift away from protest material established him as a bona fide commercial artist.

Beyond the folk genre, as will be seen, a similar phenomenon is reoccurring in the realm of rock music with the emergence of the "underground" and Top Forty audiences. Many underground groups such as Country Joe and the Fish damn the American Establishment while Top Forty artists either ignore politics or give credence to the general values of economic success.[37]

Portions of this chapter, in somewhat different form, appeared in *Journal of American Folklore*, 79 (October-December 1966). Reprinted with the permission of the *Journal of American Folklore*.

CHRISTIANITY,
COMMUNISM
AND
COMMERCIALISM:
THE SONG OF
PERSUASION REVISITED

Songs, since the ancient Greeks, have been seen as powerful weapons to win the minds and hearts of men. Plato, in *The Republic,* first warned that: "any musical innovation is full of danger to the whole State and ought to be prohibited."[1] This sentiment was echoed throughout the centuries by noble lords, clerics, and politicians. During the violent years of the Reformation, priests and ministers wrote ballads to prove the justness of their view of Christianity. English monarchs attempted to control those ballads and broadsides which did not fit their religious beliefs.[2] Less theologically minded political men such as Jeremy Collier saw ballads as being "as dangerous as gun powder."[3] Andrew Fletcher described song as more effective as a weapon than the power to legislate.[4] Across the Atlantic Ocean politicians were no less aware of propaganda songs. Every presidential campaign had *its* song. Every war its "Yankee Doodle Dandy" or "Star Spangled Banner." In time of internal crisis song also was considered a weapon. Herbert Hoover turned to Rudy Vallee for a lyric that would ease the sorrow of the Depression.[5] Revivalists and ministers echoed the sentiment that song could achieve results that speeches could not.[6] Recently popular entertainers such as Peter, Paul, and Mary observed that they could sway a presidential election through their popularity and music.[7] In 1968 they put their boast to empirical test and failed. Peter, Paul, and Mary's

19

choice for president, Senator Eugene McCarthy, lost. Their predecessors in folk music, Woody Guthrie and Pete Seeger, strongly advocated the power of music to destroy fascism and the forces of hate and bigotry.[8]

The Radical Right has launched many drives to combat the influence of song. Originally, the Right focused its attention upon folksingers such as the Weavers, whom they successfully had blacklisted in the mass media during the McCarthy period. The advent of the Hootenanny craze of the early sixties found the Right again charging a Communist conspiracy to subvert American youth. Few folksingers escaped the wrath of the Christian Crusade and the John Birch Society who equated guitar picking with revolutionary activity. Many critics such as David Noebel, Jere Real, Susan Huck, Gary Allen, and entertainer Art Linkletter have charged rock music stars with carrying on a Machiavellian plot to "hypnotize" and "subvert" young people.[9] A more prestigious source, Vice President Spiro Agnew, charged that rock music is "brainwashing" listeners into entering the drug culture. The Federal Communications Commission (FCC) warned radio station operators that they would be held responsible for the content of the songs they played. After considerable controversy, much of it generated by maverick FCC commissioner Nicholas Johnson, the order was somewhat modified. All this, despite several studies on the impact of Top Forty "message" songs which suggest that they are rather harmless.[10] The reason for the impotency of contemporary topical music appears to be found in the functional decline of protest material as it undergoes the homogenization of the music idiom.

Protest Songs: Process and Definition

While as of yet there does not exist a definitive work on the evolution of American protest songs, a number of studies are available dealing with religious, political, and cultural movements which have used songs for self-serving purposes. Originally, ideological songs addressed the service of man to God through the Church. After the Reformation hymns and songs were utilized to bring man into a denomination. During this period hymns became secularized, joining broadsides, as a way of evoking class oriented political expression. Here, propaganda songs in fact became statements of "them" vs. "us," or what many have been labelled "protest songs." It is well to keep in mind that propaganda is defined as the noun of "to propagate," rather than to protest. Indeed, most propaganda songs, such as deodorant commercials, hymns, and the like are not protest songs.

In America nearly all propaganda and protest songs began in the religious sphere.[11] As Greenway illustrates in his pioneer work, *American Folksongs of Protest*, most social movements prior to the 20th century patterned their songs upon religious models. The familiarity of hymns generally accounted for their use, even by groups such as the Industrial Workers of the World (IWW) and the Socialist Party (SP), who were violently opposed to organized religion. It is in this anti-establishmentarian view that we find the basic coloration of protest songs. These ballads are viewed as being tied to some deviant group customarily espousing a politically non-conformist position correlated with some extra-legal form of social action. One classic definition outlines "protest songs" as being:

> . . . the struggle songs of the people. They are outbursts
> of bitterness, of hatred for the oppressor, of determination
> to endure hardships together and to fight for a better life.
> Whether they are ballads composed on the picket line, they
> are imbued with the feeling of communality, or together-
> ness.[12]

Dunson provides a parallel view, seeing protest songs as emerging from "the unshakeable and immense feeling that the singer had discovered some truth, a plan that was going to make the world one of bread and roses."[13] As noted, a magnetic song can be viewed as a lyric written by a "folk entrepreneur"—distinguished from the rural folksinger or composer—which appeals to the listener for purposes of attracting the non-participant receiver to a movement or reinforcing the commitment level of adherents.[14]

The following verses from songs used by the IWW, the Communist Party of the United States (CPUSA), the Student Non-Violent Coordinating Committee (SNCC), and lastly from a songbook sold and written in the Haight-Ashbury by a street singer who frequently appeared on Hippie Hill in Golden Gate Park in San Francisco, will serve to illustrate the traditional protest song. An IWW song, based on a religious hymn, "The Sweet Bye and Bye," concluded:

> Workingmen of all countries unite,
> Side by side we for freedom will fight:
> When the world and its wealth we have gained
> To the grafters we'll sing this refrain:
>
> You will eat, bye and bye,
> When you've learned how to cook and to fry:
> Chop some wood, 'twill do you good,
> And you'll eat in the sweet bye and bye.

During the 1930's the CPUSA employed a number of hymns and rural work songs in an attempt to radicalize and organize industrial workers. A good portion of these songs stressed social participation for the destruction of the capitalist system. One example is "The Murder of Harry Simms":

> Comrádes we must vow today
> This one thing we must do.
> Must organize all the miners
> In the dear old NMU
> And get a million volunteers,
> Into the Y.C.L.
> And sink this Rotten System
> Into the deepest pits of Hell.

Excerpts from two songs taken from the *Red Song Book* also represent typical Stalinist propaganda songs of the so-called Red Decade.[15] The first song, "On the Picket Line," was nearly as popular in Communist circles as the "Internationale." During the Popular Front era the word "Socialist" was deleted and the Trade Union Unity League (TUUL) was disbanded. The second selection is a song designed for members of the Young Communist League (YCL).

> If you don't like scabs and Socialists and stools
> Come and picket on the picket line.
> With the TUUL we'll send them all to hell
> Come and picket on the picket line.
>
> ("On the Picket Line")

> Young comrades come and join us,
> Our struggle will endure
> Till every enemy is down
> And victory is sure.
> In struggle and in valiant fight
> We're marching to the workers' might,
> We are the youthful guardsman of the proletariat . . .
>
> ("Young Oarsman")

The labor movement of the late thirties and later decades also expressed cohesive sentiments in many of their songs.[16] One such tune, written for the founding convention of the AFL-CIO, December 1955 in New York City, concluded with the following verses:

> What's good for America, we're proud to note,
> "Is good for labor," this you may quote.
> So ring those bells and get out the vote
> To build our country strong.
>
> All together, all together, we are stronger
>   every way AFL-CIO
> We will build together, work together for a
>   better day, AFL and CIO.
>
> ("All Together")

In the civil rights or freedom movement, particularly in the deep South, lyrics unified those marching to the courthouse to demonstrate their grievances:

> Over my head, I see freedom in the air
> Over my head—Oh, Lord—I see freedom in the air
> Over my head—I see freedom in the air
> There must be a God somewhere.
>
> ("Over My Head")

Another typical hymn stressed the determination of the marchers with the lyrics "ain't gonna let nobody turn me round."

Ashleigh Brilliant (a pseudonym), under the banner of "personal platform for responsible freedom of speech and pursuit of happiness," composed a number of songs for the edification of Haight-Ashbury residents and visitors. Examples are "Marry-Wanna" and "Hippie Hill":[17]

Folk are free in Haight-Ashbury,
They can live and be what they wanna;
Wedding cake gives you stomach-ache
So the hippies take marihuana.

High, high, high, high
It's no dishonor —
Phoney matrimony's a lousy life:
If you need a wife, marry Wanna!!

Why get wed when she'll come to bed
Soon as you have said that you wanna?
It beats booze and you'll never lose
If you always use marihuana.

("Marry-Wanna")

Hippie Hill, Hippie Hill
If you've got a lifetime to kill
Millions of moments by day and by dark
Might as well spend them in Golden Gate Park;
You don't have to be mentally ill
To enjoy sitting perfectly still
Feeling so placid while tripping on acid—
It's happening on Hippie Hill!

("Hippie Hill")

The structure of protest songs is such that they are frequently put to familiar or catchy tunes which can be sung *en masse*, either without instrumentation or with a simple piano or guitar accompaniment. Illustratively, most pocket sized songbooks used by radical movements contain no musical notation. Even songbooks containing radical songs which do have music are very simple to play such as three guitar chords in one key. The key of G was used by the Communist-oriented Almanac Singers and People's

Songs Inc. quite often. The fundamental feature of protest songs has been the recurrent and clear statement of the political message, or as Lenin would have it, music was not to soothe but to arouse the listener to political awareness. In Brechtian terms the ideological message was to be dominant, with the misleading emotion and the artistic skill of the performer to be minimized. The most indicative American genre of the Brechtian style of propaganda is the folkish "talking blues" which Woody Guthrie described as "You talk this piece off. They say it's four-four time . . . just play chords and talk."[18] In actuality the "talking blues" are spoken against a steady 4/4 background where the chord progressions are simple and repetitive, usually in the key of G or C. This idiom has been used to address every conceivable subject possible, from sociology to unionization and Communism.[19]

> If you want higher wages, let me tell you what to do,
> You've got to talk to the workers in the shop with you.
> You've got to build you a union, got to make it strong,
> But if you all stick together boys, 'twon't be long—
> You'll get shorter hours . . . better working conditions . . .
> Vacations with pay . . . take your kids to the seashore.
> ("Talking Union")

> Now in the Daily Worker and the New York Times
> You've all been reading about Stalin's crimes.
> But if you view it dialectically, I'm sure you'll find
> That Uncle Joe's been much maligned—
> A product of the Trotskyite-McCarthy conspiracy—no doubt.
> ("Talking Stalin Blues")

Here, then, the verbal content becomes primary with the music playing a secondary role. Also, the song stresses the participation notion. The pronoun "we" is frequently used to suggest group solidarity as well as group participation as the solution to some real or imagined social problem. This remedy most often was outside of the "common sense world" of the majority, thus placing the group using a protest song in conflict with some or all of the sectors of the legitimate institutions of the social structure. Lewis Coser, in presenting his model of social conflict, sees the notion of non-legitimacy qua deviance as central to the creation of radical consciousness and group solidarity:

> Legitimacy is a crucial intervening variable without which it is impossible to predict whether feelings of hostility arising out of an unequal distribution of privileges and rights will actually lead to conflict.

> Before a social conflict between negatively and positively privileged groups can take place, before hostile attitudes are turned into social action, the negatively placed group must . . . develop awareness . . . that it is being denied rights to which it is entitled.[20]

Within this framework the conflict which succeeds its deviant or non-conformist group is viewed as establishing and reaffirming the identity of the unit maintaining its boundaries against the surrounding, hostile external world.[21] Lazarsfeld and Merton support this addition by suggesting that propaganda is by itself insufficient for social protest. They write, "Students of mass movements have come to repudiate the view that mass propaganda in and of itself creates or maintains the movement . . ."[22] Instead, they contend that propaganda must also involve "supplementation" through some form of face-to-face or organizational contacts. An outstanding evidence of this phenomenon is the climax of a Billy Graham rally where converts are urged to come forth and make their "Stand for Christ." In the political sphere an ex-Communist describes this mode of the socialization process:

> . . . I found something in the group that I hadn't known before in civilian life. Everyone had the feeling of belonging, of being part of something, of working together for something and enjoying it. They sang songs, ones that I'd never heard before, folk songs, political agitation songs, but all the songs seemed to reflect my emotions.

> I thought that these young people were fighting for things I wanted.[23]

By combining the above elements of conflict, non-conformity qua non-legitimacy, and social action, we may then define a *protest song* as: *a socio-political statement designed to create an awareness of social problems and which offers or infers a solution which is viewed as deviant in nature.*[24] The themes of songs from the IWW, CPUSA, AFL-CIO, and other collectivities advocate "working and fighting together, in some organization, for a better day or society" and in opposition to the *status quo*. Even songs from a quasi-movement such as that once found in Haight-Ashbury present this "cultural drift" as a utopian ideal, stressing sexual and spiritual gratification.

In sum, traditional protest songs exhibit certain dominant characteristics and processes. Protest songs provide an alternative to what exists. Historically, protest songs were primarily addressed to those who already believed, acting as statements of reaffirmation. Finally, protest songs generally involved more than just a verbal communication, that is, protest songs were performed in a social gathering such as a political rally, church service, protest march, and other self supportive social environments. Beyond saying that these protest songs appear to have reaffirmed existent beliefs, it is difficult to analyze the social impact of IWW songs, or those performed at Communist Party gatherings during the 1940's. At best, perhaps, the power of music as a weapon is historically unproven.

Popular Culture and the Protest Song

The homogenization of popular culture, particularly during the 1950's and 1960's, brought together a number of musical genres previously considered deviant and unsavory to supporters of Tin Pan Alley. "Race music," "hill-billy music," "folk music," all were merged into the nebulous idiom of Rock 'n' Roll. Both proponents and opponents of this newly popularized genre saw it as innovative. One sociologist spoke of the New Sound as the expression of:

> . . . a new culture being born, and its lyrics serve as normative guidelines for youth in the process of defining and establishing a new order . . . What they are saying comes through loudest, if not clearest, in their music and it is to the music that we must turn as does youth itself.[25]

A less admiring observer notes that music is:

> . . . promoting attitudes and ideas which, if they were aware of the message, would blow the minds of most parents.[26]

As such, rock music is innovative and presents ideas and styles which are viewed as presently deviant. Yet, the question which immediately becomes important is whether the music itself is viewed as protest or is it the lyrical content which is viewed as protest.

Rock and Roll, as it is presently performed, is a blend of two genres, Negro blues and Caucasian country music. Popular Rock and Roll, according to numerous observers, was a direct spin off from "race music," later called "rhythm and blues," which originally was directed totally to the urban black ghettoes.[27] Alan Freed, a white disc jockey in Cleveland, coined the term Rock and Roll to refer to the records he played for a predominantly black audience.[28] For Freed's listeners blues and so-called quasi-spiritual group renditions reflected the values and norms of the urban black community. However, few if any songs dealt with social protest. Paul Oliver, in an examination of recorded Negro blues records, states, "the number of items that are directly concerned with protest themes is exceedingly small." He continues to argue that:

> . . . the personal character of the blues would require the singer to experience the effects of prejudice himself to inspire him to sing on the theme, and a man who had so suffered would be rather less likely to bring further attention and trouble to himself. Amongst the record companies precautions were generally taken to ensure that material likely to cause embarrassment and possible distress was rejected: a practice of censorship.[29]

Ghetto blacks were more than aware of their station and did not require creation of "caste consciousness." The so-called "race songs" did however deal in detail with the subjects of sex and other normative subjects. The Midnighters recorded songs such as "Stringy Little Thing," about a girl who did not "put out"; "Annie Had a Baby" and "Work with Me Annie." In these songs "rock and roll" most often depicted sexual intercourse, a theme *kitsch* music only hinted at.

On April 24, 1954, Cat Records, a subsidiary of Atlantic Records, released a rhythm and blues tune, "Sh-Boom," by the Chords, a black group. This song was recorded by the Crew Cuts, a white singing group, and became the first "rock" record to become a number one selling record in America. This, according to many, was the beginning of a change in the tastes of American record consumers. Prior to that time ballads of the Doris Day, Perry Como, Eddie Fisher variety were dominant sellers. Groups such as the Four Aces, Ames Brothers, Four Lads, etc., sold very well.30 Prior to the release of the Crew Cuts' version of "Sh-Boom," Bill Haley and the Comets recorded what was probably the first white version of rock based on country music, "Crazy Man Crazy," in 1951. In 1953, Haley recorded or "covered" (copied) "Shake, Rattle, and Roll," based on the urban blues composition by Big Joe Turner. The rerecording of "Rhythm and Blues" songs by large companies with name artists came to be called "covering." This process not infrequently censored the original material or changed its connotation in total. For example, "Work with Me Annie" stated "please don't cheat / Give me all my meat." The popular Georgia Gibbs version was titled "Dance with Me Henry," where the above line was changed to "if you want romancin' / You better learn some dancin'." Many other "R and B" songs were covered by Bill Haley and Pat Boone, to mention only a few.31 However, it was Elvis Presley who, with "Heartbreak Hotel," merged the white country influences with that of urban black singers. It is with Presley, and in part Haley, that the generation gap in popular music began to emerge. Adults generally associated "rock songs" with sexual gyrations and characters from the film version of "Blackboard Jungle," where "Rock Around the Clock" was the theme song. Deviance, at this stage, is found in the eyes of non-participants, but not in receivers. David Riesman, for one, saw Presley as fundamentally "anti-parent." He suggests that Elvis:

> . . . appeared somewhat insolent, slightly hoodlum. Presley was a much more gifted musician than adults gave him credit for, but he antagonized the older generation. And that gave the younger generation something to hang on to which their usually permissive parents openly disliked.32

As is suggested here, Presley was a deviant of the previous coloration of the so-called Top Forty, in that popular music as a genre primarily reflected adult tastes, featuring slow ballads, broadway hits, and novelty songs. Lyrically, on rare occasion, songs would make statements of generational conflict such as "they tried to tell us we're too young . . ." or other Romeo and Juliet themes. The musical genres employed for these sentiments bore little resemblance to either "race music" or the "country idiom." Presley's deviance, then, stemmed more from his choice of musical idioms and his stage appearance rather than his lyrical statements. An examination of Presley's early million sellers (RCA LPE 1707) shows no sign of social or political dissent outside of the realm of recurrent American romantic love rites. For example: "So, if your baby leaves/Just take a walk down Lonely Street/To Heartbreak Hotel." Some other Presley hits were "I Want You, I Need You, I Love You," "Let Me Be Your Teddy Bear," and "Love Me Tender."

The deviant aspect of Rock 'n' Roll, it appears, was tied to the emergent genre of "rock-a-billy" rather than lyrical content. Horton, in analyzing the lyrical content of popular songs in 1955, found that only 12.8 percent of the songs surveyed were not about love and courtship.[33] Johnstone and Katz found that popular music tastes reflected the norms of adolescent peer groups and geographical propinquity.[34] Coleman, in *Adolescent Society*, reaches a similar conclusion.[35]

Indeed, the music of the 1950's exhibits considerable social resignation. Songs such as found in the *Billboard* Top Fifty of 1956 stressed the love theme with "Why Do Fools Fall in Love," "In the Still of the Night," "Band of Gold," and "Love Me Tender." Doris Day's million seller perhaps best captured the political tenure of the year "Whatever Will Be Will Be (*Que Sera Sera*)."

Billboard does not gauge record sales, but airtime; however there is little doubt that lyrically the hits of the latter part of the 1950's were harmless.

In examining nearly 300 "hit" singles issued during that period, which received extensive airplay in northern California it was found that the predominant themes of the songs played evolved around the topics of dating and recreation rites ("At the Hop"), notions of romantic love, ideation of love objects or self, and a host of novelty songs celebrating flying saucers, animals, and spacemen.

TABLE 1

Social concerns in lyrics of rock and roll songs played on teenage oriented radio stations during the period of 1954-1960

Dating and Recreation Rites	30
Dancing	23
Parties	4
Dating	2
Drinking	1
Trials and Glories of Romantic Love	179
Ideation of Love Object or Self	68
Female	43
Male	24
Both	11
Instrumentals	30
Novelty	3
Social Protest	7
n-	331

As the final category in Table 1 indicates themes of socio-political protest were exceedingly rare.[36] The few songs of social discontent exhibit concerns of generational conflict, especially the rigors of attending school, employment, and differential musical tastes. The singer most often found making a social comment was Chuck Berry (Chess 15140). In several of his songs Berry stated the superiority of Rock and Roll as a musical genre in pieces such as "Roll Over Beethoven" and "Rock and Roll Music."

> Don't care to hear 'em play a tango,
> I'm in no mood to hear a mambo;
> It's 'way too early for a congo,
> So keep a-rockin that piano
> So I can hear some of that rock 'n' roll music. . .
> ("Rock and Roll Music")*

In other songs Berry questions certain values:

> Yeah, I'm doing all right in school,
> They ain't said I've broke no rule,
> I ain't never been in Dutch,
> I don't browse around too much;
> Don't bother me, leave me alone,
> Anyway I'm almost grown.
>
> ("Almost Grown")*

> Too much monkey business
> For me to get involved in . . .

> Same thing every day,
> Gettin' up goin' to school
> No need of me complainin'
> My objections overruled. . . .
>
> ("Too Much Monkey Business")**

The best selling song of social dissent to appear on the Top Forty charts of the 1950's was Eddie Cochran's "Summertime Blues":

> I'm gonna raise a fuss
> I'm gonna raise a hollar
> About working all summer
> Just to try to make a dollar.

> (chorus)   Sometimes I wonder
>   What I'm a gonna do,
>   But there ain't no cure
>   For the summertime blues.

> I'm gonna take my problem
> To the United Nations
> I called my Congressman,
> But he said quote,
> "I'd like to help you son,
> But you're too young to vote."
>
> ("Summertime Blues")***

The Coasters and the Silhouettes, two R and B groups, recorded songs denouncing the "nagging parent or girl friend" which can be, if one wishes, interpreted to mean the plight of American Negroes.

> . . . And when I go back to the house
> I hear the woman's mouth
> Preachin and a cryin'
> Tells me that I'm lyin'
> 'Bout a job
> That I never could find.
>
> ("Get A Job")

* * * * * *

> If you don't scrub the kitchen floor
> You ain't gonna rock and roll no more.

* * * *

> ("Yakety Yak")

Generally, these songs were a statement of resignation to the teenage role, or as "Summertime Blues" repeated "there ain't no cure" for the problem situation. Except, perhaps, growing up.

The exceedingly small number of songs commenting on topics outside of the romantic love situation suggests that the Top Forty was not a vehicle of social protest. Indeed, the deviance of the Top Forty was aesthetic rather than social.[37] The popular songs of the 1950's, despite their somewhat unsavory image, appear to have done little more than reflect the normative pattern of their listeners and perhaps commitments to peer groups, as Johnstone and Katz would suggest.

The interim between Elvis Presley's reign and the emergence of the Beatles in popular music was, according to most social historians of "Rock 'n' Roll," a period of uncertain drift, with novelty "teenage death" songs predominating. It was also the period which saw the so-called "folk music revival" blossom on college campuses and occasionally on the Top Forty. The relationship of folk music to the Top Forty was quite similar to that of the "race records" of a decade earlier. Popular groups once again "covered" songs recorded by lesser known artists, not infrequently changing the original lyric to exclude so-called controversial aspects. For example, the first overt politically significant song to reach the national Top Ten listing was Pete Seeger's "Where Have All The Flowers Gone?" as recorded by the Kingston Trio. The Trio, however, altered one of the most important aspects of the anti-war song, changing the last line from "when will *you* ever learn" to "when will *they* ever learn," thus removing all individual blame for the cause of wars originally cited by Seeger. In time, the same trio recorded several political tunes as novelty songs such as the "MTA," originally a campaign song in the city of Boston some ten years earlier. Other so-called "pop" folk groups also recorded songs which symbolically protested conditions of a previous decade or situation, such as Woody Guthrie's dustbowl ballads and the Merle Travis song, "Sixteen Tons," describing the conditions of Appalachian coal mining.[38] In time these compositions would serve as models for urban singers such as Bob Dylan, Phil Ochs, Tom Paxton, and many others who wished to make social comments.[39] Once again "cover" versions of protest songs became popular rather than the original piece, such as Peter, Paul, and Mary's rendition of "Blowin' In the Wind," or the Byrds' interpretations of other Dylan songs, or Trini Lopez's rock emulation of the "Hammer Song" by Seeger and Hays, allegedly written for a Communist Party rally in New York. The integration of so-called "urban folksingers" into the rock genre merged the lyrical import of folk-styled protest songs with the Beatle-oriented popular sound of the mid-sixties to produce a number of so-called protest songs on the Top Forty.

The process of covering is once again suggested by the early efforts of English rock and roll groups. The first recordings of the Beatles, the Rolling Stones, and many other groups were copies of Chicago blues pieces recorded on R and B labels during the 1950's. One classic example, noted by Keil, is Howling Wolf's "Little Red Rooster," which was recorded by the Rolling Stones and sold over a million records.[40] The Beatles likewise used "old" songs of Chuck Berry and other black singers for many of their early hits, e.g., "Rock and Roll Music," "Long Tall Sally," and "Roll Over Beethoven." Indeed, many of the more popular English rock musicians such as Eric Clapton, Jeff Beck, John Mayall are all interpreters of American blues.

Therefore, if the literature is correct, we can observe a purification process which takes place prior to the popularization of a musical genre. White singers in the 1950's popularized the songs written and performed by their Negro counterparts; urban folk entrepeneurs covered songs written by the Weavers and Pete Seeger; and finally current rock groups expanded upon the urban blues recordings of the 1950's.[41] As students of popular culture have maintained, the popularization of any art form involves co-optation, that is, appeal to as many potential customers as possible.[42] This process, it appears, eliminates much of the controversial from popular music. Songs which are presented in this idiom are not in conflict with the general values of the social order and are therefore quite legitimate and conformist in nature, suggesting that songs presented on "Big Sound" stations structurally are not protest songs in the traditional sense.

The finding that neither the musical structure nor the lyrics of songs on the Top Forty actually protest does not, however, imply that popular songs are free of non-conformity *vis-a-vis* traditional standards. Rock music, as we have seen, was thrust upon a music public which was only partially open to its appeal. The dichotomization along generational lines was more over musical style than lyrics. Indeed, a major outcry of the older generation was the "mushiness" or lack of clarity of the words of a rock song. Several social satirists did quite well recording unintelligible lyrics for pop songs.[43]

In the Summer of 1965 a number of propaganda songs with socially controversial messages began to appear on the Top Forty charts. Some of these songs were "covers" of Bob Dylan songs such as "It Ain't Me Babe," and "Mr. Tambourine Man." Other songs were written especially for popular consumption, such as "Laugh At Me" by Sonny and Cher, or "Home of the Brave," which stressed the teenager's right to wear clothing different from his parents and acceptable adult standards:

> Why do they care about the clothes I wear . . .
> If that's the fare I have to pay to be free . . .
>
> ("Laugh At Me")

> The P.T.A. and all of the mothers say
> He oughta look like the others . . .
> Why won't they try to understand him.
> Why won't you let him be what he wants to be.
> ("Home of the Brave")

These two songs, while being labeled as "deviant" or "protest songs," were fundamentally in keeping with the efforts of Chuck Berry during the 1950's which lamented the teenage role and adult standards. If one compares Dylan's first "rock" hit, "Subterranean Homesick Blues," to Berry's "Too Much Monkey Business," cited above, a number of parallelisms emerge:

> . . . get born, short pants, romance, learn to dance
> get dressed, get blessed, try to be a success . . .

Once again, the values of the teen culture are lauded and the notion of postponed gratification questioned; however, this material is still in keeping with the social commentary of older popular songs.

During this period several other socially significant songs made their way on to the Top Forty, such as "We Gotta Get Out of This Place," which outlines the feelings of a slum child who has witnessed his father's unsuccessful struggle to leave, and who fears a similar fate for himself and his girl friend. The song ends "We gotta get out of this place; there is a better life for me and you." Janis Ian's more controversial "Society's Child" is about the intervention of parents in the relationship of a Negro male and a white female. After documenting the harassments of parents, school officials, and "society" in general, the song concludes:

> One of these days I'm gonna stop my
>   listening, gonna raise my head up high
> One of these days I'm gonna raise up my
>   glistening wings and fly
> But that day will have to wait for a while
> Baby, I'm only society's child
> When we're older things may change
> But for now this is the way they
> Must remain . . . .
> ("Society's Child")*

Unlike the deviant conclusions of traditional protest songs which advocate social action to create a better society or a "new day," both of these songs either are designed to "make the best" of what exists or to "get out of this place" in a Horatio Alger manner.[44] As such, these songs, at best, may be seen as topical commentaries on the world as the songster perceives it, but do not offer any solutions or invoke any sort of political action. The one exception to this rule, it appears, was "The Eve of Destruction," which is generally seen as the ideal type of "popular protest song" by all observers.

"The Eve of Destruction" was one of the first overt expressions of political sentiment basically addressed to an adolescent Top Forty audience. It was written by a 19 year old, P. F. Sloane, and recorded by a practioneer of the *kitsch* folk music scene, Barry McGuire. McGuire was an ex-Christy Minstrel, a night club circuit folk singing group which specialized in non-political ballads. "Eve" first received airplay in August of 1965 and in five weeks became a national best seller, despite widespread opposition to it which included a blacklist of the piece by many Top Forty stations. The American Broadcasting Company also refused to have the song played on its affiliates. The song, in narrative style, cited a series of social indignities and hypocrisies, concluding that if social change was not forthcoming a nuclear holocaust awaited man. Each series of indictments concluded with the chorus:

> Take a look around you boy
> Bound to scare you boy
> You don't believe
> We're on the Eve of Destruction.
>
> ("The Eve of Destruction")*

Musically, the song was a departure from the folk genre. Belz described the piece as having "an accelerating beat which slowly developed into the impact of a forceful marching song."[45] While the Sloane composition included the classic qualities of grievances and musical momentum, it ended without a solution. Sloane urges that some action must be taken, but does not specify a given course, program, movement, or political party. The broadness of

the indictment in part may explain why in a sample of under-
graduates only 14 per cent understood the total theme of the
song while 44.8 per cent partially explained the message of the
song.[46] The protest aspect of the song, it appears, was minimal;
however, its economic success being unquestionable, the song was
a trend starter of sorts.

Other topical pieces followed, either taking a similar ideological posture or expressing a counter action reminiscent of the
Country and Western genre. For example, Decca issued the "Dawn
of Correction" by the Spokesmen as an "answer song" to Sloane's
composition:

> The Western world has a common dedication
> To keep free people from Red domination
> Maybe you can't vote, boy, but man your battle stations.
> Or there'll be no need for votin' in future generations.
>
> ("Dawn of Correction")

Other anti-protest songs have been recorded by Pat Boone, Marty
Robbins (under the pseudonym "Johnny Freedom"), Frankie
Laine, and others. None, with the notable exception of the "Ballad of the Green Berets," by Sgt. Barry Sadler, based on a Spanish
Civil War march, has sold well or made any dent upon the Top
Forty charts. This fact may not be totally attributable to ideo-
logical perspectives. Nearly all of the artists aforementioned are in
the so-called "middle media" of popular music which is addressed
to adults over 35 or 40 years of age. On the other hand, topical
and protest songs have taken on a "novelty" quality on the Top
Forty as well as on the so-called FM "underground station."[47]
Songs such as "Mr. Businessman," "2 Plus 2," "Skip A Rope,"
"Fortunate Son," "The War Goes On," and "Give Peace A
Chance" all have received Top Forty airplay with relatively high
sales. Only John Lennon's "Give Peace A Chance," a chant put to
music, has actually had any success in the American political
arena, with marchers singing the piece at anti-war rallies. Significantly, "Give Peace A Chance" structurally is the only current
political song which is based on the more traditional format of
protest songs, being repetitive, easy to sing, and stressing movement solidarity.[48]

The Buffalo Springfield's "For What It's Worth" is one of the few examples of a protest song in the heart of the rock genre. Perhaps Dino Valenti's "Let's Get Together," a semi-official anthem of the hippie phenomenon in San Francisco, is another example. Nonetheless, recent overt protest songs on the Top Forty have exhibited a novelty stature.

FM underground stations, given their relative freedom from some of the economic pressures of Top Forty broadcasting, aptly described by Hirsch, play more protest material than their AM counterparts.[48] For example, Gordon Lightfoot's "Black Day In July," a bitter description of the Detroit riots of 1967, was played on FM stations and generally ignored on AM radio. Material by the Fugs, the Mothers of Invention, and Country Joe and the Fish also is confined to FM outlets, ostensibly because of its use of some four letter words. Another reason given for the higher proportion of topical songs on FM is the programming format itself. Most current topical songs, following Bob Dylan's innovative lead, are rather lengthy.[49] Eric Burdon's "Sky Pilot," depicting the role of a military chaplain, is eight minutes in duration. The "American Eagle Tragedy" by Earth Opera, attacking President Johnson as the "king in the counting house" sending young men off to die, is eleven minutes in playing time. Top Forty songs, in contrast, are customarily three minutes in length.

The length of contemporary political songs is yet another departure from the rather simplistic, easy to learn protest songs of religious and political movements. Indeed, a topical song singer, today, away from electric current would be found impotent as a propagandist.

Since the days of the early frontier circuit riders the protest song has undergone a number of important changes. Indeed, the contemporary protest song may now be little more than a novelty item on the Top Forty. Protest songs on the Top Forty, in fact, do not protest, rather they entertain. This finding suggests that perhaps a total redefinition of the protest song may be useful.

Similarly, it may be useful to consider the notion that popular songs, by their very nature, cannot be protest songs. Obviously, what is popular cannot at the same time be deviant or in opposition to the *status quo*, since popularity is the *status quo*.

URBAN
FOLK
MUSIC
'MOVEMENT'
RESEARCH:
VALUE
FREE?

The genesis of the so-called urban folk music "movement" was closely linked with the left-wing movements of the 1930's and 1940's.[1] Folklorists and other students began to investigate the city-billy phenomenon after a change in the political climate of the United States in the early 1950's. At that time any association with the Communist movement was considered subversive. An individual identified with the Communist party was socially penalized and frequently lost his job. For example, the Weavers' career was rudely interrupted in 1952 because of their alleged Communist affiliations. John Greenway's pioneer work on the political use of folk music, which appeared at the close of the McCarthy period in 1953, was an outstanding treatment of the relationship of music to social movements prior to the 1930's, but significantly he chose to ignore the political and ideological significance of folksongs for Communist and other left-of-center movements.[2]

Most students of the urban usage of folksong have ignored the Communist influence. Some have avoided any mention of the historical connection between various songsters and social movements. Others have obscured the character and intent of the utilization of the song of persuasion, preferring vagaries such as "liberal-labor movements." Ironically, extreme rightists, relying upon Congressional citations, have missed most of the objective associations of some protest singers and have pointed to folksinging in general as a "Communist plot."

Treatments of the urban use of folk music can be categorized in four major types, which reflect the evaluative assumptions of their authors: (1) segmental analysis, (2) selective avoidance, (3) sacrilegious, and (4) conspiratorial. This typology is not exclusive, however, since some of the works reviewed occasionally fit into more than one category.

The first trend found in discussions of the growth of urban interest in folk material is "segmental analysis." This approach stresses one variable as opposed to alternative factors. Josh Dunson's *Freedom in the Air* and Greenway's *American Folksongs of Protest* are two examples of this form of analysis. Dunson posits that "broad Left movements" helped bring folk music to the city dweller. He cites the influence of the Trade Union Unity League (TUUL), Highlander Folk School, Commonwealth Labor College, and the Kentucky Workers Alliance upon the working class movements of the north. He further argues that the rejection of the "organization man" ethos by college students created a new generation of dustbowl balladeers. Although Dunson's major contribution to the revival literature is his acknowledgment of the role of Communists, this is done on a highly selective basis. In comparison to the above-named organizations, the historically important Almanac Singers receive little attention. Nor does Dunson answer such significant questions as Thelma McCormick's dilemma "Just what went on in the Cumberland Mountains when the 'folk' and the Third International met face to face . . .?"[3] How did the "Third Period" of the Communist party color the musical migration of the early 1930's? What was the role of the Socialist labor colleges, such as Brookwood? Did Communist ideology play a significant role in the sectarian folk renaissance of the red decade?

Greenway's controversial pioneer work on protest songs exhibits parallel trends. While Dunson can be charged with journalistic overstatement in some areas, Greenway errs in the opposite direction. Greenway correctly associates songs with social movements, pointing to the Populists, the Industrial Workers of the World (IWW), and segments of the Congress of Industrial Organizations (CIO). But, very soon he drops this line of analysis and presents the lyrical and biographical portraits of four songmakers of protest material. Three of these performers are significant because of their membership and participation in social movements, yet this relationship is never explicitly stated.[4] Fred Beal, a Communist organizer in Gastonia, becomes a "union leader."[5] In the case of Aunt Molly Jackson, a TUUL organizer, Greenway quotes her as stating "I got all of my progressive ideas from my hard struggles and nowhere else."[6] However, as Charles Seeger later suggested, Aunt Molly's reference group was of great significance in her singing and writing: "To my personal observation, it took Molly Jackson only a few months to convert herself, when expedient, from a traditional singer . . . into a shrewd observer of audience reaction . . . ."[7]

Greenway indicates that Aunt Molly composed "The Murder of Harry Simms," which later was altered by a "foreign source" to include reference to the Young Communist League (YCL). Other students, however, contend that Mrs. Jackson was not the composer of this piece and that the original lyric did in fact refer to the affiliations of the martyred YCL worker:

* * * * * * *

> And get a million volunteers, into the YCL
> And sink this Rotten System
> In the deepest pits of Hell.

* * * * * * *

One is free to choose between the Greenway account and that found in the Guthrie-Seeger collection *Hard Hitting Songs For Hard-Hit People*; nevertheless, it appears that due to the social context of composition, New York, and several other circumstances, the YCL version may well be the original.

Woody Guthrie's politics and personality also received a historical transformation. Woody's Communist ties are generally omitted; his tenure as a *People's World* and *Daily Worker* columnist are not mentioned and his association with the Almanac Singers is almost entirely overlooked.[8] The political origins of "Union Maid," "The Rainbow Room Incident," and Guthrie's relationship to the People's Songs Inc., are equally beclouded.[9] The importance of Ella May Wiggins, Aunt Molly Jackson, and Guthrie in the proletarian revival of the late 1930's is not to be underestimated; however, their abilities as songmakers do little to edify their roles.[10] It is difficult to speculate as to why an otherwise forceful scholarly book contains these omissions and colorations. One reason may be that a ten-page appendix on People's Songs was excluded from the manuscript,[11] but this appendix, while treating the Progressive party campaign of 1948, does not elaborate on the omissions noted above. Pete Seeger offers a plausible explanation as to why an otherwise detailed work contains these errors: "I don't trust political analyses when they're made at the height of the Cold War and you can't speak the truth without getting someone in serious trouble."[12] This was an unfortunate turn of events, since most subsequent discussions have relied heavily upon Greenway's work.

The second error of omission found in the literature is that of "selective avoidance" of key variables, usually reflected in an author's use of esoteric meanings, or innuendoes. To illustrate, terms such as "radical," "progressive," "worker," "anti-fascist," "partisans," or "one big union," while they may suggest a specific meaning to students of left-wing lexicon, say little to the general reader. "Worker," "Workin Folks," and "progressive movement" in the 1930's and 1940's referred to the Communist party. Yet even the Communists would be confused by contemporary usage of these terms.[13]

An example of selective avoidance includes Ellen Stekert, who in characterizing Guthrie, writes: "He, like most of these people [Houston, Seeger, Leadbelly, Lomax, Geer] was caught up in the union and socialist movements of the time . . . ."[14] According to Oscar Brand: "Whatever the reason, the record shows an unknown number of folksingers peopling the activities of the left-wing."[15] Dunson, the most explicit of these writers, notes: "The Almanacs were part of the progressive and left movements of the time,"[16] and "Not only the Almanacs, but many traditional singers in those years identified themselves, intellectually as well as musically, with broad Left movements."[17]

Jargon such as "socialist-oriented" or "left-wing," when not used by those involved in Marxian movements, is of little value since it is applicable to a myriad of organizations ranging from Social Democrats to Trotskyists. When Guthrie speaks of "anti-fascists" or "trade unionists" or "Workin Folks" a specific meaning can be derived. Traditionally, when one spoke of "the progressive movement" or "the Left" during the 1930's, one meant the Communist party, the dominant movement of the period. However, the contemporary use of this terminology tends to obscure the variable of affiliation with the Communist movement. Given these descriptions, many other observers have characterized Guthrie, Seeger, and others as primarily labor or union singers. Seeger, in a recent interview outlined his relationship to the labor movement as follows: "Woody and I, when we went to sing for the labor unions . . . we didn't think of the union as a little protective association, we thought of it as one step to try to bring the world together."[18]

Avoidance also assumes the form of total omission of important data. For example, the musical tools of the internecine organizational battles of the red decade are excluded. Outside of the Friedland-Glazer album, no mention is made of Trotskyist material. Ray Lawless' biographies of folk performers also excludes all mention of social movements, despite the fact that a large number of the performers included in his book were politically active.[19]

Another trend found in the analyses of the city-billy phenomenon is that of "sacrilege." This posture assumes that traditional folk material has been tarnished by association and usage.[20] As Willard Rhodes comments: "Folklorists and musicologists have looked askance at the movement and regarded the new material unworthy of their scholarly academic consideration."[21] This attitude is quite understandable since most aspects of the urban folk progression are outside the traditional definitional and typological criteria of folklore. This, however, has not inhibited folklorists like Wilgus, Dorson, James, and Stekert from taking open issue with the urban political use of folksong.

One of the most powerful statements encompassing the sacrilegious position is Stekert's article in *Folklore and Society*. Stekert begins by noting that folksongs were imported into the urban milieu by "conscientious and adamant left-wing political groups." Also, "unskilled performers" such as Woody Guthrie and Aunt Molly Jackson appeared on the scene to further the "politically oriented folksong movement of the 1930's."[22] The events of this decade eventually led to the commercial revival of the 1960's which supports Dunson's thesis. In examining two of the dominant figures of the respective revivals, Stekert indicates that Woody "produced reams of abominable prose and ditties . . . only the smallest fraction of which is aesthetically worth anything either in the folk culture from which he came or in the urban culture to which he wanted at times to belong."[23] Dylan, on the other hand, "sings to eulogize the chaos of his own private hell, a hell he feels reflects the ambiguous and hypocritical world about him."[24] These two psychologically and artistically based statements fall into the realm of Weberian "value judgments" and add little to the understanding of the urban folk "movement" under consideration.

The final approach, the conspiratorial, is evidenced in the argument that folksingers are conscious tools of a domestic or foreign conspiracy.[25] While major advocates of this position are to be found in the ranks of the extreme Right several articles and books treated above also toy with this theme. The demonological thesis is best summarized by Fred Schwarz of the Christian Anti-Communist Crusade who has pontificated that "The Communists have been using folk singing for years . . . [and the folksingers] are now being used by the Communists."[26] Most objective observers of the recent folk scene would readily discount at least part of this argument. Certainly, folk material has been utilized by numerous rural social movements of the polar Right.

The most sophisticated exposition of this view is David A. Noebel's *Rhythm, Riots, and Revolution*. Noebel, relying upon governmental sources, asserts that the Proletarian Musicians Association in Moscow ordered the use of folk music, a command carried out by the People's Songs Inc.[27] The author continues his hypothesis indicting performers and musical outlets of folk materials, both traditional and political, as subversives attempting to indoctrinate American youth. Bob Dylan and most revival folk entrepreneurs are viewed as vital links in a Communist-inspired web of propaganda. Dylan is presented as one who has attained a status that was "never . . . available to one not steeped in the traditions of Communists . . ." While Dylan, at one time, did aid the civil rights movement and comment on the military-industrial complex, he certainly was not a Communist, as the disapprobations of the old and new Left testify.[28] Another illustration of Noebel's work is the use of discredited Congressional testimony. He claims that the Weavers are all members of the Communist party, despite the fact that his source, Harvey Matusow, disclaimed this assertion in 1955. Matusow recalled:

One of the members was listed in *Red Channels*, but there was nothing that could be pinned on the group specifically —they could not be placed in the Communist Party . . . I triumphantly said [to the House Committee on Un-American Activities] "I know them, and they are Communists."[29]

A number of "superpatriots," such as the Fire and Police Research Association of Los Angeles and Jere Real, writing in *American Opinion*, have made similar claims.

Another interpretation can be subsumed under the conspiratorial view. This position assumes the "innocent dupe" position advocated by Lyons in the *Red Decade*, that is, Communists did play a part in the development of folk music interest to further their revolutionary aims. Josh White, in "I Was a Sucker for the Communists," employs this trait. Others like Burl Ives and Oscar Brand present cases against Communist party policy.[30] Brand recalls: "I had been blacklisted in 1946 . . . having refused to perform for Communist Party programs . . . [after] some unpleasant experiences at leftist programs where I had been admonished for singing songs contrary to that week's party line."[31]

When these allegations were originally made, *Sing Out!* replied: "Since Oscar was active with both of these groups [People's Songs Inc. and People's Artists], it seems strange that there was never any mention of 'influential censorship' of his song material at that time."[32] Which account is correct is not important; nevertheless, both White and Brand, in their descriptions of the 1940's, invoke the demonology and rhetoric of anti-Communism, which furthered the standardization of error.

Karl Mannheim, in developing his thesis of the sociology of knowledge, suggested that the societal conditions of a particular era give rise to ideology and thought. Consequently several of the above treatments can be placed within a context of ideological and opportunistic anti-Communism based on the precepts of Radical Rightism and overt fear of media blacklists. Other students plagued by the nightmare of "red-baiting" charges have both correctly and incorrectly avoided the political and ideological aspects of the urban folk music growth. Illustratively, Woody Guthrie's association with the Communist party has deliberately been avoided by most scholars outside of the Radical Right.[33]

To label folk music as intrinsically Communist is to ignore history; to deny the association between the CPUSA and urban folk interest is to falsify history. To sum up, one is led to agree with Archie Green that little objectivity has been accorded

> . . . the role of Communists in unions before and after World War II. Woody Guthrie, Leadbelly, Pete Seeger (and their fellow People's Artists partisans) were important figures . . . To date students have shied away from this trio's politics in favor of accounts of charisma or conquest.[34]

Reprinted from *Western Folklore,* 28 (July 1969), Urban Folk Music "Movement" Research Value Free by permission of The Regents of the University of California.

RELIGIOUS ROOTS OF THE SONG OF PERSUASION *

The propaganda song in America, as in Europe, appeared originally within a religious framework. Hymn or "psalm" singing was the singular musical expression sanctioned by the rigid Puritans since, "Musick is the good gift of God."[1] Instrumentals featuring a violin or fiddle were seen as tools of the devil and associated with witchcraft. Certainly fiddling conjured up the image of a musical Pied Piper leading the innocent down the road to damnation. For early American Christians music was to serve and praise God. Hymns in this austere milieu reflected the structure and purpose of the Catholic "morality play" found in medieval theocracies, and indicated the dominant role of churchmen in the New World. Here, propaganda songs were primarily a means of moral reaffirmation or support rather than conversion.

This doctrinal supremacy, however, was transformed with the continuing process of settlement and immigration. Indeed, some resettlement in the New England area was caused by intercolonial creedinal disputes. Concurrently, the secular tastes of colonists expanded. One minister in Massachusetts published a commonplace book of English ballads. Some selections dealt with "earthly" subjects and themes. In 1720 Reverend Symmes argued that songs would have ". . . a tendency to direct young people . . . from learning idle foolish, yea pernicious songs and ballads and banish all such trash from their minds."[2]

To further dissuade youth from the ways of the devil, religious proctors injected instrumental innovations into church

48

liturgy. With the growing complexity of religious music, the church songbook or hymnal developed. This introduction made congregational or "regular singing" a standard part of church services, much to the dissatisfaction of conservative elements in the community.

The evolution of the hymn in the original thirteen colonies was minor when compared to the musical innovations introduced by the followers of John Wesley. Wesley learned the technique of balladry from the Teutonic style of song. The founder of Methodism believed hymn singing to be a major force in the process of conversion, and in 1737 he published a songbook directed to this end. Conversion for Wesley was not an intellectual commitment, but rather an emotional response to his declarations. He evoked all devices to precipitate passionate reactions.[3] For example, Wesley used tunes of the songs best known in taverns to communicate his religious message, and was one of the reformers said to have stated, "Why should the devil have all of the good tunes?" Chase observed: "Wesley found that the singing of hymns by his congregation was one of the most effective means of spreading the glad tiding of salvation."[4]

In 1761 Wesley prophetically defined seven precepts for the singing of propaganda songs: "(1) Learn these tunes before any others, (2) Sing them exactly as printed, (3) Sing all of them, (4) Sing lustily, (5) Sing modestly, (6) Sing in tune, (7) Above all, sing spiritually . . ."[5] Despite these admonitions, American Methodists strayed from this formula and improvised some material. These revivalists favored a more spontaneous approach to hymn singing, thus further involving the listener in the "religious experience." Hymns were to integrate religious dogma and serve a cohesive function by creating a "we" feeling among a community of believers.[6]

In the United States, Methodism spawned many of the methods of protest singing used by left-wing social movements.[7] The introduction of fundamentalism and the creation of the American frontier brought the emergence of a new native rite: the "camp meeting." The inhabitants of a region would come together at a predetermined time and place to hear the local circuit rider or itinerant preacher. The camp meeting generally continued for several days owing to the distances which had to be traveled by the plainsmen. At these gatherings songs were sung at fever pitch. One circuit rider commented: "They may have enjoyed themselves, but they were not singing for the sake of singing. What they were there for was to hammer on the sinner's heart and bring him to the mourner's bench."[8]

The practice of camp meetings is significant in that this frontier phenomenon was adopted by other movements such as the Abolitionists, Grangers, the Populists, and rurally based segments of the American Socialist Party. To illustrate, consider Bell's description of a Socialist Party camp meeting:

> A typical encampment would be opened with a rousing horseback parade, followed by a pickup mixed chorus which sang socialist versions of old populist songs to the tune of well-known religious melodies. Then followed the fire and brimstone oratory . . . So went the week with a tumultuous round of singing, concerts, speeches, campfires, and memories to last for the next few months of dreary labor.[9]

In time, members of Brookwood labor school used similar techniques to bring individuals to the bench of "social justice." Tom Tippett, in recalling a scene from the Marion textile strike, wrote: "Thus everybody would envisage a new kind of religion and a new kind of enemy. Many a prayer went up from the Marion strike lot that summer asking God Almighty to 'help us drive the cotton mill devil out of this here village.' " And: "The women and men stationed there chanting re-written Negro spirituals across the darkness to inspire faith and courage."[10]

One of the artifacts of the camp meeting was the *Pocket Hymn Book*. This book was the prototype of many others utilized during the revival era and was also the predecessor to the *Little Red Song Book*, the *Red Song Book*, and the *AFL-CIO Song Book*. The songbooks were generally 4 by 6 inches, making them easy to carry. On each page was a hymn without music, since the melodies were based on popular standards that everyone already knew. In other instances the tunes were simplistic and catchy, consequently easy to learn.

In opposition to urban Methodism, the Salvation Army argued that God must be taken to the people rather than having parishioners find their way into a church. This organization urged its workers to resort to any method, however spectacular, to communicate with potential converts. One attention-getting device they used was the parade, featuring the brass band. The off-key street bands took the songs known to the people and changed the words to transmit their message to both the willing and reluctant passerby. This practice did not go unnoticed by those opposed to organized theology as the "opiate of the masses." The syndicalist Industrial Workers of the World (IWW) adopted these tactics and used them for recruiting purposes.

Greenway suggests that the Wobblies stumbled upon this modus operandi as a means of combating the street bands of the Salvation Army and the Volunteers of America, who frequently would drown out Wobbly speakers in a "cacophony of cornets and tamborines." One enterprising IWW organizer, wishing to combat the forces of obscurantist "pie in the sky" theology, "retired long enough to organize a brass band of his own."[11] Wobblies performed biting parodies of religious hymns and practices of the "starvation army," such as having to "sing for your supper." Using the model of the Army, the IWW published a songbook to fan the flames of discontent, with each song designed to "illustrate and dramatize some phase of the struggle."[12] These Wobbly songs in turn would have a large impact upon the protest songs of the 1930's and after. As Archie Green has noted, "The Communist movement with its interest in 'people's songs' retained and extended Wobbly lore."[13]

The prime function of the revival song was emotional response. The songs were based on the appeal of "singing ecstasy," that is, total physical and emotional involvement. Songs, following the dictum of Wesley, were constructed to attain "an effective opportunity for mass participation and all-out shouting." Secular movements frequently emulated the methods of religious indoctrination. The Socialists and the Wobblies patterned many of their organizing methods, particularly songs and songbooks, upon the religious prototype. The Communist party, a major force in urban protest song development, incorporated many of these same techniques. As ex-Communist functionary George Charney notes in his autobiography, the party stressed that "A people who can sing will make revolution; a people without spontaneous song will never defy the gods."[14] Another religious source which contributed to the "spontaneous songs" of the Stalinists and other social movements was the Negro spiritual.

In a pioneer study of Negro folk songs, Odum and Johnson made no mention of songs of protest, despite the inclusion of several songs which are certainly suggestive of protest.[15] Early observers posited that Negro songs are comparatively free of "protest and discontent."[16] More contemporary treatments have pointed to the protest elements of hymns and spirituals. Glazer and Fowke have voiced this opinion, pointing to a spiritual such as "Go Down Moses": "In the trials and tribulations of the children of Israel they saw the pattern of their own bondage. Thus they could do full justice to one of the great Bible stories of liberation: The story of Moses who stood up to Pharoah and said: 'Let my people go.' "[17] Greenway compares the spiritual of the slave culture with the symbolic protest found in the Dark Ages.[18] Songs such as "Run To Jesus," "Didn't the Lord Deliver Daniel," "Steal Away," and "Free My Lord" are the more obvious examples of spirituals containing statements of dissent. A verse from "Steal Away" is illustrative:

> O Steal away, steal away
> O Steal away to my Jesus
> Steal away, Steal away
> For I ain't got long to stay here.

The words to this spiritual are very similar to "Run To Jesus," the song believed to have inspired Frederick Douglass to escape from slavery.[19] Slaveowners, not unlike English monarchs, perceived some of these hymns as a threat and jailed Negroes for singing "We Shall be Free."[20]

With the advent of the Civil War, spirituals were found with much more overt statements of protest, stimulated by the conflict and the imminent prospect of freedom. Songs such as "Oh Freedom" and "No More Auction Block For Me," which date from the year of Jubalo, were sung by Blacks who fought with the Union Army. As the lines from "Oh Freedom" indicate:

> No more moaning Lord for me
> And before I'd be a slave,

I'd be buried in my grave
And go home to my Lord and be free.

Shortly after the end of World War I, social movements began to take interest in the black spiritual. Marcus Garvey's Universal Negro Improvement Association employed a hymn as the base for its official anthem:

> Advance, advance to victory
> Let Africa be free
> Advance to meet the foe
> With the might
> Of the red, the black, and the green.[21]

In the late 1920's and 1930's the American Communist party idealized the Negro population as the most oppressed segment of the capitalistic society and therefore a very promising group of candidates for the working class cause.[22] Articles in the Communist press began to extol the music and culture of the Negro. His music was viewed as an effective and ideologically pure tool in the mobilization of the unorganized masses, both white and black. In the *New Masses*, Richard Frank wrote:

> When the American Revolutionary Movement finds expression in Negro music it is expressing itself in a medium capable of arousing not only the twelve or fifteen million Negroes of America, but also all the toiling masses of America, who for generations in one form or another have made Negro music their own.[23]

Frank continues to argue that Negro hymns are a valuable recruiting device:

> . . . among the Negroes, it will be to a great extent through singing that recruiting will be done for the masses of Negro workers held at illiteracy. Leaflets cannot appeal to them. But singing is their great form of artistic expression. In order to win the Negro people most effectively the revolutionary movement will have to make use of this instrument.[24]

As early as 1932, Mile Gold reported a transformed hymn "Gimme That New Communist Spirit," stating, "At mass meetings their religious past becomes transmuted into a Communist present."[25] Several months later the *Daily Worker* published a Stalinist parody of the Garvey movement anthem:

> Sing a song full of the strife that the dark past has taught us
> Sing a song full of the hope Communism has brought us.
> Facing a Red! Red! Sun of a new day begun
> Let us fight on till victory is won.[26]

On another occasion the spiritual, "My Mother's Got A Stone, A Stone That Was Hewn Out of the Mountain," was changed to "the bosses hate the stone that was hewn out of history," or "the workers need that stone . . . ."[27]

In 1936 Lawrence Gellert and Elie Siegmeister published 24 Negro songs of protest.[28] For Gellert these songs were symbolic of black class consciousness, unrest and despair.[29] Some of the songs included in the collection were "I Went to Atlanta," "The Preacher's Belly" and "Sistern and Brethern." "The Preacher's Belly," collected in a small Alabama church, according to Gellert, follows a pattern originated by Wobbly composers:

> Religion is something fo' de soul
> But preacher's belly done git it all . . .
> He eat yo' dinner an' take yo' lamb
> Givin' you pay in de promised lan . . .

The student of protest songs will quickly recognize the similarity of this lyric to that of "The Preacher and the Slave" and Woody Guthrie's dustbowl ballad, "So Long, It's Been Good to Know You." The anti-religious motif of the Gellert collection and other factors such as the inability of others to duplicate them has suggested that these songs are unique. However, they were extremely popular in left-wing circles for a time. Siegmeister noted ". . . *Negro Songs of Protest* has been received with tremendous enthusiasm by certain audiences as 'good' because they express the deepest feelings of an oppressed people."[30] Other contributors to the Communist press frequently took note of spirituals and hymns as a "cry for justice" or "people's music." Lee Collier lauded the alternation of "Joshua" to the following: "Black and white together we'll win the vote (3)/The Communist Party will lead the fight (3)."31

Lee Hays, in "Let The Will Be Done," argued that spirituals were ideal weapons for working class organization.32 Hays cited "Let The Will of The Lord Be Done," "Come To Jesus," and "Jesus Is My Captain" as highly suitable for use as "union songs." To illustrate: "The parody of 'Jesus Is My Captain' has traveled from a North Carolina textile strike throughout the agricultural movements of the South and even into the far reaches of New York City's May Day parades. . . ."33 One agricultural movement which extensively utilized hymns for organizational purposes was the Southern Tenant Farmers Union (STFU). A number of STFU songs eventually became popular standards in the songbag of many urban protest singers.34

STFU meetings were typified by their religious fervor, singing, and the use of biblical phrases as slogans. The rallies commenced with a prayer followed by hymns. H. L. Mitchell, one of the co-founders of the rural union recalled:

> . . . there was a lot of singing, especially among the Negro members who were quite good singers. They would sing the old Negro spirituals. Many of them are songs of protest that grew out of conditions that existed before slavery was abolished. Some of the spirituals seemed to fit in with the union program. One of them for instance, was selected as the official union song. It was "We Shall Not Be Moved."35

The musical bards of the Tenant Farmers were two local preachers, A. B. Brookins and John Handcox. Brookins was similar to camp meeting evangelists, previously discussed, who had the ability to exhort people to sing. John Handcox, also a preacher, wrote many of the labor protest songs of the STFU, including "Raggedy," "There Are Mean Things Happening in This Land," and "The Man Frank Weems." His best-known composition was "We're Going To Roll the Union On." This song was based on the hymn "Roll the Chariot On." Several of Handcox's songs were collected by persons associated with Commonwealth College, and later by John and Alan Lomax. "Roll the Union On" was included in the Almanac Singers' collection of labor songs, *Talking Union*

(Keynote 304).

While the Wobblies, Communists, and other secular movements have used religious models "shamelessly," the civil rights movement rarely used songs not based on church hymns. To illustrate, nearly every selection found in the Carawan's collection, *We Shall Overcome*, has a religious base.[36] The use of spirituals by southern Negroes, however, was more a function of familiarity and heritage than of imitation and parody. Robert Sherman, in describing "freedom songs," noted:

> The freedom songs are heard everywhere in the South now—at mass meetings, on the picket lines, during street demonstrations. They are sung in the jails, and often composed in the jails. They are dramatic emblems of the struggle and mighty weapons in it. Their steady, surging rhythms, their lilting melodies (taken usually from familiar hymns or spirituals already well known to the Negro community), and their simple, inspirational words, repeated over and over again, generate a fervor that can only be described as religious in its intensity.[37]

Within the civil rights movement "freedom songs" served to create unity and solidarity in the rank-and-file membership. The inner-directedness of the songs in great measure explains the use of hymns, since religion for the rural Black was a keystone of his culture and social structure.[38]

Emile Durkheim, in the classic work, *Elementary Forms of Religious Life*, argued that sacred ceremonies and rites served four social functions: (1) instilling individual self discipline; (2) creating and reinforcing cohesion; (3) perpetuating tradition; and (4) establishing a sense of personal well-being. Social movements, even more than established institutions, must invoke these functions in order to survive.

Leaders and monitors must be able to control and direct their followers when strolling to the metaphorical "gates of hell." As the late Rev. Martin Luther King suggested: "There are so many difficult moments when individuals falter and would almost give up in despair. These freedom songs have a way of giving new courage."[39] The utilization of religiously based songs gives the propaganda material an aura of sacredness, thus further legitimiz-

ng the authority of leaders and the sanctity of the cause. Songs
stating the justness of the cause or movement tend to unify that
entity, especially when employing an idiom familiar to the people.
Indeed, as the author has suggested elsewhere, religious parodies
sung by Wobblies and Stalinists frequently alienated the very
people these movements desired to mobilize.

The use of religious music adds an appeal to tradition which
social movements generally require. Movements, by their very
nature of advocating social change, are generally not tied to tradi-
ion. Hymns, in part, appear to tie the movement to a national
heritage, regardless of the programs they advocate.[40] Finally,
group singing encourages the individual to feel himself a part of
the group or movement, and therefore important, allowing the
participant to carry on. As one Georgia NAACP organizer put it:
"The people were cold with fear until music . . . [broke] . . .
the ice."[41]

Ironically, as Lipset reports, ". . . many Communist meetings [in Europe] . . . actually begin with religious hymns."[42]
The incorporation of religious hymns and spirituals into socio-
economic movements of political change is but one aspect of the
similarity between collectivities oriented to theology and to ideology. Many secular, even anti-religious, social movements owe a
great deal to organized religion for providing models and means
for social action.

Reprinted from *Western Folklore*, 1970, Religious Roots of the Song of Persuasion,
p. 175-184, Vo. 29, by permission of The Regents of the University of California.

**CLASS
CONSCIOUSNESS
AND
THE
SONG
OF
PERSUASION** *

The relationship between songs of persuasion and social movement is a subject needing examination. The role and function of
the propaganda song has in the past received little attention from
sociologists and social scientists as a whole. The primary usage of
the propaganda song is to create political or social consciousness
favorable to the position of the movement or individual using the
propaganda song. The original interpretation of the concept
"political consciousness" connotes a predisposition for social
change.[1] Lenin derived the concept of political consciousness from
Marx who viewed class consciousness as the subjective means of
facilitating change in the social structure. For Marx, class membership was originally an aggregate of persons in a given economic
strata or "a class in itself." Class consciousness emerges when
members of a class (the proletariat) identify themselves with the
class (the proletarian class) and their position in the stratification
system and when the members of the class are aware of their
historical role in the Marxian theoretical scheme, or a change-
oriented "class for itself." Mills correctly defines three elements
essential for class consciousness to exist:

> (1) a rational awareness and identification with one's own
> class interests; (2) an awareness of and rejection of other
> class interests as illegitimate; and (3) an awareness of and
> a readiness to use collective political means to the collective
> political end of realizing one's interest.[2]

Lenin made explicit this postulate in *What Is To Be Done* by suggesting that the proletariat was not and could not be conscious of the irreconcilable antagonisms of their interests. Workers, according to Lenin, are singularly engaged in "outbursts of desperation." Therefore, an organization must be formed and maintained to "take up the political education of the working class, and the development of political consciousness."[3] Lenin, hereby, injected the factor of a mobilizing force—social movements—generally ignored in the structural-psychological tenets of class consciousness as perceived by Marx. One means of creating class consciousness, especially by political and social movements familiar with the writings of Marx and later Lenin, has been the use of the propaganda song performed or composed in the folk idiom, that is, songs performed employing the instrumentation and presentational techniques traditionally manifested by non-professional folk singers.[4] Few folklorists consider contemporary propaganda songs as being folk songs. Although there appears to be some disagreement among observers as to the elements constituting the definition of a folk song, the following characteristics are consensually submitted: (1) the author of the song is anonymous; (2) the songs are orally transmitted from one generation to the next; and (3) the song must experience verbal alteration during generational transmission. Generally propaganda songs of the twentieth century have not met the definitional criteria. The vast majority of these songs suggest the following properties in varying degrees as being present: (1) the author of the song is publicly identifiable; (2) song transmission is through audio-visual aids, such as the printed page, e.g., songbooks, or in contemporary times, records; and (3) few propaganda songs survive beyond their historical *genre* or organizational milieu. This truncated comparison of the characteristics of folk and propaganda songs indicates that generally propaganda songs are not folksongs in the definitional sense and therefore the two terms cannot be employed interchangeably.

A propaganda song or "song of persuasion" in the folk idiom can be defined as a song which functions to communicate an idea, a concept, or a total ideology to the listener, employing the structure of a folk song.[5] (Note: this definition in the context of this paper refers to those propaganda songs dealing with socio-political ideologies and events in the framework of the polity.)[6] Propaganda songs function to achieve six goals: (1) the song solicits and arouses outside support or sympathy for a social movement or attitudinal orientation; (2) the song reinforces the value system of individuals who are a priori supporters of a social movement or ideology; (3) the song creates and promotes cohesion and solidarity in an organization or movement supporting the singer's and/or composer's ideological position; (4) the song attempts to recruit individuals to join a specific social movement; (5) the song invokes solutions to real or imagined social phenomena in terms of action to achieve a desired goal; and (6) the song directs attention to some problem situation or discontent generally in emotion laden terminology.[6] These six usages of the propaganda song are to be achieved by two categories of songs of persuasion.

The first type of song of persuasion is the magnetic song. The magnetic propaganda song is defined as a song written by a "folk entrepreneur"[7] which appeals to the listener and attracts him to a specific movement or ideology within the ranks of adherents by creating solidarity in terms of the goals expressed in the propaganda song. Two essential factors are contained in this definition: the song persuades, both emotionally and intellectually, individuals into supporting and/or joining the movement or goals of the writer and of the organization for which the song is written; and, the ballad creates social cohesion or a feeling of solidarity among the membership or supporters of a given movement or ideological set. Hearing the protest song is not enough. There must be opportunity for social action. The song should blueprint successful alternation of existent power relationships. A social movement is the most common vehicle for such change since it appeals to the frustrations of the down trodden and promises a "new day" or millienium. The concept of a magnetic propaganda song may be operationalized as the Marxian view of a "class for itself" or Lenin's view of political consciousness. The magnetic song contains the three elements of class consciousness, that is, an awareness of class position, differentiation from others, as indicated in the content of the songs, and further, a desire or willingness to join a movement as suggested in the lyrics of the propaganda song.[8] In Lenin's terms left-wing political consciousness encompasses the two dominant characteristics of the magnetic song, that is, the creation of solidarity and attraction and recruitment of new members to a social movement.

The other category of propaganda song is the rhetorical song defined as a song written by a folk entrepreneur and is designed to point to some social condition, describe the condition, but offers no ideological or organizational solution such as affiliating with a social movement; the rhetorical song poses a question or a dissent in relation to the institutions of the social system, e.g., Wall Street. The rhetorical song may point to an event which is endemic to its geographical or historical context and may require little commitment of the listener. This type of song can be equally useful as the above category in promoting cohesion within the membership of a social movement, but may have little effect on non-members and in some circumstances may negatively affect non-participants.[9] Rhetorical songs also can be divided on a historical continuum as being universal or specific. For example, "Kevin Barry" transcends time and geographic boundaries and political movements, whereas propaganda songs dealing with a specific event such as a strike may not transcend the historical context of the song, e.g., "Pretty Boy Floyd" or "Dreadful Memories." The latter category associates or correlates with the Marxian stage of "a class in itself" in that only a question or a protest is suggested within the context of the songs and the organizational solution of class unity and action is omitted. Rhetorical songs are thusly defined as "outbursts of desperation" rather than mobilizing factors or problem solving devices in the historical sense of consciousness as delimited by both Marx and Lenin. These definitions suggest that the political or class consciousness of a social movement and its membership, to the degree that they support the leadership, may be indicated in terms of the propaganda songs produced by a social or political movement. The structure of these songs indicated organizational trends in the Marxian sense and a unity of collectivity, therefore making propaganda songs operational vis-a-vis class and political consciousness. In this work, the former conceptualization will be treated.

In the present century four periods have manifested a significant amount of propaganda song activity: (1) 1905-1915 dominated by the Industrial Workers of the World; (2) the period of 1935-1943 dominated by the C.I.O. and the American left-wing; (3) the period of 1945-1950 dominated by the People's Songs Inc.; (4) the period of the so-called folk song revival, 1957-1964. These periods of historical spectrums represent the peak years of heightened propaganda song activity employing the folk idiom. Also, the selection of these periods on a historical continuum allows a presentation of a representative sample of propaganda song content.

Historical Background
Period I

The Industrial Workers of the World (IWW) was formed in 1905 to introduce industrial unionism or syndicalism during this period into the United States; the "one big union" would in turn bring about a socialist economic system. The occupational composition of the membership primarily included lumberjacks and miners in the West, wheat and stockyard workers in the Midwest, and textile workers in the East. The movement attained a maximum membership in 1910 of 100,000 adherents and from this point declined after the beginning of the First World War due to several factors: (1) the repression of the movement by governmental agencies and vigilante groups, such as the American Legion; (2) the transference of support by IWW members to other organizations.

Period II

In the mid-thirties John L. Lewis withdrew from the American Federation of Labor and formed the Congress of Industrial Organizations (CIO). This labor reorganization created various tactical difficulties which Howe and Coser define:

> . . . there was precious little glory and still less comfort in organizing for the CIO, and as a rule, only men moved by a conviction that unionization of mass-production industries was a step toward a larger social end were willing to take the risks that came with the job.[10]

One group willing to undertake the deprivations of the role, labor organizer, was the American Communist Party, which was accepted by some of the leadership of the CIO, anxious to have organizers.[11] The injection of the Lewis element of organizers—

miner workers with a rural tradition—and the personnel from the Left injected or reintroduced the propaganda song employing the folk structure. The Party used similar songs of persuasion in its recruiting drives. Songs advocating participation in the Spanish Civil War, urging non-intervention in the European conflict, and espousing a greater effort in defeating the Axis, were utilized by the Left to communicate a specific interest orientation.

Period III

The People's Songs Inc. (PSI) was formed from the ashes of the pre-war activities of the labor movement and the political Left. The major function of the group was to provide propaganda songs to the labor movement and left-of-center movements such as the Progressive Party in 1948. The substantive differentiation of this organization, and others like it, from the above was that PSI was to provide and perform propaganda songs for other social movements rather than to recruit members for the PSI. People's Songs disbanded in 1949, after achieving a peak membership of two thousand adherents, because of a lack of funds, the change of attitude in the CIO as to the type of tactics and organizers the labor movement desired to have, and attacks upon the group by several legislative committees.[12]

Period IV

The final period under consideration saw the disappearance of the cited movements from the realm of functional significance. The CIO was legitimized and institutionalized, the CPUSA and other Marxist groups had declined into political oblivion, and the IWW consisted of several small offices maintained by a handful of members, remnants of the 1910's. However, the folk music revival, the emergence of the New Left, and intensive civil rights activity in the South renewed interest in "protest songs," originally those of the cited periods. This rebirth of interest evidenced itself in the form of folk entrepreneurs who composed and performed material dealing with specific events and perceived grievances. These songs are representative of Gusfields' "expressive politics," that is, political expression without a function, e.g., protest for the sake of protest.[13] The civil rights movement employed songs in a traditional pattern with several contemporary adaptations, specifically in the Southern states.

These four periods may be "idealized" in the Weberian sense according to the dominant traits, structures, and ideologies of the social movements of these eras. Periods I and II are characteristically "structure-directed" in that social discontents were frequently defined within the confines of 19th century "grand cosmic schemes." The latter two periods are typically "event-oriented," that is, evidencing topical concern or free floating protest aimed at specific problem situations such as racial discrimination or recently the Vietnam War. For example, the IWW and the CPUSA viewed system change, based on the ownership of the means of production, as the remedy for their consciousness of dysfunction. In juxtaposition, the New Left desires specific outcomes of conflict situations, which differ from one *ad hoc* protest group to another.

Methodology

In this work different songs are typologized and utilized as indicators of class consciousness, i.e., the songs have been categorized in terms of the extent to which they reflect the Marxian conceptualization, through a content analysis of the songs of the periods under consideration. This index will then be applied to the above historical periods during the twentieth century where songs of persuasion were used by social movements left of the relative political center.[14] Magnetic songs, therefore, are operationalized as being indicators of class consciousness social movements. Conversely, rhetorical songs are associated with the absence of change oriented entities. The magnetic song reflects a high degree of class consciousness as opposed to the rhetorical ballad. It is, therefore, expected that there will be a greater than chance association between social movements exhibiting working class orientations, and songs that reflect a high degree of class consciousness; rather than songs that reflect a lesser degree of Marxian consciousness, see Table IV.

Sample

In 1906, the IWW during a Seattle membership campaign adapted the techniques of the propaganda song from the movement's religious rival, the Salvation Army. One observer visualizes the competition in this manner:

> . . . the revolutionary philosophy that Walsh (an IWW organizer) was peddling conflicted with the principles of religious complacency being preached simultaneously up the street by the Salvation Army and the Volunteers of America, and the two bands marched down surrounded Walsh and proceeded to drown him in a cacophony of coronets and tambourines. Walsh . . . retired long enough to organize a brass band of his own . . .[15]

From this encounter, according to Greenway, emerged the *Little Red Song Book* with the preamble "to fan the flames of discontent." The pocket sized book featured parodies of "Starvation Army" songs which subsequently have been transmitted into thirty editions as of May, 1962. This latter edition indicates the manifestation of class consciousness in the IWW.[16] Table I suggests that the IWW was primarily concerned with recruiting new adherents and maintaining cohesion in the movement. The number of cases in the rhetorical song classification of the table indicates a small percentage (.29) of propaganda songs outside the magnetic category. In the sub-category of rhetorical songs the majority of songs dealt with a specific strike situation or a martyred hero in the movement, e.g., the execution of Joe Hill. The majority of propaganda songs are indicative of class consciousness in that the supplementary variable present in the songs correlates with the Marxian typology.

To cite all of the magnetic and rhetorical songs found in the IWW song book is outside the scope of this chapter, however, we offer one example of each classification and sub-category:

Magnetic Songs

song to recruit outsiders:

Workers of the world, awaken!

Break your chains, demand your rights
All the wealth you make is taken by
    exploiting parasites. . .
Join the union, fellow workers,
Men and Women, side by side. . .
            ("Workers of the World Awaken")

song to promote solidarity:

Fierce and long the Battle rages
But we will not fear,
Help will come when 'er it's needed
Cheer my comrades, cheer.
                ("Hold the Fort")

song to achieve both new members and solidarity:

Come and join in the fray
Come and join us today
We are fighting for Freedom and Bread
            ("Now Awaking")

Rhetorical Songs

specific event:

High head and back unbending—fearless
    and true
Into the night unending; why was it you?
Heart that was quick with song, torn with
    their lead;
Life that was young and strong, shattered
    and dead.
            ("Joe Hill" by Ralph Chaplin)

universal theme:

They go wild, simply wild over me
I'm referring to the bedbug and the flea—
They disturb my slumber deep and I murmur
    in my sleep,
They go wild, simply wild over me.
                ("The Popular Wobbly")

A like pattern of propaganda songs occurred during the re-cruiting drives of the thirties and early forties as employed by the labor movement, especially the C.I.O. and the American Left-wing. Both movements were greatly affected by the organization-al methodology of the IWW in part because discontented members of the IWW who left the movement in the late twenties and joined the Communist Party and other dissidents, as well as integrated Communist Party members, served as organizers for the newly formed CIO. The transmission of techniques that occurred between the Salvation Army and the IWW was partially replicated in terms of the IWW and the CIO and the American Left.

A total differentiation of segments of the American Left and the CIO during the late thirties and early forties is a difficult task due to the fact that the CIO, especially in the person and staff of John L. Lewis, welcomed *all* support and personnel into the indus-trial workers union, thus minimizing and obscuring the influence of the left-wing vis-a-vis the so-called labor song of protest.

The Communist Party in the late thirties published the *Red Song Book* which was employed extensively at Party rallies.[17]

The content analysis of the *Songs of the People* suggests that the movement conformed to the Marxian definition of a class con-scious movement. The composition of the song book in relation to rhetorical songs indicates a specific orientation toward the Loyalist movement in Spain during the Civil War, and the CIO. The increase of rhetorical songs points to the issue orientation of the Party in contrast to the movement orientation of the IWW or Wobblies. The following verses are representative of the typology suggested in this chapter:

Magnetic Songs

songs to recruit members:

> So, workers, close your ranks
> Keep sharp and steady
> For Freedom's cause your bayonets bright
> For worker's Russia, the Soviet Union
> Get ready for the last big fight.
> ("Red Army March")

songs to promote solidarity:

> Lenin is our leader
> We shall not be moved
> Lenin is our leader
> We shall not be moved
> Just like a tree that's standing by the water
> We shall not be moved.
>
> ("We Shall Not Be Moved")

songs to achieve both new members and group solidarity:

> Young comrades, come and join us,
> Our struggle will endure
> Till ev'ry enemy is down
> And victory is sure.
> In struggle and in valiant fight
> We're marching to the workers might.
>
> ("Youthful Guardsmen")

The rhetorical songs found in the *Songbook* deal primarily with the Spanish Civil War. For example:

> Spain darkens under a cloud
> Where sun should light the land
> Spain thunders out clear and loud
> To stop the fascist band.
>
> ("Spain Marches")

The function of the lyrics, as noted, is that the Party during this period was primarily oriented to maintain its membership while recruiting neophytes to the movement. The rhetorical songs included in the song book deal primarily with events where the Party had an interest, e.g., the Loyalist movement in Spain. Similarly, the Party's preoccupation with the labor movement was a dominant theme in the songs.

In 1939 the CPUSA, while continuing in its support and activity in the labor movement, shifted emphasis with the signing of the vonRibbentrop-Molotov Pact and concentrated its efforts to keep the United States out of the European conflict. In this historical context two forms of propaganda songs were sent to the fore, the labor union song and the anti-intervention songs. (See table III)

In the first magnetic sub-category two songs are specially designed to recruit new members—"All I Want" and "Talking Union." The former includes the following excerpt:

> Take the two old parties, mister
> No difference in them I can see
> But with a Farmer-Labor Party
> We could set the people free.

"Talking Union" (spoken words put to music) contains these verses to illustrate the role of a magnetic song:

> If you want higher wages let me tell you what to do
> You got to talk to the workers in the shop with you
> You got to build you a union, got to make it strong
> But if you all stick together boys, it won't be long
> You get shorter hours. . .better working conditions. . .

The internally directed song is found in the lyrics of "The Union Maid" and "Get Thee Behind Me, Satan":

> Get thee behind me, Satan
> Travel on down the line
> I am a union man
> Gonna leave you behind.
> ("Get Thee Behind Me, Satan")

and

> Oh, you can't scare me,
> I'm sticking to the union,
> I'm sticking to the union,
> I'm sticking to the union.
> ("Union Maid")

Ballads which encompass the joint characteristics are "Which Side Are You On," "The Ballad of Harry Bridges," and "The Union Train." The latter propaganda song, representative of the magnetic song, contains the following verse:

> It (the union) has saved many a thousand, etc.
> It (the union) will carry us to freedom, etc.
> ("Union Train")

In the appeals directed at industrial workers and members of labor unions, the Almanac Singers employed magnetic songs, as Table III suggests, however, in their political and issue presentations the reverse was the case. In the anti-intervention campaign of 1939-1940, the Almanacs recorded the album *Songs For John Doe*, which contained six songs whose basic thesis was that the United States should remain neutral vis-a-vis the European conflict; all of the ballads included in this collection were rhetorical and specific. Two verses from "Washington Breakdown" and the "Ballad of October 16th" are illustrative:

> Wendell Willkie and Franklin D.
> Seems to me they both agree
> They both agree on killing me.
> ("Washington Breakdown")

and:

> Oh, Franklin Roosevelt told the people how he felt
> We damned near believed what he said
> He said "I hate war and so does Eleanor, but
> We won't be safe 'till everybody's dead."
> ("Ballad of October 16th")

In this type of song the goal is to elicit tacit support or establish an attitudinal set on the part of the listener by raising questions in the receiver's mind, rather than attempting to recruit the individual to a movement, that is, to make the listener aware of his position, but not to invoke collective action as defined by the concept of class consciousness.

In 1941 the type of propaganda songs performed by the Almanac Singers changed in relation to the events in Europe (the invasion of the Soviet Union by the German Army); subsequently, the non-involvement orientation of the songs also changed. In 1942 the Almanacs released an album titled *Dear Mister President*, which advocated support for the war. The majority of these songs were parallel to the propaganda songs described; however, the function of these war songs was more to promote solidarity and increase commitment to the war effort, rather than to convince the listener of the rightousness of the cause or commitment to a movement. Pearl Harbor had already accomplished this task.

The propaganda songs of the war period, be it from either pole of the political spectrum, urged national unity and greater devotion or commitment to the international conflict. One song designed to further labor union support for the war production program is illustrative:

> There'll be a union label in Berlin
> When the union boys in uniform march in
> And rolling in the ranks
> There'll be UAW tanks
> Roll Hitler out and roll the union in.
> ("UAW-CIO")

Another propaganda song frequently performed in the Columbia Broadcasting System was The Almanacs' "Round and Round Hitler's Grave" put to the tune of an old square dance melody:

> Round and round Hitler's grave,
> Round and round we'll go.
> Gonna lay that poor boy down
> He won't get up no more.
> ("Round and Round Hitler's Grave")

Yet another form of propaganda song in the folk idiom is that invoking the concept of duty or social responsibility:

> I'm a gonna cross the ocean wide
> With a Springfield rifle by my side
> When Hitler's beat you can be my bride
> And I told her not to grieve after me.
> ("Sally, Don't You Grieve")

These songs of the "duration" evidence the national ethos of consensus during the war and mobilization, where patriotism transcends organization goals, i.e., radical political movements supported the war effort.

A comparison of the material from the *People's Song Book* to that of the above illustrates the rise of the rhetorical song with organizational (magnetic) songs remaining relatively constant; however, if we calculate only the songs written by the People's Songs which appear in the songbook we find a decline of the magnetic song and a significant rise in the rhetorical propaganda song.[18]

TABLE I

Magnetic-Rhetorical Songs in the *People's Song Book* (1948)

Magnetic songs	25
songs to recruit outsiders (external)	9
songs to promote cohesion (internal)	6
songs to achieve both new members and cohesion (both)	10
Rhetorical songs	18
specific	15
universal	3
	43

Magnetic-Rhetorical Songs Written by PSI in
People's Song Book

Magnetic Songs	6
external	3
internal	0
both	3
Rhetorical songs	14
specific	12
universal	2
	20

Similarly, in the *People's Songs Bulletin* reprints—a collection of songs from the *People's Songs Bulletin* over a three year period—the material supports the original finding, if songs not written by PSI are held constant. (Writer's note: examples of songs from period III and IV are excluded due to the fact that the structure of songs is identical to the above.)

TABLE II

Magnetic-Rhetorical Songs by PSI members in *Reprints*

Magnetic songs	7
external	1
internal	3
both	3

Rhetorical songs	15
specific	11
universal	4
	22

An analysis of the PSI songbook indicates that a decline of class consciousness in the Marxian sense has occurred and that an organizational decline was in progress. Historically, the failure of the Progressive Party and the decline in left-wing membership during this period suggests this hypothesis of class consciousness is correct. In 1949 the PSI disbanded and was partially incorporated into the People's Artists.

The latter part of the fifties witnessed the folk music revival, the emergence of a militant Southern civil rights movement, and *ad hoc* protest "publics." The propaganda songs popular in the initial stages of this period were most frequently those noted.[19] The injection of the propaganda song into a sector of the mass media, outside of the civil rights milieu, altered the traditional transfer of material process. Urban, northern, protest publics, while sporadically employing traditional songs of persuasion, placed predominant emphasis on the compositions of successful folk entrepreneurs of the revival, e.g., Dylan. Recent "teach-ins" and rallys have featured singers such as Phil Ochs, Joan Baez, and others to communicate rhetorical indignation to an audience. Ochs' rendition at a Vietnam Day demonstration at the University of California is illustrative:

> Here's to the cops of Mississippi
> . . . behind their broken badges, there are
> murderers and more.
>
> ("Here's To the State of Mississippi")

Another excellent example of the kind of thing that was being carried on in this trend is provided by a piece which was widely popular in the underground Top Ten of several years ago. This one was written by Bob Dylan:

I hope that you die and your death will come soon,
I'll follow your casket by the pale afternoon,
and I'll watch while you're lowered down to your death bed,
Then I'll stand over your grave 'till I'm sure that you're dead.

(
"Masters of War")

The two examples of rhetorical songs index the ethos of the New Left, that is, individual dissatisfaction or alienation in relation to the social structure, while lacking an ideological or organization alternative.[20] The New Left outside of the context of marches has almost totally abandoned propaganda songs for the symbolic protest material of rock and roll as performed by the Beatles, Rolling Stones, Bob Dylan in his post protest song period, and groups such as Moby Grape, the Fugs, and the Jefferson Airplane.[21]

The Southern civil rights movement musically annexed to its northern counterparts, functionally utilized propaganda material from periods I and II. Labor songs such as "We Will Overcome," and "We Shall Not Be Moved" were adapted to the cohesive needs of the Movement.[22] Other songs, generally alterations of Negro religious hymns, were incorporated into conflict situations. While some interaction and transfer of songs between the North and South does take place—the use of civil rights ditties such as "We Shall Overcome" in northern marches and in the repertoires of folk entrepreneurs—propaganda songs in the main appear endemic to organizational and geographic boundries.[23]

Broadside magazine was established to report and circulate propaganda songs in the fashion of the *People's Songs Bulletin* emphasizing the material of northern song writers and songs from the "Freedom" movement. A sampling from twenty-five issues of the magazine reflects a diminution of class consciousness and an organization decline in social movement oriented propaganda songs. Seventy-seven percent of the propaganda songs are rhetorical. Of these 81% are specific as contrasted to that of the IWW where 29% of the songs fit this classification of which 57% are specific.

The sample shows a specific issue orientation rather than organizational prerequisites. Twenty songs connote the theme of world peace, while the civil rights question, a dominant concern of this period, was treated rhetorically in a majority of the songs, 38.

Rhetorical songs treating the topic of civil rights as contrasted to those emanating from the Movement are to be differentiated. The rhetorical ballads of the northern folk entrepreneur such as "Here's to the State of Mississippi" functionally point to the composer's view of the plight of the Negro in America, whereas civil rights songs are generated from Negro musical tradition and actual protest activities.[24] "Ain't Gonna Let Nobody Turn Me 'Round" is an adaptation of a spiritual by Rev. Ralph Abernathy of SCLC during the Albany demonstrations. The song has subsequently been utilized in a myriad of protest situations. In Albany, Georgia (1962):

> Ain't gonna let Chief Pritchett, Lordy turn me 'round. . .

In Selma, Alabama (1964):

> Ain't gonna let Sheriff Clark, turn me 'round. . .

and, Chicago, Illinois (1966):

> Ain't gonna let mayor Daley, turn me 'round. . .

The genesis of Southern civil rights songs has rendered the selection of a representative collection of this type of material difficult to amass due to the number of versions existant and the spontaneity of composition endemic to specific protest milieu.[25] The only anthology of these propaganda songs, at present, is *We Shall Overcome,* compiled for the Student Non-Violent Coordinating Committee (SNCC).[26] This songbook was functionally edited for use in conflict situations.[27] As a result, 90% of the songs are magnetic, stressing solidarity and cohesion. However, only 5% of this category are overtly structured to appeal to outsiders. Three songs (5%) of the rhetorical style are found in this collection, one of which is a popular song written by two urban folk entrepreneurs, "The Hammer Song." The functional role of propaganda songs was underlined by Martin Luther King in a television interview:

> . . . they invigorate the Movement in a most significant way. . . . These freedom songs serve to give unity to a movement, and there have been those moments when disunity could have occurred if it had not been for the unifying

force of freedom songs and the great spirituals. The Movement has also been carried on by these songs because they have a tendency to give courage and vigor to carry on. There are so many difficult moments when individuals falter and would almost give up in despair. These freedom songs have a way of giving new courage and new vigor to face the problems and difficulties ahead.[28]

The utilization of magnetic songs by the Movement, however, is not comparable to those of periods I and II due to the absence of recruitment or external direction as suggested by the definitional criteria of consciousness as summarized by Mills or treated by Lenin. Therefore, the songs are limited to "Public Witness" phenomena, rather than a specific racial or class orientation.[29]

TABLE III

MAGNETIC-RHETORICAL SONG DISTRIBUTION BY PERCENTAGES

	(N)	MAGNETIC	(N)	external	internal	both	RHETORICAL	(N)	Sp.	Univ.
1. I.W.W.	(48)	70.8	(34)				29.1	(14)		
				35,2	26.4	38.2			56.8	42.5
2. *Songs of the People* 1937	(46)	67.3	(31)				32.6	(15)		
				28.8	14.7	28.8			60.0	40.0
3. Almanac Singers 1941	(7)	100.0	(7)				0			
				28.5	28.5	42.8			0	0
4. *People's Songbook I* 1948	(43)	58.1	(25)				41.8	(18)		
				35.9	23.9	39.9			83.6	16.4
5. *People's Songbook II* 1948 (control)	(20)	30.0	(6)				70	(14)		
				50.0	0	50.0			85.4	14.2
6. PSI Reprints 1946-1948	(22)	31.7					68.2	(15)		
				14.4	42.8	42.8			73.0	26.3
7. *Broadside* 1962-1964	(138)	23.1	(34)				76.8	(106)		
				28.1	28.1	43.7			81.1	18.8
8. *We Shall Overcome* SNCC songbook 1964	(80)	95.0	(57)				5.0	(3)		
				5.0	50.8	49.9			33.3	66.7

As Table III suggests, a percentage increase in rhetorical songs has occurred with an inverse decline in magnetic songs. This is with the exception of the material from the SNCC songbook.

However, these songs are primarily internally oriented. This decline is found to be associated with the decline of so-called working class social movements, as noted.

A chi square test was made in order to distinguish the differences between the periods exhibiting activity by working, leftist class social movements and the two periods in which they were on the decline. The rationale for the usage of X^2 is that this measure of association indicates whether or not the degree of association between these variables departs significantly from an association that might be expected on the basis of chance alone. Thus, the greater the difference between the theoretical (expected) number of types of songs from the actual (observed) number of songs associated with each type of social movement—the more significant the relationship will be.

TABLE IV

	Songs		
	Magnetic (external, internal, and both)	Rhetorical (specific and universal)	
Movements			
structural	72° $(52.2)^t$	29° $(50.1)^t$	101
event	102° $(121.8)^t$	138° $(116.9)^t$	240
	174	167	341 =N

$$X^2 = 23.53$$

As this table suggests, we can conclude that the association of working class movements to magnetic songs is highly significant, since the probability of obtaining a X^2 value this large may be attributed to chance only one out of 100 times.

Also a greater than chance association is to be expected between social movements that are class oriented, and songs that reflect a high degree of class consciousness (magnetic) and that are designed to appeal to listeners outside the movement; rather than songs that exhibit a high degree of class consciousness (magnetic) and that are not designed to appeal to receivers outside the movement.

TABLE V

Movements	Songs Magnetic external	internal	
Structural (IWW to Almanac Singers)	23° $(17.6)^t$	24° $(29.4)^t$	47
event (PSI^c to SNCC)	16° $(21.4)^t$	41° $(35.6)^t$	57
	39	65	104 =N

$X^2 = 4.83$

As the table suggests, the findings are significant at the .05 level of significance. A derived X^2 of 4.83, as against a tabled value of 3.84 could have been obtained only five times out of a hundred, on the basis of chance alone. However, given 4.83=6.635, the results are not significant at the .01 level, i.e., a X^2 of 4.83 could have been expected on the basis of chance alone at this level.

The survey of propaganda songs as manifested in the four periods of maximum song activity suggests the following: (1) a marked decline in the magnetic propaganda song and a rise in the rhetorical song; (2) propaganda songs have become increasingly specific in terms of issues and events, rather than universal; (3) propaganda songs as an indicator of class consciousness find a decrease in the class orientation of social and political movements; (4) the usage of propaganda songs suggests a sharp decline in working class or proletarian movements in the United States.

The change in emphasis in propaganda songs on a longitudinal scale suggests several fundamental changes in the polis and the degree of class orientation or class consciousness in social movements considered left-of-center on the American political continuum. The change of orientation from the magnetic song to the rhetorical song correlates with the decline or virtual extinction of numerous ideological movements. The Industrial Workers of the World, the militant industrial unions of the thirties, and the sectarian Left, that is, ideological movements adhering to the philosophies of Lenin and Trotsky, have all experienced their influence and membership peaks and have been dissolved into radical political obscurity. The labor movement appears to have been legitimized into a "respectable" social institution. The sectarian Left today has little if any political import, even amongst the members of the so-called "new left." The decline of these social movements, in the sense of significance, correlates with the reduction of class consciousness found in the content analysis of the songs. The data suggests that class consciousness in relation to radical social movements has tended to point in the inverse direction from the Marxian model, that is, from the second phase of a "class for itself" to "a class in itself." This phenomenon may be approached from two directions: (1) the decline of class consciousness movements; (2) the lack of success of class oriented movements due to the false class images found in the United States by students of social stratification. The material or song content implies a correlation with a reduction of ideological movements, e.g., the *Broadside* sample contains 5 labor songs.

The emergence of contemporary "protest publics" and reformist movements, such as the civil rights movement, does not alter the fundamental position of this examination. Songs identified with the "new left" are predominantly reflective of individual, rather than collective consciousness. Further, following the lead of several folk entrepreneurs—Bob Dylan, Joan Baez—rhetorical songs are rapidly being replaced by songs of symbolic introspective protest, rock and roll. The songs of the civil rights movement are internally directed to adherents, emphasizing the unity function of "we shall overcome" as contrasted to *class fur sich*.

This work suggests that propaganda songs might be used as suggestive indicators of the organizational and ideological orientations of social movements. However, the overall results of songs as tools of mobilization are difficult, if impossible, at this writing to ascertain.

*Reprinted with minor alterations from *Sociological Quarterly*, IX (1968), 228-247, by permission of the Midwest Sociological Society.

PROTEST
SONGS
AND
SKITS
OF
AMERICAN
TROTSKYISTS

On October 27, 1928 the Political Committee of the Communist Party of the United States (CPUSA) expelled James Cannon, Max Shachtman and Martin Abern from its movement because of their support of Trotsky's Russian Opposition, which denounced Stalin's leadership and Soviet foreign policy. These outcasts and their supporters were labelled by the party faithful as "Trotskyites." In May of 1929, the Trotskyists, as they preferred to be called, organized themselves into the Communist League of America (Opposition).[1] For some years thereafter, the Opposition Left was fundamentally a "faction" with less than 200 adherents concerned with "trying to bring the official communist movement to an acceptance of the 'correct' position."[2] As most observers indicate, the Opposition Left or Trotskyists did little until the mid-1930's to build any sort of political organization or to participate in the creation of the industrial trade union movement.[3] But later Trotskyist attempts at movement-building or union organizing resulted in an interminable series of splits which effectively hampered the long-range development of a Trotskyist party.[4]

In spite of its opposition to Stalin's regime and policies, some CPUSA influence was present in American Trotskyism. Much of the latter's polemics, culture, and entertainment, indeed, was drawn from the more successful Communist movement, particularly in New York.[5] Paul Jacobs in his political autobiography *Is Curley Jewish?* recalls:

*(with Richard A. Reuss)

> . . . we were culturally dependent upon the Communists
> and their web of peripheral and supporting organizations
> for the American Trotskyist movement had no folksinging
> groups . . . nor any of the . . . activities which made the
> [*Daily Worker*] 'What's Doing' column . . . so long every
> day.6

In more specific terms, Jacobs continued ". . . we stood to sing revolutionary songs, much the same as those I had learned in the [Young Communist League] except that Trotsky's name was substituted for Stalin's."7

Several historical and sociological factors help to explain this dependency. First, the Trotskyists were a "spin-off" group from the Third Internationale. The ideological focus of their adherents, as noted, centered upon the departure of Stalinists* from Marxist-Leninism as defined by Trotsky before, during, and after his losing struggle for power with Stalin; otherwise, Trotskyists continued to view themselves as communists in the Bolshevik tradition. Also, the Trotskyists and the Stalinists frequently were drawn from the same City College of New York (CCNY) subculture of New York City, a fact which accounted for the degree of hostility between the ideological factions as well as their curious interrelationship.8 Consequently, before examing the songs and drama of American Trotskyism, it is well to review briefly the Communist position on art and culture.

Like other Marxist groups, Communists conceived of art in all its mediums as a weapon for the furtherance of the class struggle. Artistic forms and expressive content which enhanced the people's cause were seen as beneficial for the masses, and encouraged; those perceived as harmful were disparaged and, where possible, eradicated. Over and above purely agit-prop considerations, however, the more thoughtful Marxist-Leninists dreamed of creating a truly "proletarian" culture to complement the envisioned classless society. In the early 1930's, the CPUSA attempted to found such an art expression based on the militant creations of European

---

*The term "Stalinist" frequently was regarded by Communists of the Old Left as a derogatory epithet. We use the term here, however, merely as a descriptive term to differentiate that part of the Communist movement under Stalin's leadership from the Trotskyist and "opposition" Communist groups.

proletarian artists, for example, the musical compositions of the German composer Hans Eisler. Little material rooted in the indigenous scene was heard in the American Communist movement until 1935.[9] Some Wobbly (Industrial Workers of the World) and Socialist songs were sung at Party gatherings; however, the staple musical favorites remained imports. Yet laments for the lack of an "American Eisler" or "Communist Joe Hill" were not uncommon and increased as the decade of the thirties progressed.

Until the mid-thirties, the Trotskyists did not share the Stalinist interest for actively building a "proletarian" music. Even singing of an agit-prop character was limited. Nevertheless, some singing did take place within the Trotskyist ranks occasionally for the purposes of social camaraderie, rallying the spirits of members, promoting group solidarity, or for other reasons. As part of their Bolshevik heritage, Trotskyists learned such songs as "Bankers and Bosses," "The Red Flag," and the "Internationale." From the American labor experiences of the 1920's and early 1930's, shared in part with the Communists, they absorbed "Picket on the Picket Line" and Maurice Sugar's popular Depression composition "The Soup Song."

But in 1934, following their leader's "French Turn" (Trotsky's phrase for building a mass organization), Trotskyists began to move out of their isolation. They attempted a series of alliances with other anti-Stalinist socialist groups, among them the followers of A. J. Muste, a reform oriented social democrat, and later leader of the left-wing of the Norman Thomas-led Socialist Party. Since the chief concern of the Trotskyists and their allies was their common opposition to Communist policies, nationalist ideology, and tactics, it is not surprising that many original Trotskyist compositions in this period were addressed outwardly to the hated Stalinists. For example, when during the Popular Front era (1935-1939) Communist leader Earl Browder repeatedly appealed for unity on the Left with all socialist and democratic liberal organizations (except Trotskyists) against fascism, Alton Levy wrote "Our Line's Been Changed Again" to celebrate the CPUSA's shift from a militant proletarian stance to quasi-cooperation with bourgeois capitalism:

United fronts are what we love,
Our line's been changed again.
From below and from above,
Our line's been changed again.
The party says the time has come,
Our line's been changed again.
Don't call a socialist a bum,
Our line's been changed again.

I knows it, Browder; I knows it Browder,
I knows it, Browder, our line's been
  changed again.[10]

Another song heard in these years was "Land of the Daily Worker," lampooning the doctrinaire and *ex cathedra* style of said Communist newspaper:

Oh, all around our Union Square
is the land of the Daily Worker,
You'll see them standing everywhere,
reading the Daily Worker.
You go in the door of a soda store,
and talk to the soda jerker,
He knows the truth about the war—
by reading the Daily Worker.

You go to a dance to look for romance
at waltzing or majurka,
You have a chance to catch their glance—
by reading the Daily Worker.
The Eskimo, the Hottentot,
the Chinaman and the Turka,
They know exactly what is what—
by reading the Daily Worker.

Trotskyists, like most other protest groups from time immemorial, fashioned their songs out of whatever musical material lay at hand and was apt to be understood or accepted by their listeners. Not surprisingly, the tunes in the Trotskyist repertoire thus were drawn from the patriotic, popular, show, and standardized folk melodies familiar to most Americans. But unlike their Stalinist counterparts of the 1930's and afterwards, Trotskyists never paid court to the folk idiom as an idealized medium of "people's" art expression.

Beginning in the Popular Front period, folksingers and singers of folksongs began to appear at Communist rallies and social gatherings in large numbers. The lore of rural American, especially southern societies, was hailed as the true people's culture, nativistic in style and content, democratic and largely anti-fascist in character. While the fine and popular art mediums were not neglected in these years by Communists, their movement definitely placed a higher priority on the perceived folk and folk-like expression of the masses and encouraged its own artists to emulate them.[11]

Trotskyists, however, never developed such a theory of culture and continued to model their songs on the old agit-prop principles. They seldom commented upon the Communist use of folk music and if they were aware of the latter's worldview here they regarded it with amusement, curiosity, or amazement. Though largely unexpressed, it is apparent that Trotskyists on the whole basically were hostile to any *en masse* glorification of the artistic products of unenlightened "cracker culture."[12] Likewise, they held no special interest in Negro songs of protest, popular in the Communist movement at this time, for unlike the Stalinists who postulated a "submerged nation" of blacks which by right ought to be made independent, Trotskyists called for the integration of Negroes with whites everywhere in a united proletariat.[13]

To be sure, Trotskyists did not fully escape the "folk" ethos of the Communist movement of the 1930's, for the impact of the latter permeated the entire Left to some degree. Most of the few folk-styled parodies which did appear in Trotskyist literature were gleaned and sometimes reworked from Stalinists and their sympathizers. For example, several talking-blues-styled songs appeared in Trotskyist skits after Woody Guthrie and the Almanac Singers introduced this type of folk expression into New York radical circles. One, by Gene Brooks, jibed at Stalin's heavy-handed interference with the musical efforts of Prokofiev:

> Now come along comrades, listen to me,
> I'll sing of the death of the Bourgeoisie.
> The proletariat coming to power:
> The struggle for the state in a single hour:
> The party in music, the party line
> Comrade Stalin is doing fine
> For music really must express

> The hopes of the masses I confess . . .
> What else? . . . Hm? . . . So now I'll sing
> about Peter and the Wolf.[14]

Succeeding verses mocked Stalin's bureaucratic meddling in the work of artists in allegorical fashion using Prokofiev's familiar "Peter and the Wolf" story.

In similar fashion, the music of the Detroit branch of the Almanacs may have had a like impact upon post-war Trotskyist "colonizers" in the United Auto Workers union. In Los Angeles, Trotskyists reprinted Woody Guthrie's "Union Maid," set to the traditional "Redwing," in one of their mimeographed song sheets.[15] In general, however, these borrowings from the Communists took place because of the agit-prop value of the songs to the Trotskyists, not because they were deemed to have an importance as folk or folk-styled items.

Most Trotskyist protest songs actually were modeled on the show tune idiom popularized during the 1930's in labor circles, for example, by the International Ladies Garment Workers Union in their successful musical *Pins and Needles*.[16] The Broadway show genre particularly appealed to one splinter sect, known as Shachtmanites, which split off from the main body of Trotskyists over the Soviet invasion of Finland which Trotsky and many of his followers supported.[17] Opposing this action as well as the Stalin-Hitler Pact and other Communist policies just prior to World War II, the Shachtmanites wrote and performed numerous parodies and skits in "Pins and Needles" fashion attacking the Stalinists. One piece, "Doing the Demonstration," was lifted from the Communist songbook *Songs For America*, whose words were originally:

> Now's the time to get together
> This is anti-fascist weather

The second line of this text was changed by the Trotskyists to:

> Be prepared for stormy weather

And further:

> It's shaking the fat of Hoover's new brat
> And the bund right out of their uniform.[18]

Other productions came from the so-called "Jacobin Jerques" or the Staten Island unit of the Shachtmanite Young People's League (YPSL). One of these, *Reunion In Berlin*, originally presented at a picnic held on Staten Island in 1941, began with a parody of the Hitler Pact put to the tune of "Deutschland Uber Alles":

> Deutschland, Deutschland, uber alles,
> Uncle Joe we all adore,
> With his hammer and his sickle,
> He lays down der Fuhrer's law!
> Hurrah, hurrah, U.S.S.R.!
> We'll call them when we want some more!
>
> Deutschland, Deutschland, uber alles,
> First Berlin, and now Moscow!
> We're all just one big happy family:
> Uncle Adolf and Uncle Joe!
> Hirohito, and Benito,
> We told them both where they could go!
>
> Deutschland, Deutschland, uber alles;
> Profound thinkers all are we;
> We spend our time in concentration . . .
> Camps![19]

Still another condemnation of the Stalin-Hitler Pact was Walter Cliff's (a pseudonym) "In Old Moscow," set to "Clementine":

> In Old Moscow, in the Kremlin, in the fall of '39,
> Sat a Russian and a Prussian, writing out the party line.
> Chorus:
> Oh, my darling, oh my darling, oh my darling party line,
> Oh, I never will desert you, for I love this life of mine.
> Leon Trotsky was a Nazi; oh, we knew it for a fact,
> Pravda said it; we all read it, BEFORE the Stalin-Hitler Pact.
>
> Once a Nazi would be shot, see; that was THEN the party line,
> Now a Nazi's hotsy-totsy; Trotsky's laying British mines
>
> (Chorus)
>
> Now the Nazis and der Fuhrer stand within the party line;
> All the Russians love the Prussians; Volga boatmen sail the Rhine.
>
> (Chorus)

A second song penned by the same author during this period indicated that Shachtmanites forewent sectarian polemics in favor of other matter, though they still did not lose the Marxist rhetoric. The following is entitled "I Wanna Marry A Trotskyite."

> O Mama, I saw one on the Square, heck-el-ing a Y-C-Ler there.
> I could see that she was doing fine, for she had better
>   twists and curves than any party line.
> Chorus:
> A Trotskyite, a Trotskyite, I wanna marry a Trotskyite.
> The bourgeoisie, they don't appeal to me,
> A Yipsel girl must keep me company.
> O dearie, no Y-C-L for me,
> I only want a Trotskyite to bounce upon my knee.
>
> The Yipsel girls have given their consent to Marx's laws
>   of full development;
> My, how dames and dialects, Trotsky, love and Lenin
>   and sex appeal can mix.
>
> I know about Joe Stalin's Comintern, and "surplus value"
>   is just what I should learn,
> My education has never gone above, beginning of
>   "Utopian and Scientific Love."[20]

The Detroit Trotskyists during the 1940's, staged several musical skits mostly composed by Kuppy Scott. One effort, *On To City Hall*, dealt with the Shachtmanite technique of pamphleteering, and the ideological problems involved in buttonholing passersby on a street corner. The first of its songs concerned Shachtman's unsuccessful mayoralty campaign and was put to a calypso tune. It was called "Vote for Shachtman":

> Now if you want to be a silly man
> You vote Democrat or Republican
> But if you are a real smart workingman
> Don't waste your vote on them
> You better
> Vote for Shachtman
> The Workers Party man[21]

Another song from the same skit was based on a favorite from the highly successful Garment Workers stage play, *Pins and Needles*. "Love Will Be Sweeter Under Shachtman" stressed the non-political benefits of a Marxist city administration.

Love will be sweeter under Shachtman
Everybody knows that his administration will
Make every lover twice as potent
City Hall will give every man a certain little pill
And if you find that your love just won't endure
And you know that you've got a neurosis
Our Mayor Shachtman's clinics will give you a cure
Guaranteed by the dialectical process
Yes, love will be sweeter under Shachtman

He will see that every nook and cranny in our parks
Will be for lovers' use protected
He will have them shaded by the whiskers of Karl Marx.
Oh, Lulu Belle, O Lulu Belle, you can tell those
    cowboy lovers
They can go right plumb to hell
For love will be better in the City
When this fellow Shachtman to the Mayor's chair
    mounts
He'll make our city's lovers pretty
And they will be thicker, slicker, quicker where
    it counts.[22]

Following the fall of the Axis, the general ethos in the American Left was "let us continue." In Detroit, Shachtmanites again attempted to elect their candidate to public office. In 1946, Benson opposed the incumbent Mayor Jeffries. The tune of "Hard Times" was used to provide the basis of "The Benson Campaign Song."

Come listen a while and give ear to my song,
An election is coming and I'll not steer you wrong.
Detroit is a town full of workers who know,
Who work in the shops and who sweat for their dough,
A working class mayor will fight for you strong.

The landlord will swear that he's losing his dough:
Repair bills are high and the rents they are low.
Now Jeffries he says he will investigate,
But during this time we get kicked out the gate,
But Benson will move us back out of the snow.[23]

Besides supporting Benson, the Shachtmanites put on an "anti-bosses, anti-capitalist" skit based on the format of the popular radio drama, *Sam Spade: Private Detective.* In this skit written by

Kuppy Scott, Howard Duff—star of the Spade series—is hired to find a lost union leader, last seen on the "only streetcar line in the city." The rest of the skit chronicled and ridiculed the operation and condition of the Detroit streetcar system. It included four songs, "Oh Won't You Move Back," "Oh We're In the Red," "We Want A Girl," and "Everybody Has to Ride the Clairmount." This latter song best captures the thrust of the playlet.

> You will hear a famous broken record
> When you have to ask your way around
> Though your path be wide, diverse and checkered,
> And you're going all around the town.
> They'll say take the Clairmount, take it going east
> Then you take it when you're going west.
> Take it north or south, but they don't tell you why
> Surely not because the Clairmount's best.
> Oh no, oh no.
>
> Everybody has to ride the Clairmount
> No matter where it is you want to go
> You'll reach your destination on the trolley car
> If you can stand a ride that's mighty slow.
>
> Second verse:
> Nothing ever changes on the Clairmount
> The cars are never anything but old
> You can always wager that the trains will make you late
> Or else a traffic jam will stop you cold
> You call always transfer off the Clairmount
> If you don't fall asleep and ride too far
> Going out to Chevrolet to Plymouth or to Ford
> Don't look for a different line, climb right on aboard
> Unless you own a motor car it's all you can afford
> It's the orphan of the DSR
> It's the orphan of the DSR[24]

In theme, this song is similar to the 1948 Steiner-Hawes composition, "The M.T.A.," which was directed against the Boston Metropolitan Transit Authority and later popularized by the Kingston Trio.

In 1949, Trotskyists, "fulfilling their historic" mission, attempted to colonize and organize the Dodge plant in Hamtramck, a suburb of Detroit. Kuppy Scott wrote the following song, set to the tune of "The Streets of Laredo," to create political consciousness.

> As I walked on the streets of Hamtramck,
> As I walked out in Hamtramck one day.
> I spied an old worker all wrinkled and weary,
> All wrinkled and weary with a head that was grey.
>
> "I see by your outfit that you are a worker,"
> This old fellow cried as I slowly walked by.
> "Come sit down beside me and hear my sad story,
> For I'm too old to work and I'm too young to die."
>
> "It was once to the fac'try I used to go daily,
> Once in the fac'try I worked for my pay.
> Twenty long years for the same corporation.
> Now I'm too old to work and I'm starving today."
>
> "For when I reached sixty the line was too speedy,
> And I couldn't keep up at my usual rate.
> The boss was hard-hearted and that's when we parted,
> The company kicked me right out the gate."
>
> "Now, who's going to hire a man that's past sixty,
> Who will believe that he's willing to try.
> Who's going to feed him and keep the roof o'er him,
> When he's too old to work and he's too young to die."
>
> "Now listen young feller, and learn from this story,
> So you don't meet my fate as the years pass on by.
> Fight for those pensions so you can retire,
> When you're too old to work and you're too young
>   to die."[25]

Trotskyist protest songs were generally at their artistic best when addressed to the sectarian polemics of the Left. An outstanding illustration is another Scott skit, *Moby Dick*, attacking the super-intellectualism and abstractness of the so-called "Johnson-Forrest tendency," a position which viewed the Shachtmanites as right-wing deviationists. Professor William H. Friedland described *Moby Dick*, as being:

> . . . understood by only a handful of people. It was Kuppy's catharsis following a lengthy involvement with the Johnson grouping, which split out of the Shachtman group, went into the SWP for a while and later—after Kuppy left it—went independent as the 'Johnson-Forrest tenden-

cy,' Kuppy staged the skit as the cruise after the great
white whale—Moby Dick—and, of course, Captain Ahab
symbolically represented Johnson.   Moby Dick was, of
course, the revolution which was pursued with relentless
determination and with the same success as Melville's Ahab.

The choice of Moby Dick was not fortuitous but delib-
erate since Johnson had, at some stage earlier, come up
with an absolutely delightful notion that Melville has symbolically dealt with the rise of capitalism in *Moby Dick*.
There were some absolutely remarkable songs in this skit
including 'Everybody's Got A White Whale to Chase,' and
'Politics Make Strange Bedfellows' to the tune of 'Muss i
denn.'[26]

The title song, put to the tune of the spiritual "Rock-A-My
Soul," summed up the thrust of the dramatic polemic.

> 1st and last chorus:
>
> Everybody's got a white whale to chase,
> Oh Moby Dick
> But each one looks in a different place,
> Oh Moby Dick
>
> 1.   The penniless poet's an ambitious fellow, it
>   Isn't the art but to be T. S. Eliot
>   And reap the acclaim of a great poet laureate,
>   He's got a white whale.
>
>   To be immortal's his fondest hope, that's his white whale.
>   To rank with Shelly or Byron or Pope, his private whale.
>
> 2.   The theoretician who dabbles in politics
>   Wants a career just like the old Bolsheviks,
>   He spends all his time composing his polemics,
>   He's got a white whale.
>   He thinks he'd make a good commissar, that's his
>   white whale.
>   He dreams of rising very far, his private whale.
>
> 3.   Ahab expounds on his evaluation
>   Of politics and in his estimation
>   There's socialism in each situation,
>   He's got a white whale.[25]

With the advent of the McCarthy period, the white whale of
capitalism had totally eluded the Trotskyist Ahabs. By 1950, the
Shachtmanites had come to regard themselves primarily as demo-

cratic socialists and now called themselves the Independent Socialist League (ISL). The ISL, however, was a far cry from the original Trotskyist Workers Party as one observer suggests:

> They now [ca. 1952] regard themselves not as Trotskites at all (though they still sell publications by Trotsky and treat his name with respect) but as "independent socialists" . . .27

During the early 1950's many Shachtman followers drifted into academe, a good number becoming sociologists who championed the End of Ideology argument.28

Outside the campus walls, the satirical *Bosses' Songbook: Songs to Stifle the Flames of Discontent,* edited in part by Trotskyists, espoused essentially the same point of view. First published in New York in 1958, this songbook lampooned the old topical songs, ideologies, and internecine warfare of the Left in the 1930's and '40's. Exhibiting the basic ahistoricism of the late 1950's, it reflected no strict dogmatic posture except anti-ideologism generally and anti-communism more specifically. As Dave Van Ronk, one of the editors, observed in the forward to the first edition:

> These songs have been written and passed along by people from every conceivable political and apolitical tendency and sometimes they don't even express the serious views of the writers themselves.

In the second, expanded edition, Dick Ellington, another editor, added: "THESE SONGS ARE SATIRES!!! They were done for fun and meant to be sung for fun."

However, despite these political disclaimers, the contents of both editions were highly partisan in their anti-Stalinism. Most of the songs satirized and parodied came from the repertoires of the Almanac Singers, People's Songs, Inc., and People's Artists, Inc., groups sympathetic to the Communist positions of the 1940's and early 1950's. "Talking Management Blues," for example, was based on the Almanac classic "Talking Union":

> If you want higher profits let me tell you
>   what to do,
> You got to talk to the people who work for you,

> Got to bust up the unions. They're much
>   too strong,
> Fire anybody who dares to belong.
> Get rid of the agitators,
> Hire friendly people
> Willing to work for an honest wage.

People's Songs Inc. and People's Artists, likewise, bore the brunt of several satirists. The following verses from two songs are illustrative:

> Sing a song for People's Artists,
> Balladeers unite!
> Buy your latest People's Songbook
> There's a hoot tonight
>
> Organize and Fertilize
> And sing your little song
> You are right on every issue
> All the rest are wrong.
>   ("Hold The Line")

> Well, it's a long, long haul
> From 'Greensleeves to Freiheit,'
> And the distance is more than long,
> But that wonderful outfit they call the
>   People's Artists
> Is on hand with those good old People's Songs.
>   ("Ballad of a Party Folk-Singer")

Most of the songs published in the *Bosses' Songbook* were written in folk style, partly because the material parodied was couched in this idiom, and partly because most of the editors and contributors to the volume were much younger than previous Left polemicists and very much involved with the mushrooming folksong revival of the late fifties.

A more traditional type of musical expression, also historically rather than currently oriented for the most part, was the long play album *Ballads For Sectarians*, issued in the middle of the same decade.[29] Sung by Joe Glazer and Bill Friedland, two ardently anti-communist labor minstrels, one an ex-Trotskyist, the record contained a number of older parodies stemming from the Trotskyist repertoire. Among them were "Our Line's Been Changed Again," "Land of the Daily Worker," and "In Old Moscow." It also included the "Old Bolshevik Song," a humorous parody of the "Queen's Nav-y" song in Gilbert and Sullivan's *H.M.S. Pinafore* cynically noting the disappearance of first generation Communists in Russia during Stalin's reign:

> When I was a lad in 1906, I joined a band of
> Bolsheviks,
> I read the Manifesto and Das Kapital and I
> even learned to sing the "Internationale."
> And I sang that song with a ring so true,
> that now I'm in the prisons of the
> Gay-Pay-Oo
> [GPU or Russian Secret Police] (repeat
> last line)
>
> When Lenin and his boys the insurrections made,
> I found myself on the barricade,
> On Kerensky's troops I turned my gun, and I
> didn't stop shooting till the Reds had won,
> And I shot the gun with an aim so true, that
> now I'm in the prisons of the Gay-Pay-Oo.
> (repeat last line)

The album was not widely distributed, however, and those who did encounter it needed to be well-versed in the ideological polemics of the previous two decades, or pay careful attention to the copious explanatory references to unfamiliar events and personalities, if they were to extract much meaning from it.

As numerous observers of the American Trotskyists have repeatedly noted their propaganda was self contained and legible only to those in a given faction.[30] In terms of the Left movement of the Depression era versus outsiders the protest songs of Trotskyists generally were esoteric in character. In all, they were few in number and mostly addressed to the despised Stalinists and their foibles. Few compositions could be said to be aimed at the urban proletariat as a whole. Generally, Trotskyists tended to view music and singing as something of a waste of time. Paul Jacobs recalls: ". . . party meetings in Minneapolis [ca. 1934] didn't usually end with singing revolutionary songs—that was kid stuff, not for real Bolsheviks."[31] Thus little songwriting was undertaken, at least in the New York milieu. One correspondent noted:

> Considering all the literary talent around, it is in fact a

> sad commentary on the lack of imagination we displayed
> . . . . There were two satires [of Communist songs] . . .
> written by Bernie Wolfe and Ben Lieberman, and very good
> ones too: 'I Am A Dialectic Dope' and 'I Haven't Had My
> Worthy Cause Today . . .' And about six people actually
> learned the verses.[32]

This last observation is significant also in that it underscores another factor which limited the dissemination and impact of Trotskyist songs: most Trotskyist compositions were written in the more complicated and involved show business song genres rather than the simple but militant airs used by most American protest groups to rally the faithful and convert nonadherents. Indeed, it is hard to envision a mass audience singing spontaneously such lyrics as:

> Bill Bailey belonged to every radical party that
> ever came to be,
> Till he finally decided to start his own party so
> he wouldn't disagree.
> He got himself an office with a sign outside the
> door, with 'Marxist League' in letters red,
> And to everyone who came around, these were the
> words he said:
>
> 'Oh, you may be a friend of Max Shachtman, Jim
> Cannon and you may agree,
> You may get along with Norman Thomas and
> with Algernon Lee.
> You may be an old-time Wobbly, and think Jay
> Lovestone's fine,
> Yes, you may be a comrade to all of these folks,
> but you ain't no comrade of mine.[33]

And so on, with a different cast of personalities in each succeeding chorus.

To be sure, the Shachtmanite faction of American Trotskyism did sporadically direct its musical and dramatic appeals to mass or exoteric audiences, as seen in the post-war election and other skits in Detroit and in the songs written by Kuppy Scott. But as Trotskyism never developed a *raison d'etre* of its own except to offer an opposition to Stalinist Communism so its cultural products have little meaning or purpose outside of this context. As such, the songs and skits of American Trotskyism remain largely a footnote to the more viable and dynamic arts of the Communist movement of the Depression years and after.

PROTEST
SONGS
OF THE
OLD
AND
NEW
LEFT

Social movements and 'protest publics' have historically utilized song to promote ideology and to achieve organizational cohesion.[1] These world changers have drawn upon the musical idioms of their sphere of operation. Social movements have employed popular standards such as "Casey Jones" and the "Battle Hymn of the Republic" to communicate themes of social discontent and *esprit de corps*. Ralph Chaplin, an I.W.W. organizer, wrote militant lyrics to the "Battle Hymn of the Republic" and produced "Solidarity Forever," the official anthem of the American labor movement.[2] Michael Quin, a Communist writer, employed the same tune for a May Day celebration as follows:

> We will end their greedy system which is rotten to the core,
> It has trampled out the souls of men and slaughtered them in war,
> It shall make the lives of working men a hell on earth no more:
> We Swear to Change the World
>
> Build the Farmer-Labor Party,
> And Change the Lousy World
>
> We are marching from the factories, the offices, and fields,
> With the hammer and the sickle carved upon our flaming shields,
> We have joined our might in common cause, our courage never
>   yields
> We Swear to Change the World . . .[3]

In recent years, college students and street people have composed pieces such as "Epistomology Forever," "Glory, Glory Psychotherapy," and "Structural Functionalism Forever," to disparage metaphysics, psychology and sociology to the tune of "Battle Hymn." "Structural Functionalism Forever," written at San Francisco State College, is illustrative of campus usage:

We have ignored the theorists from Durkheim on to Marx
We have studied all the trivia from scrabble to children's parks
We never suggest solutions to avoid all social sparks
For sociology is value-free.

Structural functionalism forever,
Terminology so clear
Journal articles now or never,
For the career it must go on.

We spend all our energy in a sterile white class room
While sociologists speculate on interaction on the moon,
They sit and feed it to us on an imaginary spoon
For the text books must be sold.

"Battle Hymn," like other standards and so-called American favorites, has received numerous alterations and treatments in keeping with what Greenway and others have labeled "ease of communication," that is, familiarity of the material.[4] Songbooks popular with both religious and political movements in the 19th and 20th centuries, generally printed only the lyrics, assuming that the melody was known to both the membership and potential converts. The structure of a song may also lead to repeated usage. "We Shall Not Be Moved," as previously noted, has been a standard with social movements because of its simplicity in adding verses and telling the story of a conflict situation or lauding a leader. The West Virginia Miners Union,[5] The Southern Tenant Farmers Union,[6] the Communist Party, and many other movements used the hymn to praise their political personalities. More recently, popular songs have been written by rock and roll stars such as John Lennon and "Country" Joe MacDonald in opposition to the Vietnamese War. Lennon's "all we are saying, is give peace a chance," and MacDonald's "Fixin To Die Rag" have become standards at marches and demonstrations. Both were first introduced in the mass media partially because of the prestige of the performers. Familiarity, consequently, is an important element in the choice of protest songs by social movements. The use of folksongs outside of the rural milieu is, however, a deviation to this pattern. Folksongs, illustratively, were disdained and avoided by Wobbly composers. Similarly, until the commercial folk music revival, they were generally unknown or considered as "novelty material" by the general public. As several observers have noted, "folksinging" is believed to be antithetical to the industrial urban scene.[7]

Kaplan, in one of the few sociological treatments of urban folksinging, describes the practice as "deviant in mass society."[8] The advent of the revival of the late 1950's somewhat colors and dates Kaplan's work since the introduction of folk material into the mass media legitimized segments of this genre into "mass culture."[9] In the context of social movements and protest publics, the use of folk material by the Sectarian Left of the 1930's and the New Left of the 1960's is to be considered a deviation from the familiarity pattern generally found in other vehicles of social change. Therefore it is of value to ask the question, "What factors were operative in the societal and organizational environs which engendered this deviation we shall call Folk Consciousness?" Folk Consciousness refers to an awareness of folk music which leads to its use in a foreign (urban) environment in the framework of social, economic, or political action. The addition of social and organizational themes to traditional tunes, the emulation of rural attire, and the idealization of folk singers as "people's artists" are all aspects of Folk Consciousness. Folk Consciousness, while generally endemic with the Left-wing, has exhibited a number of alterations and patterns of usage. The use of folk material by the Marxian Left of the 1930's and the New Left has differed sharply. One differentiation between the radicals of the "red decade" and those of the contemporary era has been ideology. Ideology according to the functional approach:

> . . . is to build solidarity and solidarity is the moral basis
> of society. Society is for Sorel a moral system based on
> class and held together by myths . . . Solidarity-produc-
> ing myths are 'good' when they lead to a higher morality.[10]

Social movements can easily replace the term "society" since ideology in the framework of social change relates to a "collective view of reality and its alteration."[11] Erikson, in discussing youth, sees ideology as explanatory and a means of identity resolution.[12] It then follows that identity resolution, vis-a-vis a given ideology, creates a "limited collective conscious" endemic to those partaking of it. As such, a social group denouncing ideology should be individualistic and multi-directed as juxtaposed to an ideologically committed collectivity or movement. This appears to be a key variable between the radical generation of the 1930's and that of the present.

Sociological Origins of Folk Consciousness

Folk Consciousness can be seen as a gestalt predominantly found in the Communist sub-culture of the thirties and forties. In a Durkheimian sense it can be considered an emergent reality (*sui generis*), that is, a whole different from the sum of its parts. The first ingredient of Folk Consciousness was tactical. During the Gastonia strike of 1929, as Shannon suggests, "the Communists discovered folk music in the person of a little hillbilly striker named Ella May Wiggins."[13] This "discovery" was transmitted through the articles of Margaret Larkin describing the Gastonia conflict and the role of the martyred Mrs. Wiggins. Larkin wrote in the *Nation*:

> These songs that begin 'Come all ye workers' and end 'Let's stand together, workers, and have a union here' are destined to be the battle songs of the coming industrial struggle.[14]

Several years following the Loray conflict in Gastonia, the Communist-led, dual National Miner's Union brought Molly Jackson and Jim Garland to New York to sing of the hardships of the Kentucky hard rock miners. The Third Period, or "dual-unionism" phase of American Communism introduced the song of persuasion into the urban milieu. The composition of the movement at that time, predominantly foreign, hampered the acceptance of this genre until the Popular Front Period, or "Browder era."

Another segment of this gestalt was ideological. Marxists, in treating the class struggle, saw art as being class-oriented, that is a cultural form was associated with social location. Art could be perceived as a "tool of the bourgeoisie." In juxtaposition, the proletariat was to have evolved its own artistic preferences. Therefore, in the 1930's Marxists and their adherents saw music as dichotomized vis-a-vis strata. Popular music was considered an obscurantist ploy of Tin Pan Alley.[15] Other musical expressions, including the classics, according to Louis Harap and Sidney Finkelstein were used to maintain the "status quo."[16] Consequently, the choice of "people's music" was ideologically focused. The Almanac Singers, in discussing their philosophy stated:

> People know inwardly that these 'hits' are no part of their working, slaving, worrying, and no solution to their troubles.[17]

and

> We are trying to give back to the people the songs of workers. Their songs have been stolen from them by the bourgeoisie.[18]

In the early 1930's a number of writers began to argue the need for proletarian music.[19] Music for these observers was a weapon in the class struggle and not to be ignored by radicals. However, as Charles Seeger suggested, "The proletariat has not produced any music of its own."[20] He suggested that music must be, "National in form: and revolutionary in content."[21] One of the few musical forms fitting this criteria was the folk based song of persuasion. Richard Frank, writing in the *New Masses*, synthesized ideology and practice by noting:

> When the American Revolutionary Movement finds expression in Negro music it is expressing itself in an idiom capable of arousing not only . . . [the] . . . Negroes of America but also all the toiling masses of America.[22]

and

. . . Negro workers are held at illiteracy . . . But singing
is their great form of artistic expression. In order to win
the Negro people most effectively the revolutionary movement will have to make use of this instrument.[23]

Woody Guthrie, the Marxian Will Rogers, at the beginning of the
proletarian renaissance supported this notion:

. . . most people don't seem to realize that there are still
thousands on thousands of folks that go more by singing
than they do by reading.[24]

A complementary variable in this awareness of folk material
was the tradition of mass singing in the Communist Party. Mass
singing in the CPUSA prior to the late thirties was centered around
Bolshevik material, English versions of European propaganda
songs, and some Wobbly (IWW) material. The staple of the movement was the "Internationale." An examination of the songbooks
of the period, such as the *Red Song Book* (New York, 1932), and
the youth oriented *Pioneer Song Book* (New York, 1933), show
a nearly total exclusion of so-called folk material. In the *Pioneer
Song Book* children's songs were given revolutionary meaning.
For example, "Sing A Song of Six Pence" was changed to "Mother
Goose on the Breadline, Sing A Song of Six Percent."

Sing a song of six percent
that is where all my labor went
whom was I working for
I worked for the Queen in the parlor
the King in the counting house
The King was counting dollars to clothe his lazy spouse,
My wife was worn with worry so the Queen could have no woe . . .

The song, after many verses, concludes,

What are we
What are we waiting for some day
when set before them with many a groan and cry,
They find a hammer and sickle is carved on every pie.[25]

One adaptation of a folk song is reported by Lasswell and
Blumenstock in the Negro neighborhoods of Chicago:[26]

That New Communist Spirit

Gimme that new Communist spirit,
Gimme that new Communist spirit,
Gimme that new Communist spirit,
It's good enough for me.

It was good for Comrade Lenin,
It was good for Comrade Lenin,
It was good for Comrade Lenin,
And it's good enough for me.[27]

It was not until the advent of the *front populaire* that the "Internationale" was joined by the "Star Spangled Banner" and American folksong. These coupled with songs from the Loyalist army of Spain, replaced the time-honored Bolshevik songs. Woody Guthrie, a major spokesman for Folk Consciousness, noted:

The best way to take a left hook at Wall Street's chin is to get the Union Folks [Communists] to a knowing the folks outside . . . and the best way . . . is to play them some music . . . John L. Lewis . . . said the Singing Army will be the Winning Army.[28]

As Oscar Brand and others have argued it was the Spanish Civil War that popularized the folk genre in sectarian Left circles.[29] Lawrence Lipton, in recalling this period writes:

Later in the decade the army songs of the Spanish Civil War, brought back by young veterans of the Lincoln Brigade, were sung . . . Anyone who could sing 'The Four Insurgent Generals' in Spanish was sure to be the life of the party.[30]

While Brand's and Lipton's casual assertions are dubious, it was during the Popular Front period that the above elements of tactics, ideology, theory, and personnel entered into the world-view we have called Folk Consciousness. Folk music, or its urban variation, for the adherents to this view, was the People's Music. The fact that Benny Goodman, Glenn Miller, and crooners Russ Columbo and Frank Sinatra were best known by the working class did not alter this sense of reality. Instead, these practitioners looked to the Spanish Civil War, and past rural industrial conflicts, such as Harlan County, as the indices of People's Music. Upon the concept of Folk Consciousness was elaborated an ideology which argued that "folk music was People's Music" since the People (urban radicals) used this genre. As a result, a "new folk community comprised of people's artists" was created in New York City, centered around Almanac House, the home of Left-wing hootenannies. A number of songsters put forth this position. Marjorie Crane (a pseudonym) in discussing the Almanac Singers wrote:

> Tunes that people know that are the body of their folk memory, carry words that tell of their daily life and struggles.[31]

The use of folk material in the urban milieu and in the context of social movements is seen as a continuation of previous usage. Empirically, as noted above, this position is difficult to validate. Indeed, numerous articles in reviewing the songs of the Almanac Singers suggest that the reader send ten cents or more for a copy of the material. Communist publications printed the words and music.[32] This then was the context of the proletarian renaissance.

Structure of The Proletarian Revival

The proletarian renaissance was collectively oriented. Performers were perceived as part of a class. Practitioners such as Woody Guthrie, Pete Seeger, Lee Winters, Molly Jackson, and others, were characterized as "people's artists" or interpreters of working class culture. One columnist wrote:

> Sing it Woody, sing it! Karl Marx wrote it, and Lincoln said it, and Lenin did it. You sing it, Woody, and we'll all laugh together yet.[33]

Other *People's World* writers typified performers of folk material as:

He has probably never heard of Marx or Lenin, but there can be no doubt where his roots lay, as he [Jilson Setters] sings.[34]

or,

People's Artist the first recipient of the title, Lee Winters will sing Earl Robinson's "May Day Song . . ." . . . this is the best way I can be a worker and serve the working class, and I think it is right now.[35]

The collective ethos of the period minimized the importance of the individual performer. Several folk entrepreneurs employed pseudonyms, and performers generally appeared as part of a total program. The structure of the left-wing hootenanny focused on a round-robin form of performance, where one performer sings and gives way to another. The Almanac Singers, the ideal type of the renaissance, have been described as an "amorphous aggregate." The reason for this is that the members of the group were highly interchangeable. One night in New York City three different groups, all calling themselves the Almanac Singers, appeared at various radical functions and rallies. When one member was involved another took his place. This group structure during the revival was unthinkable, since members of the Kingston Trio and the Limeliters, etc., were frequently celebrities in their own right.

The form of communication equally was collective. The practitioners of the proletarian renaissance interacted primarily with ideologically supportive audiences. Indeed, several uncommitted performers adapted the values of the sectarian Left through these interaction sequences.[36] Public appearances and exposures were predominantly in face-to-face situations such as meetings, rallies, and picket lines. Media exposure was minimal, with sporadic radio appearances and occasional recordings for the esoteric Keynote label. The renaissance can best be described as a self contained, organizationally sustained phenomenon, centered in several urban enclaves such as Detroit, Los Angeles, and the radical mecca of New York City. The self-containment of this activity can best be seen as a form of self-imposed and structurally-directed isolation. Performers such as Woody Guthrie refused to accept the offering of radio, for example, due to the censorship of the medium.

The collective factor and that of isolation is also attributable to the centralization of folk singing during this time. While various performers occasionally made national tours, the loci of this activity was New York City. Here traditional white and Negro performers altered their material to fit the ideological demands of the Left. Middle-class intellectuals discarded their backgrounds to become "working class" or members of the "leather jacket set." As will be explicated below, this was a far cry from the diffuseness of the commercial revival which arrived with force throughout the country during the early sixties.

The ideology of the songs of the isolated Left was acceptable only to selected segments of the society. This isolation is evidenced in the Almanac Singers position on the Stalin-Hitler Pact, where they opposed intervention with the album "Songs For John Doe," and shifted their position with the invasion of the Soviet Union, with the musical collection "Dear Mr. President." Consequently, the propaganda impact of folk entrepreneurs in this period was exceedingly small.

Folk Consciousness and the Commercial Revival

The commercial folk music revival took place in the United States commencing with the Kingston Trio's rendition of the southern murder ballad, "Tom Dooley." In its early years the revival was primarily apolitical, rarely treating controversial subjects. In the early 1960's the Kingston Trio recorded several satirical pieces such as the "MTA" and the "Merry Minuet," and finally the protest-oriented "Where Have All the Flowers Gone," an anti-war song. Concurrent with these developments was the rise of the civil rights movement and the "new left." The civil rights movement, following in the tradition of southern protest movements, used religious hymns such as "We Shall Overcome" in their meetings and demonstrations. Northern protest publics, such as the City Hall demonstrators in San Francisco, used some traditional movement songs such as "We Shall Not Be Moved" in opposition to the House Committee on Un-American Activities. It was not however, until the rise of Bob Dylan that protest songs were adapted in toto by northern protest publics. This incorporation also brought several survivors of the proletarian renaissance into prominence once again. Pete Seeger, although blacklisted until 1967 from television, was able to reach a far wider audience than in years past. The songs of Woody Guthrie and other singers of the 1930's were revived to some extent prior to Bob Dylan. Dylan, Paxton, Ochs, and others, while utilizing the folk genre, composed and altered the words and melodies of many traditional pieces, as well as writing their own.

The term "revival" in the sociological literature is derived from the religious movements of the 19th century in America, and suggests an "awakening." This entails the elements of discovery or rediscovery of an existent phenomenon or behavior pattern. Smelser, for one, suggests that, ". . . social changes in the recent past have reduced the churches' access to large bodies of potentially faithful who, it is felt, need the spiritual services of the church."[37] The notion of revivals, however, has in recent decades been secularized and applied to the fields of art and entertainment; for example, the jazz revival of the early fifties and the folk music revival in the latter part of that decade. The notion of revival will be utilized here to refer to the transfer of folk music from an esoteric series of "publics" to that of a mass audience, which in turn changes the elements of the original product into an "emergent reality" in Durkheimian terms.[38] As noted, folk songs and propaganda songs were generally confined to the isolated sub-cultures of the Left during the thirties and forties, although some entertainers did venture from this milieu into the mass media such as Burl Ives, Richard Dyer-Bennett, John Jacob Niles, and finally, the Weavers. The Weavers, prior to being blacklisted "out of existence," were the first urban folk-singing group to reach the number one position on the country and western charts and Hit Parade with their recordings of "Goodnight Irene," "So Long, It's Been Good To Know You," and "Tzena." While folk music enjoyed sporadic bursts of popularity with the record buying public, it was mostly considered a novelty until the Kingston Trio, Ernie Ford, and others demonstrated to the record industry that it was a saleable commodity.[39] As students of mass communication have suggested, success breeds emulation. Other record companies began signing folk entrepreneurs—the Limeliters, Brothers Four, Mitchell Trio, *ad infinitum*—and the revival began. Ironically, the custodians of the "people's music" were generally ignored in the early periods of the revival, and it was only after the supply of clean cut, well scrubbed college fraternity men had been exhausted or found lacking in public appeal that singers of songs of persuasion began to find acceptance in segments of the mass media. For example, Peter Seeger was signed by Columbia Records.[40] The songs of persuasion utilized in the early stages of this revival were most frequently those of the left-wing periods noted above. Union songs and "Dustbowl ballads" by Woody Guthrie and others were being performed by middle-class college students.[41] It was also during this time that middle-class college students were becoming the foci of the political phenomenon termed the New Left.

The New Left, despite the claims of its publications, was not a social movement at least within the context of traditional sociological definitions of this phenomenon. A synthesis of definitional statements reflects several dominant motifs: (1) movements are a group or organizational phenomenon; (2) social movements function in relation to some form of change; and (3) the members of social movements possess a definable form of societal awareness or ideology.[42] With the exception of the second element, the New Left did not fulfill the requirements of a social movement.

The lunch counter sit-ins conducted in North Carolina by SNCC (Student Non-Violent Coordinating Committee) in 1960 are widely regarded as the organizational birth of the New Left.[43] However, SNCC was but one segment of the New Left which was comprised of middle-class students, "dropouts," intellectuals, militant Negroes, and others, most of whom felt affected by some structural problem of American society. Unlike the movements of the thirties and forties, this collectivity of personnel did not possess any common solution or indeed, definition of the problem situation.[44] Jacobs and Landau, in their description of the New Left, point to the diffuse issue orientation by stating, "What began perhaps as a rebellion against affluence and liberal hypocrisy grew in a few years into a radical activism that protested injustice at the very core of the society."[45] As such, while the dominant orientations of segments of the New Left were civil rights, civil liberties, "democracy and equalitarianism," and peace, a common social awareness, best expressed by Mario Savio, dominates this aggregate:

There is a time when the operation of the machine becomes
so odious, makes you so sick at heart that you can't take
part, you can't even tacitly take part, and you've got to put
your bodies on the gears and upon the wheels, upon the
levers, and you've got to indicate to the people who run it,
to the people who own it, that unless you're free the
machine will be prevented from working at all.[46]

For the New Left social problems existed, and the "solution" to
this situation is within the realm of tactics, rather than ideology.
As most observers of the New Left suggest, the dominant characteristic of this phenomenon is dissent and in many cases disaffiliation. This last motif is found in the so-called "psychedelic or
hippie phenomenon," a group much in the contempt of activists,
but which provides personnel for many protest activities such as
demonstrations and marches.

The folk music revival and its impact on publics which are
considered a segment of the New Left—intellectuals and college
students—created a contemporary emulation of the performers of
the thirties, both in style and not uncommonly in dress and attitude. However, the role of the propaganda song in two decades
had changed drastically. Also, the injection of the propaganda
song into a sector of the mass media outside of the civil rights
milieu altered the traditional practice of transfer of material.
Urban northern protest "publics," while sporadically employing
traditional propaganda songs such as those of the thirties, placed a
predominant emphasis upon the material presented by successful
folk entrepreneurs, that is, the name performers of the revival,
e.g., Joan Baez, Bob Dylan, Phil Ochs, et al. Contemporary
"teach-ins" and other New Left demonstrations have featured
performers such as Phil Ochs, Joan Baez, and others to communicate their rhetorical indignation to an audience.[47] Ochs' rendition of protest songs at a Vietnam Day teach-in at the Berkeley
campus found him in one song berating the state of Mississippi
and in another American liberals.[48]

Most rhetorical songs indicate the ethos of the protester,
that is, individual dissatisfaction or alienation in relation to
the social structure, while lacking ideology or organizational alternatives.[49] In recent years, the Left, outside of the context of
marches, has almost totally abandoned propaganda songs for the

symbolic material of rock and roll as performed by the Rolling Stones, Beatles, Bob Dylan, in his post-protest period, and groups such as the Fugs, Country Joe, the Mothers of Invention, the Grateful Dead, and the Jefferson Airplane.[50] Several members of the last sextet, when interviewed, stated that their music was "apolitical."[51] The final death knell for the traditional protest song may have occurred at Berkeley in December, 1966 when at a student strike meeting someone shouted, "Let's sing 'Solidarity Forever.' " According to one account, "No one seemed to know the words. Then from the back of the lecture hall, a hoarse voice shouted 'Yellow Submarine,' a song popularized by the Beatles. A thousand voices took up the song as the students floated from the building."[52]

The southern civil rights movement, functionally utilized propaganda material adapted to hymns and spirituals. While some interaction of material between North and South does appear to take place—the usage of civil rights songs such as "We Shall Overcome" in northern marches and in the repertoires of folk entrepreneurs—propaganda songs in the main appear endemic to organizational and geographical boundaries.[53]

The Structure of the Protest Revival

The protest revival was patterned upon a hybrid of the proletarian renaissance merged with the structure of the mass media. The protest segment of the revival mirrored the 1930's with a twist of Thoreauvian individualism. The perceived style of life or rural "folk" and Dustbowl migrants, was emulated. The "Seeger-Guthrie" tradition was invoked and filtered through a sense of individualistic or existential reality. Peter Krug, a Berkeley folksinger, summarized this ethos:

> From this situation [the commercial revival] which has come to be called the Folksong Revival movement has grown another movement, shunning the 'folkniks' for their strenuous insistence on authenticity and at the same time condemning the commercialists for their crass insipidness and lack of artistic principles. These young artists either modify existing traditional material to fit their needs of self-expression or create their own material in the folk mode.[54]

The protest revival, as opposed to the renaissance of the "red decade," operated at several levels. The dominant framework was the commercial revival which had a wide diffuse audience being served by all segments of the mass media. Magazines, records, and visiting performers were to be found in all geographical areas. The primary appeal was commercial, as the success of the Kingston Trio, Limeliters, and Peter, Paul, and Mary illustrate. Within this context, remnants of the previous decades come to the fore, followed by contemporary adapters. Pete Seeger and the Weavers were "rediscovered" by socially conscious college students who employed folk material to nihilistically comment on contemporary events. For this group the organizational genre of the past became an individualistic social statement. This individualism, however, was merged with the charisma of media, that is, the star system. Dylan, for example, in rejecting the "cry for justice" ethic led a considerable number of "folkniks" into the idiom of folk-rock, much to the consternation of political ideologues.

The protesters of the revival emphasized individualism and commercialism. One index of the Thoreauvian individualism is found in the perceptions of the so-called "folk thinkers" of the revival. Singers such as Woody Guthrie, Pete Seeger, and Leadbelly, were treated in print and in song as charismatic individuals, apart from the ideological climate of the proletarian renaissance. Contemporary writers such as Tom Paxton, Phil Ochs, and Bob Dylan, idealized "the folk" in songs.[55] One Dylan composition, "Song to Woody" paid tribute to Cisco Houston, Sonny Terry, Leadbelly, as well as Guthrie.[56] A west coast songwriter illustrated this identification function:

> I never knew him personally
> And yet I feel I've known him more intimately
> Than the silver-tongued preachers who called him their friend
> And used his affection as means to an end,
> Their secret derision couldn't trouble his mind
> He was bound for a glory all of his own kind
> He laughed all his laughter, he wept all his tears
> And he loved all his life through his rich rolling years.
>   He is a man I wish I'd known.[57]
>   ("The Man I Never Knew")

While revival singers, with several exceptions, canonized individuals, the response to the ideology was negative. In 1959, *The Bosses' Songbook, Songs to Stifle the Flames of Discontent*, was published, which parodied and attacked the ideology of the old left.[58] An example of a song from this book is the following parody of Guthrie's "This Land Is My Land":

> As I was standing a mile long breadline,
> My landlord gave me a one week deadline,
> The *Daily Worker*, it ran this headline,
> This land is not for you and me.
>
> This land is their land
> This land is not our land
> From the plush apartments
> To the Cadillac car land.
>
> From the Wall Street office
> To the Hollywood star land
> This land is not for you and me.
>
> So take your slogan and kindly stow it
> If this were our land you'd never know it
> Let's get together and overthrow it
> This land is not for you and me.[59]

One singer derisively described protestors as "folk singers turned folk thinkers." The orientations of the performers of the revival also differed from their predecessors. Phil Ochs, one of the major musical protestors of the revival stated, "I'm only singing about my feelings, my attitudes, my views."[60] Another singer, Tom Paxton, in an interview indicated that many of his songs were personal statements of discontent. Paxton wrote the "High Sheriff of Hazard" because the law officer "was a bastard." Paxton further commented, "Every artist's first responsibility is to himself." Bob Dylan, on a number of occasions indicated that his main responsibility was to himself, and that protest songs were a means to an end, that is, a way of launching his career. This is a far cry from the collective ethos of the proletarian renaissance where performers "sang everywhere for all sorts of causes" in order to change the social structure. Guthrie and the Almanac

Singers on several occasions rejected commercial offerings due to the lack of opportunity to express their ideology.[61]

The Rejection of Folk Consciousness

The most striking differentiation found in the protest revival was the rejection of Folk Consciousness for that of folk-rock, which was a hybrid of popular music.[62] This repudiation was both political and aesthetic. As noted, Folk Consciousness was a deviation from the "ease of communication" aspect of propaganda songs. The adaption of folk-rock was a return to the familiarity theme. The socially conscious "folkniks" or the "voices of the new left" were products of media. They were raised on the Top Twenty offerings of Elvis Presley, Chuck Berry, rhythm and blues and rock and roll. Much of their musical knowledge stemmed from the recordings and radio broadcasts of the Kingston Trio and other media commercial offerings. This music of their milieu was "popular music." They did not reject, as did the "working class intellectual" of the 1930's, the offerings of mass media as obscurantist ploys. Nor did they desire to create a "people's music." As a result their musical attention span mirrored the caprices of the Top Twenty. Therefore, variation between the two periods under consideration is suggested by participation and media. McLuhan, in *Understanding Media*, suggests two types of phenomena based on participation:

> Hot media are, therefore, low in participation, and cool media are high in participation or completion by the audience.[63]

McLuhan illustrates this view by suggesting that radio is a hot medium as opposed to the telephone, since the first medium does not require participation as opposed to the verbal interaction of conversation. A similar argument can be made regarding the songs of persuasion in the proletarian renaissance as opposed to the material of the commercial revival. In the late thirties the notion of "mass singing" and audience participation were stressed and most songs stressed the "collective" aspect of protest. For example, Woody Guthrie, in describing a benefit held for migratory workers in New York City, wrote:

> In several places the whole audience joined the singers and
> the theater rang like the hammer of a blacksmith . . .
> [this] . . . shows that songs can be useful.[64]

One member of the Almanacs lamented to the writer that audience participation in UAW meetings in Detroit was confined to the "singing of 'Solidarity.' "[65] The medium of transmission in the 1930's and 1940's was primarily oral in an auditorium, meeting, picket line, etc. One index of this participation notion is the songbooks utilized during the period. The songbooks used in the proletarian renaissance were:

> designed to solve the problem of those people who hum
> through songs at meetings with that 'I wish I knew the
> words' look on their faces![66]

The contents stressed Spanish civil war songs, traditional labor hymns, Soviet songs and others. The Almanac Singers, in appearances as well as several albums, stressed the issue of labor and non-intervention.[67] The tenure of their songs were structural, that is, opposition to bosses and government policy with solutions of "organization" and "we won't go."

The revivalists exhibit a lack of continuity and individualism generally associated with mass media, which many of them were part of. Phil Ochs and Bob Dylan both disdained audience participation in their performances. Also, their appearances at political affairs did not parallel that of the Almanac Singers. The musical structure also excluded participation. The Almanac Singers described the structure of their songs as:

> saying the truth as simply as you can and repeat it as many
> times as it has to be repeated.[68]

The structures of most contemporary songs are patterned upon the lyric poem, long, rambling, and non-repetitive. Some of Dylan's songs, such as "With God On Our Side" contain ten verses without a chorus. The key variable, here, follows McLuhan's argument of media, that is, the revival artists used the medium of recordings, predominantly, as opposed to the collective mass meeting emphasis of the 1930's. Therefore, each recording must have ten or more selections. Equally, the marketplace prescribes a given frequency of record production which in effect saturates the mass culture with issues and individual statements of protest. In paralleling these two periods one striking element is that the proletarian renaissance did not exhibit media offerings of the revival. It was not until the publication of *People's Songs Bulletin* in 1946 that a "folk" magazine was sold in America. This mimeographed publication served three years, to be replaced by *Sing Out! Sing Out!* during the revival which was joined by a plethora of magazines glorifying the events and personalities of the "movement." A similar phenomenon is found in the recording industry. Only *Keynote* and *Disc Records*, followed by *Folkways* issued the products of the Almanac Singers, Leadbelly, etc. In the early sixties every American recording company marketed some folk and protest material. The effect of this deluge created an "underground top twenty" reflective of the popular music format.[69] Evidence the career of "Blowin' In the Wind." Dylan recorded his composition, *Sing Out!* and *Broadside* published the words and music. Peter, Paul, and Mary, and other popular groups pressed the ballad. Other protest-oriented singers learned the song and performed it until a new album or song caught their fancy. As such, the life span of the composition is relatively short. It is significant that of the thousands of songs written during the revival, few, if any have become standard fare. During the 1930's, however, the career of songs, such as those from the Spanish Civil War, showed some durability. Indeed, some songs of the period by the Almanacs and from Spain are still sung today. This media influence, coupled with ideology, may in part suggest two main differences in the orientations of adherents to Folk Consciousness.

Analysis

As Mannheim suggests in his essay on generations, age-groups can be interpreted in the framework of location and societal conditions. He argues that rapid social change alters the perceptions of generational units, fitting McLuhan's arguments in *Understanding Media*. Mannheim writes:

> The quicker the tempo of social and cultural change is, then the greater are the chances that particular generation locations will react to changed situations by producing their own entelechy.[70]

This position is quite valid in the Durkheimian sense of "emergent," that is, the musical statements of protest in the 1960's assumed a hybrid form based in part on the practices of the Old Left coupled with contemporary media. Media are seen as altering both the *Zeitgeist* and the entelechy of songs of persuasion. The songs that came from the generation of the 1930's reflected the organizational and collective feelings of "unity and power" for social change. As Dunson suggests:

> The songs came out of the unshakeable and immense feeling that the singer had discovered some truth, a plan that was going to make the world one of 'bread and roses.'[71]

The Communist oriented ballads of the time gave answers and solutions such as sinking "the system," "joining a union," or "coming down to the picket line."

The young protest singer of the revival was sparked by disillusionment and dissent in the entelechy of his time. The essence of his material frequently was fragmented by immediate 'outrages' shown him by the media:

> Here's to the land you've torn out the heart of,
> Mississippi find yourself another country to be part of.
>
> ("Here's to the State of Mississippi")

The tone of these songs also suggests that songs of persuasion may be correlative with economic conditions. During the Great Depression work was glorified in both American interpretations of Marxian theory and concrete reality. The Communists and other left-wing groups urged full employment and the nationalization of economic institutions. Many of Woody Guthrie's writings speak of a 'good job of work' and the role of Wall Street in preventing the attainment of this goal. The economic conditions of the decade may be seen as engendering a form of class consciousness in the musical material.

Conversely the ethic of the revivalist may be reflective of the middle class affluence of the 1960's, where the question of jobs or basic necessities of life are rarely raised. Instead, issues pointing to the imperfections of the social order are raised. Dylan's "Hollis Brown," for example, speaks of the plight of the rural dweller in the midst of plenty. Other writers hit upon issues of war and peace, civil rights, and a host of other societal contradictions. This differentiation suggests that economic contradictions may point to a singular focus, as opposed to those in the super-structure which do not immediately impact upon the individual or aggregates of society. Further research on this tentative finding, however, is indicated.

Finally, the above suggests that despite differentiations in world view, role of media, and generations, the tools of social and political protest remain remarkably similar. Tactically, the notions of separatism, mobilization of the urban and rural poor, and other programs of the "new left" can be traced back to the Communist drives of the "dual-unionism" period. In sum, a musical comparison of the "old left" and the "new left" suggests some similarities, which are out-weighed by differences based on ideology, media, and social location.72

Portions of this chapter, in somewhat different form, appeared in *British Journal of Sociology*, 20 (December 1969). Reprinted with the permission of *British Journal of Sociology*.

FOLK
ROCK:
FOLK
MUSIC,
PROTEST
OR
COMMERCIALISM *

"I can't get no satisfaction," blares a jukebox in a coffee house; "Look out kid you're gonna get hit," interjects itself from a hastily contrived speaker system at a hippie or collegiate party; and a beleaguered appearing group echoes the theme first penned by Bob Dylan, "for all the hung up people in the whole wide universe," at the psychedelically symbolic and visually narcotizing dances held weekly in San Francisco's Fillmore Auditorium. This, for the "love generation," is the anthem of both protest and hedonism. The label given this music is folk-rock, or as its critics have called it "folk-rot."[1] Folk-rock popularly refers to a fusion of material and traditions derived from the "folk music" idiom combined with the instrumentation and beat of the rock 'n' roll genre.[2] However, as several writers have suggested, folk-rock is generally a nebulous term. The use of the term "folk" is provocative since the "folk" elements present are manifestations of the revival interpretation of the idiom as opposed to any traditional genesis. As Dunson suggests:

> Entwined in the music and words of folk-rock are the segregated field of race music, white rock and roll, pop music values, and the protest singers and songs generally associated with the student movements of the 1960's.[3]

Bob Dylan, the so-called progenitor of the hybrid idiom, equally dissents from pat definitions. He is quoted as saying, "We're not

118

playing rock music. It's not a hard sound. These people call it folk-rock—if they want to call it that, something that simple, its good for selling the records. I can't call it folk-rock."[4] Most music labeled euphemistically as folk-rock is a hybrid of a number of genres and stylistic schools. Commercially, the term refers to anything an A and R man wishes it to. Nevertheless, folk-rock can be seen as an eclecticism of the Dylanesque "folk" style, the early Liverpool sound, Negro strains, rock-a-billy, and the so-called San Francisco drug sound. Definitionally a great deal of what generically may be termed rock 'n' roll is frequently called folk-rock.

During the early 1950's, the music industry was taken over by one type of music or "mass cult"—Rock 'n' Roll or rock-a-billy. The record buying public—the teenage or adolescent culture—focused on the offerings of Elvis and his many imitators. Upon leaving the adolescent culture and the musical values it upheld, the young adult frequently experiences the status requirement to differentiate his new role from his past reference group and values, in the context of Erikson's argument. This appears to be true of some individuals attending college. In the campus environment, folk music, in the revival phase, was a musical form bearing structural resemblances to rock 'n' roll. For example, the instruments used and the composition of groups in folk music were similar to those found in rock-a-billy aggregates. Folk music took on an aesthetic differentiation and past cultural associations.[5] As such, it can be argued that a dichotomization of cultural attitudes existed, based upon educational and class factors prior to the 1960's.[6] The disenchantment of the sixties manifested in the "new left" and the withdrawal or disaffiliation of the Beats altered this pattern of differentiation. At first, the cleavage appeared in the form of protest songs or songs of persuasion, versus the commercialized "folk singing" of the Kingston Trio and the Brothers Four. However, as typified by Dylan, the performance of protest songs in the folk idiom did not alter the social structure.[7] Consequently, Dylan, the pied piper of the folk revival, led his camp followers back into the teen-age musical culture of rock 'n' roll. This transformation of stylistic pattern also was correlative with a growing political sense of futility and apathy, in the organizational sense, by the "new left." Illustrative are the articles in "new left" literature condemning adherents to the psychedelic "astronauts of inner space" and the like. Irwin Silber, in *Sing Out!*, the dominant folk music magazine, attacked Dylan in similar terms.[8]

This musical stratification phenomenon can best be viewed in terms of Almond's differentiation in *Appeals of Communism*.[9] Rock and roll originally was "exoteric," while folk music via the individual was esoteric or "in." For example, prior to the revival urban interest in folk music was generally confined to academics and political partisans.[10] The popularization of the latter genre created a further cleavage of the esoteric. Dylan, Paxton, Ochs, and others were "in" while the offerings of the Kingston Trio were exoteric or "out." The shift of the former group—mainly Dylan—merged the esoteric with the exoteric qualities of rock 'n' roll, thus leading to the idiom of folk-rock. Here, there also emerged a new status differentiation in terms of "in" and "out." This differentiation, with time, has become increasingly complex and sophisticated. Songs which are played on the top twenty stations exhibit several perception levels. The Beatles' "Lucy In the Sky with Diamonds" has evidenced a multitude of interpretations including the acronym "LSD."

Folk-rock can therefore be perceived as a transitional phase from folk music to the mass cult of Beatlemania. The term encompasses protest songs and compositions such as "Eve of Destruction," "Mr. Tambourine Man," and "Subterranean Homesick Blues," made exoteric by the instrumentation and style of "mass cult." This form was popular in 1965, and is still found in some of the performances of Dylan, Simon and Garfunkel, and the Flying Burrito Bros. The mergence of "folk" with "rock," however, is not due *in toto* to the change of style attributed to Bob Dylan Several historical patterns reminiscent of dialectic progressions have become clearly visible. The major trend is found within the nebulous confines of the political-professional folk music "scene."

The "common-sense" image of folksinger invokes the stereotype of an untidy individual with a guitar and a bomb inside the guitar-case. Professor Charles Seeger frequently tells the tale of two Spillane-like officers walking into the Archive of Folksong in the Library of Congress demanding to see the person in charge of writing revolutionary songs. Similarly, Congressional committees and private vigilante groups, such as the Police and Firemen's

Research Association of Los Angeles, have pointed to folk music as a tool to subvert the minds of American youth. Within the urban folk music "movement" an analogous identification has occurred. Sophisticated urbanities, who perform songs of protest, are viewed as "people's artists" and therefore ipso facto "folk." Despite the classic view of folklorists as taken by Wilgus, Dorson, and others, prior to the revival of the late fifties, as dominated by the personages of the Kingston Trio, there were elements which justified the identification of protest songs with the "people." One reason for this was the fact that most early songs of persuasion, although frequently written by the intellectually oriented, were composed in the verbal symbols of the so-called "mass man." Moreover, as in the thirties and forties, songs of persuasion did reflect certain cultural sub-groups in the society, and their conflicts and sufferings, such as the coal and textile industrial struggles of the early thirties. During the Depression, sub-groups also revolved around social movements such as segments of the embryonic C. I. O., the declining Socialist Party, and the dominant Communist Party. The brief common focus of these organizations produced political songs of ideological protest pointing to the social system as being in need of change. Also the songs stressed the magnetic aspect of recruiting and maintaining cohesion and solidarity within the movements for which the pieces were written.[11] Performers of propaganda songs, such as the Auvilles, Molly Jackson, Sarah Ogan, and later the Almanac Singers, ably carried out this function. These songs, however, were limited to specific audiences and groups which customarily supported the values espoused within the framework of the songs. Access to the mass media of the day was limited, as the publication difficulties of the Almanac Singers and Earl Robinson suggest. People's Songs Inc. in a sense was a counter community to Tin Pan Alley. Songs preceding the revival stressed the organizational or "magnetic" aspect of social movements. In the early fifties, due to the excesses of political "patriotism," and opportunistic politicians coupled with the international power struggle, few of the movements of the past decades existed in their militant form or were allowed to function in a meaningful sense. The singer of folk and protest songs, who rarely had access to the mass media, was totally blacklisted by the efforts of *Red Channels* and other xenophobic publications. Only those performers willing to turn informer were exempted. It was not until the folk song and later the protest song became economically profitable that any of the giant recording companies employed singers of protest material, and this was only after the supply of clean cut, well scrubbed college fraternity men had been exhausted or found lacking at the cash register. Only then did Columbia and its peer record companies realize that protest songs did have some public appeal, however fleeting. In part, to return straying and more politically minded record buyers to the labels of the major companies, protest songs were included in the albums of the popular trios and quartets. Another reason for the introduction of the protest song was that the so-called "traditional" well had nearly run dry due to the ferocious appetite of the mass media. The trough of protest songs had yet to be significantly tapped. The Kingston Trio's watered down rendition of "Where Have All the Flowers Gone," which became a "hit," was a directional step. The song of protest, however, was legitimized by Dylan's somewhat unexpected success, and the simple fact that "it sells."

The growing exposure of the protest song and the then subtle change in the American culture away from the ethos of other-directedness, the Social Ethic, and the "silent generation" equally appear to have accounted for the success of the song of persuasion, according to Dunson.[12] The demand created by a growing audience of politically conscious students forced the reintroduction of singers previously confined to the campus circuit and the New York "hoots." An army of emulators followed. The introduction and rate of acceptance reflected the long standing cleavage within the folk music "movement" which only a handful of artists such as Pete Seeger have transcended, that is, specific rather than mass appeal. Dylan was known to a mass audience while others, such as Phil Ochs, were only supported and known by delimited audiences, as the cold record charts in *Variety* show. This isolation is not dissimilar to that experienced in the forties by urban folk singers whose main audiences consisted of militant labor unions, the supporters of Henry Wallace, and occasional radio audiences. The similarity, however, ended after two decades. The song of protest became a commodity in the fickle market place, to be replaced by the "Yellow Submarine" and "Grand Funk Railroad."

Folk music, in its broadest sense, is now a part of popular music and therefore subject to the frailties and fickleness of the idiom. As a consequence, protest songs in the folk idiom were increasingly at the mercy of the value system of the top twenty. Songs were discarded and accepted with the issuance of a new record or a fresh issue of *Sing Out!* or *Broadside*. This was a far cry from the historically minded audiences that the song of persuasion appealed to in the 1930's and '40's. Another effect is that in popular music, audience building is essential, and therefore, protest songs, due to their success in the folk music form must be exposed to a larger record buying public, in a word, the teenager, and his musical correlate: rock 'n' roll.

Rock and Roll is a hybrid musical form, purely American, incorporating nearly every lyrical tradition of the country. Long before the time that artists of folk material and protest songs, such as Dylan, discovered "folk-rock" during the Beatlemania, this form of musical expression was viewed as symbolic protest. The first time Elvis Presley shocked the viewers of the now defunct Sunday night Steve Allen program letters from indignant parents decried the corruption of youth. As observers argued in the fifties, Presley was the symbol of adolescent rebellion against the values of conformity. Some songs of the early rock-a-billy era did overtly protest, such as Eddie Cochran's "Summertime Blues" and Chuck Berry's "Roll Over Beethoven," matching the symbolism of Elvis in advancing the values and tastes of the teen world over those of their parents. Generational conflict, however, is a classic theme (e.g., "They Tried to Tell Us We're Too Young"). Yet it was only the emergence of the Liverpool craze, centered on English rock 'n' roll quartets and groups, at a time featuring social change, that protest became more than just a generational conflict of values set to music.

The popularity of folk styled songs, especially those found on the top twenty charts, recommended themselves both to rock 'n' roll artists and their recording companies, who are constantly in search of new material. One of the earliest of these attempts was made by Trini Lopez, who adapted "The Hammer Song" to rock-a-billy and sold over a million records. Again the precedent of success has been set, and in the world of popular music success is only to be imitated. One manager of a West Coast folk-rock group told the author, "We record what the A & R man sees is selling." Soon other traditional and topical songs were put through the amplifiers of electric guitars. On the other hand, folk entrepreneurs, frequently in satire, performed rock 'n' roll songs, such as Joan Baez's version of "Little Darlin" which was originally popularized by the Diamonds. Indeed, some well-known artists, at private parties, sang rock songs remembered from their teens. A point, all too frequently forgotten by advocates of "folk-rot," is that the contemporary city-billy grew up in the heyday of Haley and the Comets, Little Richard, Ray Charles, and others, not to mention the thousand and one over-night sensations such as Jimmy Bowen and Dale Hawkins. Also for the urban folknik rock and roll was a further extension of the blues tradition of Blind Lemon Jefferson and Leadbelly. "White Negroes," to use Mailer's expression, copied and preserved the styles of jug bands, blues singers, and finally rhythm and blues as performed by John Hammond. Given these factors, it is not surprising that folk and protest singers should employ rock 'n' roll as a form of rebellion, and, in juxtaposition, that commercial rock 'n' roll groups should use folk-styled material to make money. However, by the fusion of the two styles and value systems, the identifying features of the two became blurred, especially in the case of Bob Dylan and the Turtles, the Animals and the Byrds.

Dylan's role in the origins of "folk-rock," particularly his impact upon folkniks, is not to be underestimated. Dylan did open a new idiom for many of his imitators and followers; however, his defection from the folk scene cannot be explained without mention of the "Liverpool sound" or the Beatlemania of the mid-sixties which evolved into a serious intellectual concern of the late 1960's.

Exoterically, the Beatles revived rock 'n' roll in America after its corruption by the fast-buck mills of payola, Dick Clark, Fabian, and other fleeting "nubie" heroes. ("Nubie" is a trade term referring to the 9 to 12 year-old segment of the record buying public.) Europeans, as numerous observers have noted, have been greatly impressed with the offerings of Negro-American culture, to a much greater extent than native white Americans. Jazz in the twenties, illustratively, was an art form as opposed to background music in the speakeasies of America. Similarly, blues was both musically and intellectually treated abroad, while being considered "race" music by a large portion of the domestic population. As a result, when American markets closed to efforts of urban bluesmen and Negro hard rock singers such as Chuck Berry and Muddy Waters, they were still imitated and supported in Europe. One product of this interest was the so-called English rock-a-billy performed by artists like Lonny Donagan (e.g., Leadbelly's "Rock Island Line"). The emergence of English rock-a-billy and American rock led to a so-called "Liverpool Sound" best illustrated by the early efforts of the Beatles. The "hard-rock" sound, primarily derived from Chicago blues bands, was further popularized by the Rolling Stones.

Numerous interpretations of early Beatlemania have been offered by both social scientists and interested observers. These perceptions are of course confined to the "I Want To Hold Your Hand" era, prior to the consciousness-expanding *Sgt. Pepper*. The most popular explanation of the Beatles' original success falls under the heading of generational conflict, that is, a revolt against parental authority. Conceptualizations such as "adolescent revolt," "economic success by those under twenty-one," and "identity crisis" have all, at one time, been used to causally treat this subject. David Riesman suggested:

> It's a form of protest against the adult world. These young-
> sters are hoping to believe in something, or respond to some-
> thing new they have found for themselves.[13]

Another sociologist, Fox, indicated that the popularity of the Beatles stemmed from the dual roles of both adults and children: "They appear to be good boys who nevertheless dress and pose as bad ones."[14] Significantly, similar modes of interpretation could have been utilized in explaining the emergence of Elvis Presley as a national hero—the "hood" like singer who went to church on Sundays. Unfortunately, social scientists at present, due to a lack of hard data and in many cases lack of interest, know little about the mechanics of collective behavior, particularly in the realm of popular music.

Regardless of the cause of this mass phenomenon, English electric groups did begin a musical redirection in America, at various aesthetic levels of the social order. One observer wrote:

The likes of Frankie Avalon, Fabian and Elvis Presley sent

good rock and roll musicians running to folk music. Then absolutely the world's greatest musical blitz fell and the Beatles landed, everywhere, all at once. The impact of their music was analogous to the Industrial Revolution of the 19th century. They brought music out of the juke box and into the street.[15]

While this somewhat zealous account raises certain questions, it does point to the role attributed the English group in developing the ideology of American rock groups. This student continues:

The Beatles' ecstatic, alive, electric sound had a total sensory impact, and was inescapably participational. It was 'psychedelic music.' 'The Beatles are a trip.' Whether the Beatles or Dylan or the Rolling Stones actually came to their style through psychedelic involvement . . . is not important as the fact that their songs reflect LSD values—love, life, getting along with other people, and that this type of involving, turn-on music galvanized the entire hippie underground into overt, brassy existence—particularly in San Francisco.[16]

The "Frisco sound" is a corollary to the underground subculture of the Haight-Ashbury community. The music scene began commercially in the summer of 1965 when groups such as the Lovin' Spoonful, The Byrds, Paul Revere, The Fugs and the Charlatans, performed in subterranean San Francisco clubs such as Mothers and the Peppermint. Informally at this time Ken Kesey, author of *One Flew Over the Cuckoo's Nest,* in his La Honda home, was using rock 'n' roll with lights for psychedelic experiences, entitled "Acid Tests." In the fall of 1965, a group of individuals calling themselves the Family Dog, ("a metamorphic association of free spirits") formed to stage dances, employing the following rationales:

Rock 'n' roll is the new form of communication for our generation. We want to bring in the artistic underground, use light machines, boxes projecting a light pulse from the tonal quality of the music . . . we want to have a good time and meet people and not be dishonest and have a good profitable thing going on . . . music is the most beautiful way to communicate. It's the way we're going to change things . . . [17]

The Family Dog's first dance occurred at the Longshore-men's Hall on October 16, 1965, titled "A Tribute to Dr. Strange" (a comic book character) and m.c.'d by a local top twenty disc-jockey. Groups such as the Jefferson Airplane (named partially after Blind Lemon Jefferson), the Great Society, the Marbles (now defunct) and the Charlatans played to a full dance floor. Several weeks later a Lovin' Spoonful "Tribute to Sparkle Plenty" repeated the initial success.

The Mime Troup, an *avant garde* theater company, attempted a benefit utilizing the format originated by the Family Dog, which was equally successful, prompting business manager, Bill Graham, to rent the long dark Fillmore Auditorium for a repeat benefit. Again success, and according to music critic Ralph J. Gleason, it was a "smashing success," putting "Graham and the Fillmore into the rock business."[18]

The significance of the events in San Francisco is that an ideology was provided for the music. The ideology or ethos was provided by Ken Kesey and the three-day Trips Festival at the Longshoremen's Hall in January, 1966. Here music and lighting were used to create a so-called "psychedelic experience." The end result of these "happenings" was that a highly profitable platform was provided for the music and a quasi-religious ideology partially based on narcotics, especially LSD, was formulated. As Kaplan has noted in terms of protest songs in folk music clubs, this was a legal manner of deviation.[19]

While observers disagree on the remaining history of the "American Liverpool," it is safe to say that the Family Dog started the "scene," helped motivate Bill Graham and the Fillmore, and moved to the Avalon after "Fillmore went Graham and teeny-bopper." Equally, the Avalon today is perceived by some as more "hippie" as opposed to the "teeny-bopper" and "plastic hippie" orientation of the Fillmore. Again the notions of "in" and "out" emerge. There is nevertheless, a great deal of overlapping in this area, especially in regards to performers. For example, a so-called "underground radio station," KMPX, is mimicked by the "teeny-bopper" oriented station KYA.

Numerous other entrepreneurs have attempted to capitalize on the successes noted above, such as the Matrix, Rock Garden, and other night clubs. However, the prices of these establishments, not to mention age requirements, have made them shoestring operations.

As the so-called "hippie movement" evolved so did the ideology. The ideology added Dr. Timothy Leary's "Turn on, tune in, drop out," or in the words of its proponents, "Love, freedom, and experience." Not unlike Lenin's slogan of "bread, land, and peace," Leary's notions, especially among the teenage rebels, have heightened the previous generational conflict. The conflict in the eyes of many youths is one of normative conflict, that is, a partial rejection of the American Creed. David Boxer in describing the ideology of the music noted:

> It is a rejection of the traditional Western systems of thought. It does not make any difference that Dylan's poetry, like Blake's, defies rational analysis. It doesn't make any difference that the words of the Rolling Stones 'Have You Seen Your Mother Baby' are difficult, if not impossible to distinguish. It makes no difference at all.
>
> What is important is that the New Road is paved with 'emotional stuff' and it lets you feel what it's all about when you walk it, rather than telling where it's at.[20]

Anthony Bernard, in a paper delivered at the American Sociological Association meetings in 1967, expanded this theme by stating:

> Generally it posits a rejection of the 'order' of the parents and tries to describe a new order, one which is seen as incompatible with that already existent. *The references are quite often very subtle* and more refined than one might first admit.[21]

In the words of Marty Balin, leader of the Jefferson Airplane:

> All the material we do is about love, a love affair, or loving people. Songs about love. Our songs all have something to say, they all have identification with an age group, and I think an identification with love affairs, past, beginning or wanting . . . finding something in life . . . explaining who you are. . . .

A spokesman for another San Francisco group, the Wildflower, stated:

It is like communal love. I can't explain it any other way
and if you don't know what I mean, well all I can say is
come live with us. . . .

Recently other participants have indicated a similar inability to
verbalize the "meaning of the music."[22] Dylan told a television
interviewer the meaning of his music was "good luck."

The music under consideration has, on occasions, been perceived as a form of deviant behavior vis-a-vis adult taste. The
rationale for this perception appears to stem from political, legal,
musical, and behavioral factors, such as protest, drugs, dress, and
the idiom of communication. Ideology or content has, as we
shall see, a multitude of definitions.

Sociologically, as the above history suggests, folk-rock, analyt-
ically, can be viewed at two levels: the exoteric and the esoteric.
The former encompasses most of the elements attributed to mass
communication theory. These elements include the interactional
sequences of the market place personified by the top twenty format and highly stratified star systems. One illustration of the exoteric is found in the history of the Monkees, a group organized
especially for a television series, capitalizing on the previous motion picture success of the Beatles. The appeal of this group is to
a mass audience, primarily the "gum-drop" set. Exoteric folkrock
is *not* a deviant form of music, except possibly at the aesthetic
level of musical value judgement or a manifestation of generational
conflict.

On the other hand, esoterica may indeed be conceived as
containing elements of deviance and rebellion. Within the "rock"
idiom, songs have historically presented "in" meanings to listeners.
The rhythm and blues selections of the 1950's such as "Buick
59," "You Got To Rock With Me Annie," "Jelly Roll," and many
others employed terms like "rock" and "roll" to connote sexual
intercourse, as opposed to dancing. Exoterically, performers such
as Georgia Gibbs and other mass media singers have utilized, ludi-
crously at times, the same songs, such as "Dance With Me Henry"
referring to the dance styles of the period.[23] While the line of
demarcation in folk-rock is not as clear as the in's and out's of the
fifties, several indices are present.

The first, as suggested elsewhere, is labeled the "underground
top ten," connoting a popularity of songs which may or may not

be correlative to the selections of the top twenty.[24] However, this does not mean a total separation, since adherents to this popularity scale also comprise members of the "mass media audience." For example, "For What It's Worth," a song based on the Sunset Strip riots in Los Angeles, by the Buffalo Springfield, made both the exoteric and esoteric hit parades. Conversely, early selections by groups as the Jefferson Airplane, Cream, the Grateful Dead, Moby Grape and others were customarily popular with "insiders" as opposed to the fans of the top twenty stations. The San Francisco top twenty stations for nearly a year refused to play the material by local groups. Several factors may account for this differentiation in popularity scaling. First, esoteric songs frequently exceed the so-called three-minute structures of "popular songs" thus limiting exposure. For example, Dylan's "Rainy Day Women" was cut to meet the demands of pop stations. Only the Beatles, it seems, are exempt from this restrictive time limitation. Secondly, the definitions of both "publics" may not be similar. The artists' perceptions and meanings are differentiated, thus, acceptability is varied. Finally, the exposure factor is frequently limited by age and geography. According to *Variety*, the "nubies" purchase a majority of 45 rpm singles, yet this age group is barred from attending dances which feature many groups not found on the mass media. Therefore, this factor alone skews the popularity charts. One example of this phenomenon is illustrated by so-called "All-Time Top 300 Record" polls. Of the songs chosen a majority are always more contemporary, that is, no more than several years old. However, in the last hundred songs, a majority are of a five to ten year duration. This in part supports the age-popularity hypothesis. Another element of differentiation is found in content and perception or the definition of the situation. One observer has suggested that:

> There is plenty of disagreement over how much—if any—'Junky words' are being used, since some people hear them and others don't listening to the same song. There is some concern by some observers that so-called 'drug songs' might cause youngsters to try drugs, while others say mere lyrics have no effect.[25]
>
> . . . you know what we mean wink to teenagers while disclaiming all evil intents to adults.[26]

"Definitional songs," as we shall term these, have for years been sexually suggestive; however, songs featuring drugs are relatively new, at least in the mass media. "Take a Whiff On Me," "Candy Man," "Cocaine Blues," and other blues and folk songs were sung during the revival. However, it was Dylan who originally penned, prior to "Subterranean Homesick Blues," a drug song entitled "Mr. Tambourine Man," a pseudonym for "brother cowboy," "mother," that is, a pusher. Dylan's song was picked up by several rock groups and given an alteration in lyrics. One can conclude that they either were censored or had little conception of the original meaning. Other songs on the top twenty such as "Sunshine Superman," "Eight Miles High," "Mother's Little Helper," "Along Comes Mary," and "Rainy Day Women No. 12 and 35" also have been interpreted as being songs that deal with the drug theme.[27]

On the other hand, songs of an esoteric nature have overtly dealt with the subject. Donovan's album *Sunshine Superman*, featuring "The Trip," "Fat Angel" and others, makes little effort to disguise the intent of the songs (e.g., "we are flying at an altitude of 39,000 feet, Captain High at your service"). Equally, "White Rabbit" by the Jefferson Airplane, and a selection by Country Joe and the Fish are overt examples of the drug culture. "White Rabbit" begins "one pill makes you larger, one pill makes you small. . ." In "Bass Strings" the song opens with "I said hey there pardner, won't you pass that reefer 'round'."

Groups like the Fugs and the Mothers of Invention have made a relative amount of success in the underground exclusively stressing so-called "definitional songs." Needless to say, their exposure is banned from the mass madia. Ironically, while these groups have been segregated from commercial channels, recent innovations by their economically successful counterparts legitimized the "psychedelic" sound. However, even in this realm, only some people can totally appreciate "A Day in the Life," "White Rabbit," or "Two Heads."

In short, the degree of deviance perceived in folk-rock and in rock 'n' roll is primarily in the "eyes of the beholder." However, perception here is influenced by many factors such as understanding and exposure.

Folk-rock then is not overt protest in the historical sense. Indeed, many practitioners of the protest song are highly critical of "mind blowing" music as the editorial page of *Sing Out!* indicates. The music, however, is reflective of the social goals and aspirations of the "love generation," which are a far cry from those of the old or the new left. This may in part account for its commercial value since legitimate protest ceases to be meaningful protest. As Emile Durkheim indicated, what is esoteric one day may become exoteric the next. Not unlike the protest songs of the early sixties, the mass media has discovered that "vicarious deviance" may be profitable, or according to Lenin's dictum, "the middle class loves to be shocked." Or in the words of Phil Ochs:

> Many grew their hair down to their wallets and jumped on the Beatle bandwagon in true hands-across-the-sea-spirit. Palms upward as usual.

*Reprinted from *Journal of Popular Culture*, III:2 (1969), 214-230 by permission of Ray B. Browne, Editor.

credit: left--Cash Family Album; right--ABC-Television Network

THE NEW LOST CITY RAMBLERS

m. s. greenhill, mgr.
✳ folklore productions
176 federal street   boston 10, mass.
HUbbard 2-1827

**GLENN YARBROUGH, LON GOTTLIEB AND ALEX HASSILEV
(THE LIMELITERS)**

MOTOWN TEMPTATIONS AND MR. & MRS. BERRY GORDY, SR.,
were on hand to greet Senators Kennedy and Hart and their wives when they
arrived at the Recess Club. Shown above (left to right) Senator Edward Kennedy, Melvin Franklin, Mrs. Joan Kennedy, Dennis Edwards, Mrs. Gordy, Sr.,
Otis Williams, Mr. Gordy, Sr., Eddie Kendricks, Mrs. Janie Hart and Senator
Philip Hart. (Motown photo)

BOB DYLAN
(COLUMBIA RECORDS PHOTO)

BURL IVES

(L-R) Tony Butala; Jim Pike; Gary Pike

THE LETTERMEN

THE SHANGRI-LAS

Manuel Greenhill Folklore Productions, Inc
176 Federal Street, Boston, Mass.

JOAN BAEZ

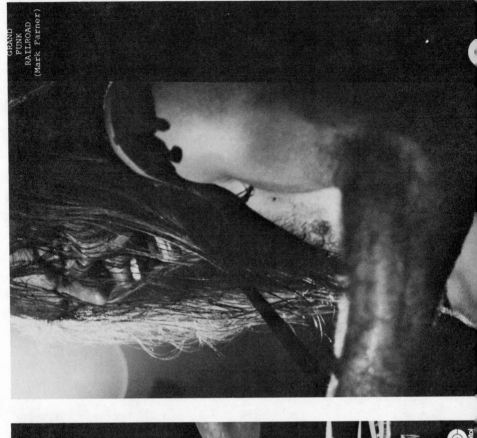

GRAND
FUNK
RAILROAD
(Mark Farner)

GRAND FUNK RAILROAD

Capitol

ED SANDERS

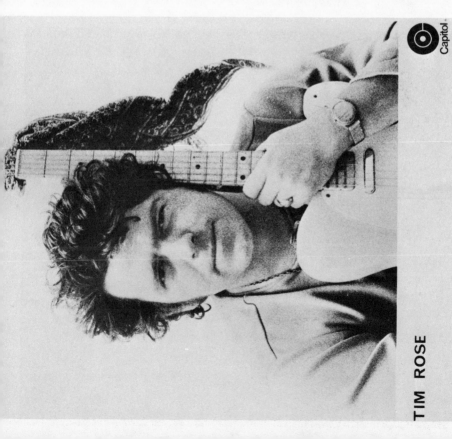

TIM ROSE

Capitol

PETER PAUL and MARY

JANIS IAN

GRAND FUNK RAILROAD

The Last Poets

On *Douglas*

PROTEST SONGS: THOSE ON THE TOP FORTY AND THOSE OF THE STREETS *

Give me the making of the songs of a nation, and I care not who makes its laws.

Conversation Concerning a Right Regulation of Government for the Common Good of Mankind [1703]

Andrew Fletcher of Saltoun

Presidents,[1] pop singers, radicals, as we have seen, have echoed this proposition.[2] Nevertheless, as we shall see, there is little, if any, concrete or empirical evidence that songs *do* in fact have an independent impact upon attitudes in the political arena. The few available studies of protest song activity appear to underline the correlation between propaganda songs and social movements such as the Populists, Wobblies, and Communists. In the context of social movements songs evidence the moral reaffirmation function rather than the one of building outside support. John L. Lewis' classic statement, "a singing army is a winning army," is indicative. Earl Robinson, Aunt Molly Jackson, Woody Guthrie, and Pete Seeger, in the organizational milieu of the Communist Party, used folk material either as part of their cultural heritage or as an ideological fulfillment of the need to identify with "the people." Although the pre-McCarthy period yielded a

133

flurry of propaganda song activity, the social impact of these tunes was severely limited by the isolation of the areas in which they were performed. Songs of persuasion in the past were little more than a "feedback" colloquy: the labor singer performed songs to audiences comprised of militant union members, the anti-interventionists sang to anti-war supporters, and members of People's Songs Inc. extolled Henry Wallace to Gideon's Army. Consequently, the songs did little more than reinforce existing attitudes.

Both practitioners and critics have, despite this fact, tended to see music as an effective external weapon. *Fortune* magazine, at one time, announced that picket line songs were comparable to corporation public relations efforts.[3] Other antagonists have labeled these ditties as "subversive ploys." The activities of Congressional committees and vigilante groups aided by *Red Channels*, a magazine devoted to "identifying Reds," and the McCarthy atmosphere banned socially significant compositions from the mass media for another decade. Protest songs were submerged and segregated to New York City "hoots" and liberal university campuses. The folk music revival, however, reintroduced protest material into the commercial media, but on a highly selective basis.

While People's Artists partisans were socially isolated in the 1950's, another segment of the urban folk music scene was not barred from the mass media. Traditional folk songs were injected into the urban complex by Burl Ives, Oscar Brand, John Jacob Niles, Harry Belafonte, and ironically the Weavers, and received some exposure. The Weavers, with their recordings of "Goodnight Irene," "So Long, It's Been Good To Know You," and "Tzena," were the first urban *folk* group to reach the much sought after number one ranking on the Country and Western charts and the Hit Parade since Vernon Dalhart's 1924 recording of the "Wreck of the 97." Right wing zealots curtailed the career of the Weavers, perhaps postponing the revival for nearly a decade, a fad which would merge protest songs with the mass media.

Prior to the revival, which was triggered by the Kingston Trio's rendition of "Tom Dooley," folk music enjoyed sporadic bursts of success with the record buying public. It was generally considered a novelty item until the late fifties. Commercial revivals, as students of mass communication note, exhibit a self-destructive consumption. Following the introduction of Southern

white ballads and Negro blues material, satirical songs were incorporated into the repertoires of folk-singing groups, and finally,
traditional and contemporary protest songs, hidden away all these
years, caught the attention of a large mass of young people. Protest songs became a means of expressing personal disdain for the
events of the early sixties. One of these dissenters in the folk
idiom was Bob Zimmerman, who changed his name in emulation
of his favorite literary figure to Dylan.

Bob Dylan, since his first show business success in a Greenwich Village coffeehouse, has gone through a number of musical
styling changes; topical and political songs, symbolic and expres-
sionist poetic songs in the folk genre, and later to a variant of rock
'n' roll, folk rock. This pace setter was catapulted into the world
of the Top Forty more by his song writing ability than by his
prowess as a singer. His early compositions were recorded by
popular folk singers Peter, Paul, and Mary, who placed his ballad
"Blowin' In the Wind," on the best-seller charts of *Billboard*.
During this period Trini Lopez's rock version of the "Hammer
Song," written by People's Songsters Pete Seeger and Lee Hays,
sold over a million copies. Dylan's direct audience was at this time
substantially limited to folkniks and a body of teenagers who
identified with the sentiments expressed in his lyrics. All of this
was altered by the issuance of "Subterranean Homesick Blues," a
rock 'n' roll number with, at first hearing, nearly unintelligible
lyrics. The electrified piece was a "hit" and some went so far as to
suggest that it was all one glorious "put on." One prominent folk
music publication, *Sing Out!*, issued an open letter to the "folk
poet" stating that he was losing sight of the fundamental purpose
of music; social protest. Dylan had chosen drums, electric Fender
guitars and amplifiers over Guthrie's inscription to convey his
thought. The end product of this transition was that a proponent
of social dissent became a force in popular music. Dylan was the
trailblazer. It was, however, a former Christy Minstrel, an apolitical commercial group, Barry McGuire, who exploded the "art is a
weapon" ethos upon the Top Forty.

A song, prophetical of the nuclear annihilation of mankind
unless social conditions change, became the best selling record in
the country in the fall of 1965, introducing the pessimism previously confined to the problems of going steady and "purple

people eaters." "The Eve of Destruction" was written by a 19 year old and designed to make people face the facts of "where the world is at." The song was more in keeping with the Brechtian notion of art, rather than the trials and tribulations of teenage romantic love. The theme of the song was that man was half an hour away from global extinction:

> Don't you understand what I'm trying to say?
> Can't you see the fear that I'm feelin' today?
> If the button is pushed there's no running away
> There'll be no one to save with the world in a grave
> Take a look around you, boy
> It's bound to scare you, boy
> But you tell me
> Over and over and over again, my friend
> You don't believe we're on the eve of destruction
> My blood's so mad, feels like coagulatin'
> I'm sittin' here, just contemplatin'
> You can't twist the truth, it knows no regulation
> And a handful of senators don't pass legislation
> Marches alone can't bring integratin'
> When human respect is disintegratin'
> This whole crazy world is just too frustratin'
> And you tell me
> Over and over and over again, my friend
> That you don't believe we're on the eve of destruction
> Think of all the hate there is in Red China
> Then take a look around Selma, Alabama
> You may leave here for four days in space
> But when you return it's the same old place
> The pounding of the drums, and pride, and disgrace
> You can bury your dead but don't leave a trace
> Hate your next-door neighbor
> But don't forget to say grace
> And you tell me
> Over and over and over again, my friend
> That you don't believe we're on the eve of destruction.

This piece, whatever its musical merits, was a breakthrough in a medium whose range of lyrical dissatisfaction was relegated to generational conflict. For the adolescent, the Top Forty was *his* music as opposed to the "straight" or "square" products preferred by his parents. Conversely, the genre itself was a form of symbolic protest. Explicitly some rock 'n' roll numbers did fleetingly point to the banalities of going to school and the interference of parents in adolescent love rites. Eddie Cochran's "Summertime Blues," the Coaster's "Yakety Yak," and Chuck Berry's "Almost Grown" may have dissented to parental control, yet none hinted at even the slightest alteration in this relationship, except "growing up."[4] The structure of "The Eve of Destruction" incorporated these elements with those previously cited to create a mild furor.

The emergence of "art is a weapon" in the rock idiom was received with mixed emotions. Tom Paxton, a major contemporary topical song writer, stated:

> The fact that there has been a response by the young to these 'protest' songs is no cause for rejoicing. Anyone who asks of these idols that they probe a bit deeper will be disappointed, because these songs never intended to tell them anything more than Mom and Dad don't understand them.[5]

A teenage folknik in Northern California protested that:

> This new concept of uniting rock 'n' roll and folk music is a debauchery of all the ideals which made folk music unique and though-provoking.

Brecht's philosophical presence on the Top Forty and the growth of social awareness in American youth did not escape the gaze of the Radical Right. In 1963, prior to the blossoming of the folk-rock syndrome, the Fire and Police Research Association of Los Angeles called for an investigation of folk music as a tool in the subversion of American youth. The insertion of a protest song into the realm of the Top Forty doubly was a call to arms. David Noebel, of the Christian Crusade, wrote that the lyrics of "Eve" ". . . are obviously aimed at instilling fear in our teenagers as well as . . . [inducing] the American public to surrender to atheistic, international Communism."[6] Groups such as Citizens for Conservative Action and the Young Republicans for a Return to Conservatism in California filed a complaint with the Federal Communications Commission arguing that "Eve" and similar songs violated the equal time proviso, and contacted popular rock 'n' roll aggregates in an attempt either to ban or refute the message of the controversial song. Decca Records jumped on the political bandwagon with the "Dawn of Correction" by the Spokesmen. The ideological antithesis of "Eve" was not a commercial success. As this outcry illustrates, neither the advocates of the Guthrie-Seeger tradition or the Radical Right were overjoyed with this type of protest on the mass airwaves. The Left objected to the aesthetic supporting the sentiment. The Radical Right partially discounted the idiom and concentrated on the content. Both agreed that music was a powerful opinion formation device. The popularity of "The Eve of Destruction" raised a question which has not generally been treated by social scientists: "Is Art An Effective Weapon?" More specifically, do protest songs on the Top Forty have any perceivable impact upon their generalized audiences? The mass exposure of "The Eve of Destruction" provided an excellent opportunity to gain some insights in this sphere.

During the period that "The Eve of Destruction" received extensive airplay the writer administered a questionnaire to a random sample of students at a junior college in the San Francisco area. The school was chosen for several features. First, the subjects were either freshmen or sophomores, thus attuned to the offerings of the Top Forty. Secondly, due to the programs offered by the college a representative sample of the general population was possible. The curriculum included both vocational and academic courses. Finally, the student body was generally conservative and apolitical as contrasted to the four-year schools in the region such as the University of California at Berkeley and San Francisco State College. For example, only the Young Republicans existed *sub-rosa* on the campus. Political groups were banned. Students the previous semester, the spring of 1965, had overwhelmingly rejected the attempts of a small band of on and off campus radicals to institute free speech reforms at the junior college. This latter factor appeared to make the sample ideal to measure the impact of a song considered left-of-center.

The students were posed questions to determine the following aspects of propaganda songs: (1) exposure, (2) intelligibility of lyrics, and (3) the responses of listeners.

The injection of protest material into the offerings of the Top Forty did, as expected, greatly increase the audience for this fare. Of those sampled, 88 percent (158) had heard "The Eve of Destruction." Eighty-six percent of the total sample were first exposed to the song on the radio. As such, the Top Forty proved to be an excellent medium for the exposure of political ideology when addressed to teenagers and young adults. "The Eve of Destruction" reached a sizeable portion of the sample, suggesting that it far outshadowed efforts in the folk genre in past decades to reach a mass audience.

A number of critical observers, especially those wedded to the people's song ethos of folk music, have argued that rock 'n' roll is a poor idiom of transmission for political propaganda. Many persons in the "over thirty" category also have expressed the view that "rock" lyrics are basically unintelligible. Others have added the notion that the selections on the Top Forty are little more than background noise. The respondents weakly supported these contentions since only 36 percent interpreted "The Eve of Destruction" in the composers' terms. Thirty-seven percent expressed some of the sentiments of the song and 23 percent entirely misconstrued the intent of the lyric. From another perspective, a majority, 73 percent, did assimilate part or all of the message, indicating that rock 'n' roll as a propaganda vehicle is capable of conveying sociopolitical thoughts understandable to the receivers.

Attitudinal answers to the efficacy of protest songs centered upon three propositions: (1) approval or disapproval of "The Eve of Destruction," (2) would the respondents dance to a song expressing a political theme, and (3) did the respondents feel that protest should be aired on Top Forty stations.

TABLE 1 – APPROVAL-DISAPPROVAL OF "THE EVE OF DESTRUCTION"

Responses

Approval	81 (44%)
Disapproval	70 (39%)
Other	3 (02%)
No opinion	26 (14%)

As Table 1 indicates support for "The Eve of Destruction"

was provided by a bare majority of the sampled collegiates. This approval was primarily couched in the rhetoric of the uplifting quality of popular music, rather than the political sentiments expressed. Dislike for "Eve," as will be seen, adopted the stance of "entertainment for entertainment's sake," and rejection of anti-war sentiments.

TABLE 2 – DANCE POTENTIAL OF "THE EVE OF DESTRUCTION"

Responses

Would dance to the song	43 (24%)
Would not dance to the song	112 (62%)
Other	2 (01%)
No opinion	23 (13%)

The non-entertainment aspect of protest song is further explicated by Table 2. Left wing critics of rock 'n' roll as a propaganda genre customarily have pointed with horror to teen-agers and young adults dancing to civil rights and anti-war songs such as "Blowin' In The Wind." The detractors claim this behavior as support for their view of the rock genre as background noise. In this study a majority stated that they either could not or would not gyrate or dance to "The Eve of Destruction." This finding suggests that either the listeners are aware of the social signifi-cance of the piece or that folk-rock is not suitable for contem-porary dance styles. While the respondents did not feel that "Eve" was conducive for dancing, this should not indicate that restraint is *ipso facto* acceptance of the sentiment expressed by the song.

The key attitudinal question was the respondents' opinion of the efficacy of the protest song, "The Eve of Destruction." The query, being open-ended, received a wide range of responses, many of which transcended the particular song under consideration. A minority of answers reflected some of the attitudes noted, such as "won't replace folk music," "commercialism," and "Communist inspired." A vast majority expressed other reactions. Of those students responding to this question 45 percent were generally favorable, while 52 percent were hostile or negative.[8] Similar arguments were presented in some instances to support both rejection and acceptance of "Eve" and protest songs in general. The most common shadings of opinion invoked were intellectual, aesthetic, and political arguments.

TABLE 3 – EFFICACY OF "THE EVE OF DESTRUCTION" AND PROTEST SONGS ON THE TOP FORTY

Responses	No.	percent of total	percent of respondents
Negative	51	28%	52%
Positive	44	24%	45%
Other	3	02%	03%
No opinion	82	46%	----

Positive responses to the efficacy of protest song exhibited three fundamental themes: the song or songs were (1) "meaningful," (2) "original," or, (3) "saying something." These replies were by-and-large focused upon the intellectual aspect of "Eve" and the Top Forty with little attention given the musical idiom itself. Several, however, did have reservations about the use of "rock" for socio-political purposes. A sample of the "meaningful" replies underlined awareness:

. . . Eve of Destruction, it makes you aware.

. . . They are good. They stop and make people think even if they may not agree with theme of song.

. . . they are a unique way of protesting.

. . . meaningful, moody, emotional.

. . . important insofar as the message they relay.

As these examples indicate a portion of those positively reacting to political material see the songs as valid. Another segment echoed the same motif more specifically in terms of the medium of the Top Forty:

. . . I think it is very good that the people rock 'n' roll music appeals to are finally listening to provocative lyrics that do or at least stimulate thought. A few years ago the lyrics were very poor and were sung so badly that you couldn't hear them anyway.

. . . I like these songs because they're a change from the

usual song.

. . . It's great to hear popular music 'saying something.'

. . . Think there should be more of them instead of whiny half baked 'love' songs which are neither rhythm and blues nor rock 'n' roll . . . folk music or songs of commentary are far better. The American audience is ready and likes music other than pop as witnessed by the popularity of Bob Dylan.

Two respondents, unaware of the Guthrie-Seeger tradition, stated:

. . . 'Eve of Destruction' was the first protest song I heard and at the time it made sense . . .

. . . these songs represent the first breakthrough in rock and roll as an art-form. Social protest should reach as wide an audience as possible—especially the young.

Some, while concurring with the sentiments expressed in the song, dissented from the above respondents, viewing the Top Forty as an inappropriate place for protest. The motives of both performers and record companies were strongly questioned:

. . . Barry McGuire as a performer or activist is to me repugnant—his personality extremely artificial.

. . . they are made to make money not to win wars and stop them.

. . . they cannot be taken seriously since they are merely putting the whole world on for a buck.

. . . too commercialized, shallow.

While some concern was voiced over the choice of genres for political transmission, these students did support the anti-war message. On the other hand, no rejoinders were evidenced which applauded the song while disagreeing with the composer's position. One of the more politically minded students supported "The Eve of Destruction" on the basis of the civil liberties issue:

I don't think they are 'Communist inspired' as has been claimed. After I heard about the things that were being said about KYA for playing "Eve of Destruction" I wrote their general manager and said that I thought he was right to keep playing it.

As will be seen, a good portion of those answering negatively did consider "Eve" and songs like it to be radically inspired, and unpatriotic.

The negative responses ranged from "they stink" to "it's a Communist plot." Rejection, however, was based on both intellectual and aesthetic grounds as opposed to affirmative statements where intellectual factors predominated. At the intellectual level a common response was that protest songs were not objective. As the following quotations illustrate, lack of objectivity provided a rationale for rejection:

> . . . They present only one side of the story. They present no concrete alternatives, and the only alternatives I can see are anarchy or World Communism.

> . . . some of these songs put out a one-sided view, and should not be taken too seriously.

Answers in the non-objective category also saw songs as either too idealistic or sensationalistic. One student wrote that songs were "sensationalist, vastly overplaying existing situations." A similarly motivated statement was that:

> . . . it is easy to tear down society and criticize but it is quite another thing to give answers to these problems. These songs are negative and offer no positive solutions.

Other informants saw protest songs as being basically ineffective, frequently parroting opinions of social critics. One student said that songs do not have "any influence over the listener." In a similar vain others invoked the background noise hypothesis:

> . . . I hardly consider them entertainment . . . if someone did listen to them it might do some good. But then after the initial shock I bet kids just laugh at them.

> . . . [protest songs] . . . always will fail anyway because the younger teen set couldn't care less about what the songs say.

A substantial number of negative respondents did care about the content of the songs, citing lack of patriotism to subversion. These dissents operated at two levels: (1) lack of support during wartime, and (2) a generalized subversive plot. The "hawks" felt that social criticism was inopportune while the Vietnam conflict was in progress:

> . . . songs come at a bad time. We're in Vietnam and they are getting much more play than they should.

> . . . they are made by guys who are afraid to help their country.

> . . . Anti-American in view of U.S. involvement in Vietnam.

> . . . when I listen to these songs, I feel another page in the story of anti-war pacifists has been written. We have a tradition to keep up, and it won't be kept up by lying down in the middle of the street or lighting yourself on fire at the Pentagon.

> . . . I don't like Peace Marchers.

A more extreme presentation of the unpatriotic view was the "Communist plot" motif:

> . . . Put them in one big pile then put the pacifists on top of the pile and either burn them or drop them in North Vietnam with the rest of the REDS.

> . . . they're pinko.

Several others, concurring with the subversive nature of the songs, stated that these ditties "should not be *played* on the radio." A majority of students objected on political or philosophical grounds to protest songs. Unfortunately at the time of the study it was impossible to gauge responses to right-of-center songs which had not yet appeared on Top Forty stations. A minority of negative subjects dissented to protest songs on aesthetic grounds:

> . . . they were composed by people that do not know anything about music.

> . . . I don't enjoy these songs because the music and singing is of poor quality.

> . . . They can't make everything rhyme and still come out saying what they really mean.

> . . . from a musical standpoint they hit rock bottom. They don't add anything to the arts.

More specifically some individuals objected to a lack of entertainment value:

> Protest songs show no class. Songs should be written for
> entertainment.

Finally, some respondents dismissed the entire subject of protest
songs with epithets such as "they stink," "idiotic," "waste of
wax," or "ridiculous." This attitude was not uncommon, given the
number of "no opinion" responses. Perhaps a segment of respondents felt that protest songs were not particularly meaningful or
significant. The employment of the Top Forty as a genre for
transmitting socio-political ideas appears warranted when exposure
is a primary goal. A large segment of the "below thirty" age group
listens to this medium. Moreover, despite the critics, receivers do
in part assimilate lyrics, if only subconsciously. Most respondents
understood part of the message and would not use the protest song
for dance music. Those lower-division collegiates responding, at
least, reacted to protest songs in a generally rationale or content
oriented manner.

The affirmative responses tended to laud the advent of "meaning" in popular music, yet only occasionally gave outright support
to the sentiments expressed by "The Eve of Destruction." A
number of supportive answers implied that political statements
were commendable when addressed to other people. Another
segment approved of the content of anti-war songs, but objected to
the corrupting influences of the Top Forty. The interdiction of
protest into a previously apolitical sphere was both condemned
and applauded by those favorably inclined to "The Eve of
Destruction" and anti-war sentiments in general. A majority, however, had no opinion in this area.

The negative respondents deviated from the "intellectual"
pattern, somewhat. Many dismissed "Eve" and other such songs
as "unpatriotic," "subversive," or in other ways emotionally dis-
pleasing. Those opposed to the content tended to view the message
as not proper either for themselves or their peers. Opposition to
"The Eve of Destruction" frequently transcended the particular
song under consideration. This suggests that the main attitudinal
function of protest songs remains reaffirmative. Those supporting
the anti-war proposition generally accepted the idea of protest
songs. As noted, unfortunately at that space in time songs decry-

ing draft card burners and Vietniks had not yet blossomed in popular music circles.

The intellectual approach to protest songs on the Top Forty suggests that listeners view this type of indoctrination as just another political message. The fact that it is an editorial put to music precludes for many its entertainment function, which in turn curtails the propaganda potential of the piece. Both proponents and antagonists posited arguments appealing to the canons of objectivity and relevance. This puts forth the notion that while political statements in the ranks of popular music reach a large portion of the adolescent and young adult community, they are no more effective than a polemical column by William F. Buckley or Walter Lippman. Indeed, the public stature of these columnists may in fact increase their propaganda potential. One can only speculate upon the impact of "The Eve of Destruction" had it been recorded by a charismatic performer with a large personal following such as one of the Beatles or Mick Jagger. It is possible that the musical endorsement of a "rock star" would lessen the intellectual aspects of propaganda songs and heighten the emotional contagion.

Protest songs on the mass media do not appear to transcend the reaffirmation function, that is, fitting previous intellectual commitments. The fact that only 24 percent of those queried advocated the use of political material on "pop music" stations, and only 36 percent correctly interpreted the meaning of the song under consideration suggests that protest songs outside of a supportive context are not overtly effective as agitational weapons. This is a far cry from the role of so-called "freedom songs" of the civil rights movement.

In 1966 urban black militants such as Julius Lester were saying that "man, the people are too busy getting ready to fight to bother with singing anymore."[9] Prior to the popularization of the Black Power slogan, in civil rights circles the "freedom song" was an extremely effective weapon if printed accounts and observations of Negro rights activists are correct. A number of observers, including the late Martin Luther King, have credited "freedom songs" with unifying the movement, giving it the will to continue, and creating new courage in the rank and file members. As one writer put it:

They are dramatic emblems of the struggle and mighty weapons in it. Their steady, surging rhythms, their lilting melodies, and their simple, inspirational words, repeated over and over again, generate a fervor that can only be described as religious in its intensity. Even the least articulate of people can join in these group songs and respond to them fully, often the music serves as the best, even the primary means of communication between the people and their leaders.[10]

The majority of these songs were adaptations of songs familiar to their constituents. They were based on the hymns sung weekly in wooden Southern churches. They, like the Psalms, were directed inwardly. As examination of the lyrics of "freedom songs" indicates that unlike "The Eve of Destruction" and other popular songs, these tunes are directed to those within a movement or picket line rather than to a general audience. The lyrics are specific, repetitive, and simplistic. They do not utilize abstract concepts as does "Eve" but rather evoke immediate situations and solutions for those in the movement. "We Shall Overcome," the anthem of the civil rights movement, has been particularly effective in marches and other situations of confrontation, since it reaffirms the valor of the marchers and the righteousness of the cause in a highly repetitive manner:

> We are not afraid, we are not afraid
> We are not afraid today.
> Oh, deep in my heart, I do believe,
> We shall overcome someday . . .
> We are not alone . . .
> The truth will make us free . . .
> We'll walk hand in hand . . .[11]

Songs like "Oh Freedom," "We Shall Not Be Moved," "Ain't Gonna Let Nobody Turn Me Round," and many more all stress the role of a collectivity, a group, in achieving social goals. As the writer has reported elsewhere, 95 percent of the songs from the SNCC songbook (1964) were directed internally to those already in a movement or on a picket line.[12] Freedom songs were, therefore, aimed at the committed at a time when social action was in progress or contemplated. Labor songs of the 1930's exhibited a similar character. They were spontaneous and appropriate in terms of a given conflict situation. The songs of the civil rights movement of the South were what members of People's Songs Inc. would call "zipper songs." Songs that were repetitive and so structured that verses could be improvised to meet any contingency. "Ain't gonna let _____ turn me round" could be sung on the streets of any community. The simplicity and repetitiveness made the song easy to learn within a matter of minutes.

In juxtaposition, "The Eve of Destruction" was not conducive to group singing given its narrative quality and the number of disjointed verses. Civil rights songs were structures for group singing as opposed to "Eve" which was primarily suited for a professional entertainer. Moreover, popular protest songs are not collective statements of discontent, but rather individualized sentiments as to what is wrong with society. Solutions are not offered, social action is not advocated, and most importantly, the songs are impersonal statements sandwiched in between other Top Forty selections of a totally apolitical nature, not to mention commercials.[13] As such, propaganda songs on the radio primarily are entertainment oriented. Indeed, some singers of "protest songs" do not accept the sentiments of the songs themselves. To illustrate, Glen Campbell, who recorded the anti-war song "Universal Soldier," is reported to have stated that "draft card burners should be hanged."[14]

In a public witness situation or demonstration, commitment is dominant. As such, songs are designed to foster the "will to continue" in the face of adversity. The following excerpts from songs used in Southern voting rights marches are indicative of this function:

> My Daddy was a freedom fighter and I'm a freedom son
> I'll stick right with this struggle until the
> battle's won . . .
>> ("Which Side Are You On")

> The time has come to prove our faith in all men's
> dignity
> We serve the cause of justice, of all humanity
>> ("Student Sit-In Song")

These songs, as contrasted to the efforts of the mass media, are designed to achieve specific goals for a defined audience, in this case blacks. They are intelligible and political, not part of the entertainment enterprise. These songs, again, are predominantly addressed to those active in fighting "Jim Crow" rather than to possible external supporters.

The Top Forty audience is both heterogeneous and diffuse, compared with the 200 to 1,000 Negroes who followed Dr. King down the main street of a hostile Southern community. Resultantly "freedom songs" make little, if any, effort to convert the non-believer. Instead, unity and the will to carry on are stressed. This is a far cry from Sloane's "The Eve of Destruction" which chronicles the nation's ills and offers no solutions or organizational commitments, which could lead to amelioration of political and economic grievances:

> . . . you're old enough to kill
> but not for voting,
> You don't believe in war,
> but what's that gun you're toting,
> And even the Jordan River
> has bodies floating.
> But you tell me over and over
> and over again, my friend,
> Ah, you don't believe we're on
> the Eve of Destruction.

In comparing the songs of civil rights adherents and those found on the popular music charts it has been suggested that the one is genuine protest and the other is symbolic or expressive discontent.[15] Protest by its very nature is outside of the legitimate avenue of political action. Freedom songs most frequently were utilized outside of legally sanctioned milieus. In the jails, in confrontations with Southern sheriffs and police dogs, and at non-sanctioned or licensed marches, the freedom song was most frequently heard. This environmental and political aspect perhaps explains the stress on unity found in civil rights songs.

While "Eve" was a deviation from the normal patter of Top Forty programming, it nevertheless was within a socially approved vehicle of communication. Political songs presented on the mass media were not tied to overt protest situations. The ideological tenets of some conservative Americans were strained by the song, but if record sales are any index, a number of other persons did not see this song as un-American or objectionable. As Malvina Reynolds, the composer of "Little Boxes" suggested to the author, "the only reason that 'Eve of Destruction' was played on the air was because the kids wanted it." It would appear that popularity invokes legitimacy. Moreover, the song itself was legitimate since it was played by radio stations, few of which could be accused of left-wing leanings.

"Eve" was not tied to a protest movement or even a demonstration. It was not written for a movement but rather as an intellectual symbolic form of discontent. "Eve" was external to direct social conflict, but structured to an idiom geared to commercial entertainment. Most significantly, neither of these features challenged the social order. The listener, equally, is not expected to be engaged in facilitating social change.

Propaganda songs, both in social movements and on the Top Forty stress the notion of reaffirmation of existent belief systems. Nevertheless, it would appear that outside of an organizational structure or a demonstration protest songs function primarily at the intellectual level when positively received. An emotional response is generally associated with a negative reaction. Surprisingly, despite the exposure afforded protest songs on the Top Forty, this medium does not have the impact some observers have suggested. For example, the Radical Right's contention that "mass hypnosis" protest songs on the Top Forty are potent weapons does not appear justified. Instead, the most striking aspect of this probe is that a large portion of college students were totally unconcerned with protest songs.[16] This is possibly due to the transitory nature of the Top Forty. Songs come and go, fads change, hit songs last for a month or two and are rarely revived. Another interpretation is suggested by several performers. Neil Diamond, for one, estimates that only ten percent of the Top Forty audience listens to the lyrics of popular songs. While the responses to "Eve" do not support this contention, it would appear that the protest song is primarily seen as an entertainment item rather than one of political significance. Perhaps Marxists (the only ones to give the subject serious consideration) are correct in pointing to popular music as basically an obscurantist tool.[17] However, a great deal more research is called for.

Furthermore, it appears that for maximum effectiveness, protest songs must be linked to some supportive organizational form such as a social movement. Otherwise, the message is intellectualized without some possible social action.

In sum, protest on the Top Forty reaches a large audience. Once the message has been received, it is subjected to a number of responses, only a minority of which are affirmative.

The opinion formation function of protest songs on the Top Forty remains unsubstantiated with the burden of proof still in the hands of the advocates of "music is a weapon."

*Denisoff, R. Serge, "Protest Songs: Those on the Top Forty and Those on the Street," *American Quarterly*, Vol. XXII, pp. 807-823 (1970). Copyright © 1970, Trustees of the University of Pennsylvania.

MANNHEIM'S
PROBLEM
OF
GENERATIONS
AND
COUNTER
CULTURE

Karl Mannheim's sociology of knowledge rests upon the notion of "relationism," where truth is predicated upon situationally prescribed values of individuals or units in any social context.[1] Generations in this schema are viewed as: "nothing more than a particular kind of identity or location, embracing related 'age groups' embedded in a historical-social process."[2] With this unique relationship to a historical time and place, generations are conceptualized as possessing a distinct awareness akin to Marx's view of "class consciousness." Each generation, Mannheim argues, has a different or "fresh contact" with custom, tradition, and political thought.[3] Furthermore, in periods of rapid social change generations are likely to develop highly distinctive outlooks and aims which conflict with those of older generations, thus leading to political youth movements as groups consciously emphasizing "their character as generational units."[4] T. B. Bottomore has applied this conceptualization to the New Left in North America, writing:

> 'Make love, not war' is hardly an exhortation directed to the elderly. The fact that radical movements are animated and led for the most part by university students is itself enough to establish that they are primarily manifestations of generational culture.[5]

This view is predicated upon several assumptions, particularly the

---

*(With Mark H. Levine)

152

"end of ideology" thesis submitted by Bell, Lipset, and recently Boorstin.[6]   Bell and Lipset, in their controversial treatise, advanced the argument that ideological movements of the Left were irrelevant after the 1950's due to the exigencies of international political polarization and the rise of the Welfare State in the West. Moreover, Marx's Law of Immiseration, it was contended, had no persuasive power in the Affluent Societies of the West. While a number of critics came forth to challenge this thesis only staunch Marxist ideologues presented reaffirmations of their maligned position.[7]   Instead, most critiques were aimed at the "pluralistic and economic" assumptions offered by Bell and Lipset, generally ignoring radical alternatives. C. Wright Mills, in his "Letter To the New Left," was one of the few to urge that "intellectuals and students" should formulate "new theories of structural changes of and by human societies in our *epoch*."[8] Despite Mills' desire for radical alternatives, he dismissed Marxism-Leninism, stating:

> Forget Victorian Marxism except whenever you need it;
> and Lenin again (be careful)—Rosa Luxemburg, too.[9]

Since this famous "open letter" to the British New Left, nearly all the studies dealing with this political phenomenon have characterized it as non-ideological. In fact, the New Left has come to idealize Camus' description of the rebel who affirms human solidarity and value without resorting to the Hegelian Absolute Truths.[10] While contemporary North American Leftists were differentiated from their Stalinist, Trotskyist, and Socialist forerunners, they were nearly always characterized as carrying on the liberal, humanistic tradition of Roosevelt's New Dealism cherished by their parents, that is, the values of Jeffersonian and countervailing power as described by Galbraith, e.g., "participatory democracy."[11]

Keniston indicates that political activists are "living out their parents' values in practice, and one study suggests that activists may be somewhere *closer* to their parents' values than nonactivists."[12] The study, cited by Keniston, of members of the Students for a Democratic Society (SDS) at the University of Chicago, noted:

> . . . most students who are involved in the movement . . .
> are involved in neither 'conversion' from nor 'rebellion'
> against the political perspectives of their fathers. A more
> supportable view suggests that the great majority of these
> students are attempting to fulfill and renew the political
> traditions of their families.[13]

Early studies such as those by Keniston and Flacks appeared to imply that Mannheim's conceptualization of "generational units" was not totally applicable to the New Left. Accordingly, the generational conflict originally was most apparent between the Old Left and their New Left children. More recently, other investigations of the political attitudes of New Left adherents have come to question the "political socialization" hypothesis. Jansen, et. al., report that continuity of ideology and political activism are strongly influenced by the prestige of a university.[14] Riley Dunlap found little support at the University of Oregon "for the socialization hypothesis, as the SDS activists do not appear to have very liberal parents."[15] In effect, these latter studies appear to indicate that while students in America's academically elite universities, such as the Ivy League schools, may be closely tied to the liberal cosmopolitan orientations of their parents, others in the same generational unit are *not*. As student discontent and anti-war sentiment are dispersed throughout the generational unit, the continuity hypothesis appears to be less valid.[16] Due to the sheer amorphousness of the present anti-establishment sentiment, extrapolation from university political groups and other organizations is limited in value. As Roszak correctly observes, there is more to the generational unit than a "card carrying movement, with a headquarters, an executive board, and a file of official manifestoes."[17] It appears that with the increasing polarization and internal fragmentation of sociopolitical publics, even what was nebulously termed the New Left is no longer a viable unit of analysis.[18] Externally, the New Left has been isolated from a number of legitimate political channels and institutions such as traditional liberal, peace, and civil rights lobbies. Only the foci of opposition to the Vietnam War has kept some segments of the New Left in touch with older protest groups. Internally, the New Left has been shattered by the emergence of the New Old Left and the so-called Counter Culture.

The New Old Left can be defined and characterized as being ideologically committed to either Mills' "labor metaphysic," the idealization of the proletariat, or the neo-Leninism of International Third World organizations, e.g., the glorification of students and minority group members as vessels of social change. This newly emerging dogmatism has led to the inevitable internecine splintering so characteristic of sectarian movements.[19] The New Left's shift to increased ideological agitation has pushed it away from its natural generation constituency. This trend was clearly evidenced at the November 15, 1969, New Mobilization Against the War (New Mobe) rallies in two central urban areas. The New Mobe marches were designed to give witness to public opposition to American participation in the Vietnamese Civil War. Demonstrators assembled in both Washington, D.C., and San Francisco, to express their opposition to the war in a manner similar to the Aldermaston East Peace March. Crowds exceeding 200,000 in number were reported in both cities. In San Francisco, the tone of the rally can best be described as anti-doctrinal and non-violent. Speakers who invoked ideological solutions, and tactics involving the use of force were soundly hissed and booed as evidenced by David Hillard, the Black Panther Party spokesman who, professing allegiance to the tenets of Marxism-Leninism, was hooted loudly when he remarked, "If you want peace, you've got to fight, fight, fight."[20] Hillard received a like response following the statement, "You won't get peace by playing guitars or holding demonstrations like this . . ."[21] Other representatives of ideological organizations did not fare better. The greatest public accolades were reserved for apolitical speakers, particularly musicians.

Paul Schrade, a union official, labeled the Golden Gate Park rally appropriately the site of the first Be-In, "Woodstock West." This reference, of course, is to a rock festival held August 15, 1969, in upstate New York, attended by 300,000 to 500,000 youths. Here the participants lived on an open hillside, listening to their rock idols for three days and nights, with no buildings or conveniences. *Life* Magazine reported:

> For three days nearly half a million people lived elbow to elbow in the most exposed, crowded, rain drenched, uncom-

fortable kind of community, and there wasn't so much as a
fist fight. The whole world was watching, and never before
had a hippie [sic] gathering been so large or so successful;
so impressive.

. . . 'There are a hell of a lot of us here. If we are going to
make it, you had better remember that the guy next to you
is your brother.' Everybody remembered. Woodstock made
it.22

Given its success, Woodstock has been recurrently presented as
evidence of the practicability of a new culture and social order.
Noteworthy is the fact that Woodstock was apolitical; attempts by
political activists to radicalize the milling throng went unheeded.
The *Rolling Stone* recorded the following incident involving The
Who, a leading rock band, and Yippie leader Abbie Hoffman:

. . . Hoffman leaped onto the stage, grabbed a microphone
and announced that the festival was meaningless as long as
White Panther Party leader and MC-5 manager John Sinclair
was rotting in prison. Peter Townshend . . . [of the Who]
. . . then clubbed Hoffman off the stage with his guitar.
That's the relationship of rock to politics (emphasis added).23

Woodstock generally has been described as a "victory for music
and peace." A similar observation could be made of the Moratorium rally in San Francisco. While the New Old Left drifts into the
political esoterica of Marxsmanship a larger entity is becoming
more potent: The Counter Culture.

The Counter Culture is an amorphous representation of the
generational unit which cuts across educational and ideological
boundaries. It constitutes a social entity which emerges *en masse*
at given social events such as demonstrations, rock festivals, love-
ins, marches, etc., and then melts away until the next such happening. As Roszak observes, the Counter Culture is:

. . . something in the nature of a medieval crusade: a vari-
egated procession constantly in flux, acquiring and losing
members all along the route of march. Often enough it
finds its own identity in a nebulous symbol or song that
seems to proclaim little more than 'we are special . . . we

are different . . . we are outward-bound from the old cor-
ruptions of the world.' *Some join the troop* only for a
brief while, long enough to enter an obvious and immediate
struggle: a campus rebellion, an act of war-resistance, a
demonstration against injustice. (emphasis added)[24]

The Counter Culture is viewed as "experiential" rather than ideological, or as Roszak describes it, "ectoplasmic Zeitgeist" in competition with "values and assumptions that have been in the mainstream of our society . . . since the scientific revolution."[25]
Thus, as Roszak sees it, the Counter Culture is a product of the
demands of technology and the New Industrial State, as described
by Ellul and Galbraith, rather than the ideologically prescribed
causes of alienation and immiseration.[26]

The hub of the Counter Culture, given its experiential nature,
is the musical genre of Rock, from where come the heroes or
"high priests" of Counter Culture, the rock musicians. At the
Moratorium the greatest audience response was to Rock music, one
report correctly noting that the ". . . most ecstatic response of
the day . . . [was] . . . to several numbers by the San Francisco
cast of the rock musical 'Hair.' "[27] The next largest outpouring
was for the rock band of Crosby, Stills, Nash, and Young. After a
prolonged standing ovation from an estimated 200,000 persons,
Steve Stills walked up to the microphone, raised his arms with the
now traditional V sign, and shouted:

> Politics is bullshit! Richard Nixon is bullshit! Spiro Agnew
> is bullshit! Our music *isn't* bullshit![28]

A sentiment nearly all of the crowd appeared to share. It is precisely this anti-political attitude which characterizes the Counter
Culture. Given the nature of the Counter Culture, even the
broadest of political movements is not necessarily representative
of the *entelechy* of the current generational unit. For example,
even the most liberal estimates of anti-war demonstrations in
America have not matched the turnout for the Woodstock Festival
nor the Rolling Stones' free concert at Livermore, California.
Similarly, the continuity hypothesis of Flacks, Keniston, and
others, while true of their samples, does not begin to picture the
generational unit described by Mannheim and later Bottomore.

Instead, we must concur with Roszak, Leary, Carey, and others that "one is apt to find out more about their ways . . . [young people] . . . by paying attention to . . . pop music, which now knits together the whole thirteen to thirty age group."29

The thrust for this assertion is that while politics as an organizational phenomenon reflects less than a tenth of the present generational unit, rock music affects over eighty percent of this group. As such, we are proposing that Mannheim's notion of generational units in conflict can best be examined in terms of life styles and cultural learnings rather than conventional political ideologies.

Moreover, we would suggest that if indeed politics between generations are as similar as the above data suggests, then the so-called generational gap must lay elsewhere, perhaps in Roszak's Counter Culture.

Generational Conflict and Rock and Roll: 1950-1970.

Rock and Roll emerged during the 1950's as an aberrant, in the Mertonian sense, deviation, in that it connoted juvenile misconduct not in the lyrics, but in the presentation of the material, such as the dress styles and stage presence of performers. The key word, here, was "roll" suggesting sexual intercourse. Lyrically, however, as will be explicated below, the notions of adolescent passage into adulthood and "postponed gratification" were stressed. The adult generation at this time objected to rock and roll as "senseless and incoherent, and as expressing consternation as to how this genre could provoke such extraordinary interest."30 As such, rock and roll was perceived by the adult generation in the 1950's as deviating from the outward symbols of respectability, not the basic normative order. Rock and roll, as opposed to the Rock music of the next decade, did not question basic values or institutions. The fact that youngsters liked "junk music" was seen as a fad, one which they would pass by upon entering adulthood.31

In the 60's Rock music was nonconformist in that it was viewed as urging social change. The stress of the music of the 1960's was upon lyrical content, setting the stage for "rock music's connection with politics and social issues."32 Rock music was viewed not as advocating a "temporary role suspension" but rather as questioning basic values and institutions. For example, the senti ment of "turn on, tune in, and drop out," found in some rock numbers, stresses total disaffiliation. Drugs, discussed in some songs, also are viewed as a barrier for later participation in the system.

More importantly rock music has in time gained an intellectual respectability lacking in the 1950's. It was only in the late 1960's that scholarly interest was directed to this musical phenomenon. In the 1950's serious musicians and adults-in-general denounced rock and roll as *declasse* in an artistic and moral sense, whereas in the 1960's rock music was seen as innovative, *classe,* but as politically and intellectually deviant.

Contemporary rock music is the product of several *declasse* sub-cultures and musical genres vis-a-vis Middle America and popular music.[33] Rock and roll was a direct spin off from "race music" originally directed to urban Black ghettoes. Another important strain of rock music is derived from "hill-billy" or the country and western genre, occasionally referred to as "shit-kickers" music, connoting the "barnyard quality" of the product. This genre until recently was primarily addressed to a rural, white audience in the southern and western parts of the United States.

The dominant or *kitsch* society's exposure to "rock and roll" was originally through so-called "cover" versions of Black material. Here popular as well as country singers would take "race material" and make it usable for their audience.[34] This practice, it was argued, was necessary because of the emphasis on "roll" or sex in these original versions. For example, the Midnighters' "Work With Me Annie" was transformed to "Dance With Me Henry." "Shake, Rattle, and Roll," was changed by Pat Boone and others to exclude "obscene passages." Covering was not always moralistic, but overtly economic. For example, the Chords, a Negro group, recorded "Sh Boom" for the ghetto market. The Crew Cuts recorded the same inoffensive lyrics, added strings, and other *kitsch* trappings, and produced a million seller in the white or "pop" market.

In the country and western sphere a similar process took place, with Bill Haley, and later Elvis Presley taking Negro blues tunes and merging them into a semi-country or "rock-a-billy" style. Haley explained this practice to one interviewer as follows:

> Bad lyrics can have an effect on teenagers. I have always
> been careful to not use suggestive lyrics.[35]

Despite the innocent lyrics, rock and roll was associated in the mass culture with various *declasse* undertones. One of the original best selling records in this genre was Bill Haley's "Rock Around the Clock," the theme song from the movie *Blackboard Jungle*. Equally, Presley's physical appearance greatly paralleled and furthered the American stereotype of a delinquent youth. David Riesman characterized "Elvis the Pelvis" as follows:

> Presley created a definitely 'antiparent' outlook. His music—and he, himself—appeared somewhat insolent, slightly hoodlum.

> Presley was a much more gifted musician than adults gave him credit for, but he antagonized the older generation. And that gave the younger generation something to hang on to which their usually permissive parents openly disliked.[36]

Presley, as an examination of his early hits shows, was not in any way a social or political dissentor. Only his outward appearance and his stage posture, or lack of it, offended adult sensibilities.[37] Yet the lyrics of Presley's songs continued the "romantic love" syndrome of less controversial crooners, as with "I Want You, I Need You, I Love You," and "Heartbreak Hotel," a classic statement of the rejected suitor. As Donald Horton's work suggests, nearly all popular songs during the mid-Fifties were addressed to ancient courtship motifs.[38]

Early rock music rarely went beyond "boy-meets-girl-loses-girl" themes. Occasionally some song dealing with adolescence or the music itself would become popular, but generally the music was totally in keeping with social norms. Chuck Berry was one of the few "stars" who recorded songs such as "Brown Eyed Handsome Man," "Almost Grown," "Monkey Business," "Rock and Roll Music" and "Roll Over Beethoven" which questioned the status quo. The latter two pieces were direct attacks upon the more traditional musical tastes of an older generation as well as a reaffirmation of rock and roll:

> Don't care to hear 'em play a tango
> I'm in no mood to hear a mambo;

It's 'way too early for a congo,
So keep a rockin that piano
So I can hear some of that rock 'n' roll music.
                    ("Roll Over Beethoven")

The song continues to urge the listener to feel or *experience* the music and to "reel and rock" to its rhythmic beat. Some of his other recordings such as "Almost Grown" and "Monkey Business" stated the problems of adolescence, but concluded "Don't bother me, Leave me alone . . . I'm almost grown." Eddie Cochran's "Summertime Blues" is universally considered the first "protest song" in the rock genre. The piece is typical rock-a-billy or Presley style, emphasizing the hardships of part-time jobs, getting the car, and adolescence in general. The only political reference, however, was to the lack of enfranchisement.

Given the rather confused institutional references—congressmen have little to do with the United Nations—and the song's ending, "there ain't no cure for the summertime blues," the protest value of this piece was symbolic at best.[39] This feature was characteristic of all of the quasi-protest songs of the early Rock and Roll period, indeed, most of the songs ended in resignation to cultural diffusion and parental domination. In fact, several knowledgeable observers, such as Barzun and Riesman, have gone so far as to suggest that rock music was little more than "background noise" selectively turned on and off.[40]

One indication of the symbolic nature of the music was the summary blacklisting of rock 'n' roll musicians for alleged "misconduct." Jerry Lee Lewis' marriage to his teenage cousin resulted in his removal from the playlists of the Top Forty stations. Yet, rock was generally viewed by adults as beyond serious consideration and structurally deviant. For many, the payola or bribery scandals of the early 1960's only reaffirmed this belief. Substantively, it was not until the so-called Folk Music Revival (1958-1965) that lyrics began to address political issues and social dissent.

Folk music, as noted, has been utilized as a vehicle for social protest.[41] In America it has been exploited especially, but not exclusively, by the working class or left-wing movements, particularly the Industrial Workers of the World and the Communist Party. It was this latter movement which sowed the seeds of the revival, although it never succeeded in popularizing the folk

genre itself. Folkniks, during the revival of the early 1960's discovered the songs of Woody Guthrie, Molly Jackson, The Almanac
Singers, and of course, Pete Seeger. In time, they wrote songs
about the social strains of their period, rather than recalling the
labor struggles of the 1930's, and the Spanish Civil War. The key
figure in this transition was Bob Dylan, who wrote countless
pieces decrying racial, political, and other social dysfunctions.

Concomitant to the popularization of "protest singers,"
particularly on college campuses, was the rise of the Beatles, who
revitalized the popular music field. The Beatles, with their
Skiffle tradition, "covered" early American blues recordings as well
as writing their own material. Originally, their material was in the
romantic-love vein of "I Want to Hold Your Hand" and "She
Loves You." Several ex-folkniks, particularly the Byrds, a rock
group, melted the Dylan lyric into a Beatle-like arrangement, thus
coming up with "folk-rock."[42] In 1965, Dylan followed suit,
giving up politics and adopting an electric rock band, a move which
severed him from his folk music mentors and the Old and New
Left. In his song "My Back Pages" Dylan dissents from those who
see song as "a cry for justice" and Left-wing ideology:

*   *   *   *   *
*   *   *   *   *

Ah, But I was so much older then
I'm younger than that now.

Dylan's new popularity among Top Forty audiences, as well as
that of the Byrds, produced a number of imitators who tried to
combine rock music with protest songs. One of the better
pieces, which was relatively successful, was Steve Stills' "For
What It's Worth" which chronicled the police abuses of the Sunset Strip confrontations of 1966.[43] Despite the sales of this
controversial song, few other blatantly political songs have
been commercially successful. Indeed, overt political propaganda
songs today are more in the realm of novelty items, both
Right and Left, than effective songs of persuasion.[44] In most
recent years only John Lennon and Yoko Ono's "Give Peace a
Chance" has gone from the Top Forty into the political arena. As
we have seen, rock music during its formative years incorporated a

number of "deviant" elements from American society into a vehicle of the mass culture. Yet unlike the classic notions of "massification" presented by Gessat and McDonald, the popularization of rock music was in a particular generational unit rather than the entire population, which in many instances did not exhibit atomization.

Strikingly, in the later part of the Sixties rock music was strongly influenced by events in the emerging Hippie movement and the model of the Counter Culture, with its stress on mind expanding drugs. Timothy Leary, the self-appointed prophet and youth leader, portrayed the "underground movement" as preaching a message of "turn-on, tune-in, drop out."[45] In the drug culture, politics were generally deemed insignificant. What was important were the week-end "Happenings" at the Fillmore Auditorium and the Avalon Ballroom. At these events one was exposed to a total experience in mixed media. Wolfe presents one description of a night at the Avalon:

> Evening at the Avalon provides plenty of the ear-splitting sound characteristic of the hippie band. Continuously changing light projections of liquid colors and protoplastic forms bathe the dancers. Their luminescent, striped and dotted clothes glow eerily amid the flashing lights. Symbols, concentric circles, and pictures of Indian and Oriental priests are beamed onto the walls.

> Suddenly, the fast, screaming music dies down to a soft love song and then gives way to a mournful Indian dirge. The light show changes. On one wall there is a picture of Buddha and on another a picture of Christ on the cross. Several hundred of the youngsters on the dance floor join hands. They sway back and forth in a trancelike state.[46]

Rock music for the Hippie cult was a religious experience in the tradition of William James, Aldous Huxley, and as described by William Sargant. One critic notes:

> . . . rock concerts are religious experiences and today's rock musicians and audience view the church in the regalness of their robes and mystical trappings.[47]

More significantly, the music became a symbol for social alternatives, that is, a counter culture. The music for both generational units became an expression or *zeitgeist* of the rejection of deferred gratification and of limiting traditional rites of passage. The music's "trance-like" quality was viewed as deterring students from scholastic achievement. Songs such as "White Rabbit" were described as urging listeners to drop out and into the drug culture. Most studies of rock music, to date, have converged upon the musical message of individual freedom, "doing one's own thing," or the "hang loose" ethic. As Carey notes:

> The overall preoccupation in the lyrics is with choice. Choice is mainly exercised in terms of freeing one's self from external constraints, whatever their source . . .
>
> The lyrics imply two major choices, urging the listener to maximize his freedom in interpersonal relationships, and to drop out of conventional society. Dropping out is viewed as a positive thing. . . . Withdrawal is a response to the coerciveness of institutions and a decision not to collaborate with them.[48]

The "freedom of choice" in rock numbers is both anti-intellectual and anti-ideological. Rodnitzky relates

> . . . Folk-rock . . . is becoming increasingly anti-intellectual. The new stress on the sensory effect of the music rather than the verbal message is one aspect of the increasing belief that truth must be felt rather than rationally grasped.[49]

At a press conference the Jefferson Airplane stated, "Don't ask us about politics, we don't know anything about it. And what we did know, we just forgot."[50] A once political musical commentator described contemporary music as "a sensual experience . . . everything but an intellectual, theatrical presentation."[51] Only a handful of rock musicians, it would appear, have strong political commitments or views which are translated into their songs. Country Joe and the Fish, the Fugs, and the Mothers of Invention were the overtly political in the rock genre.

Despite the lack of political sentiment expressed in most rock songs, spokesmen of the older generation see the music as politically and socially subversive. The stress upon "freedom and choice" cited by most observers as major tenets of the American Creed, have been described as statements of "hedonism and license." In the 1950's Rock and Roll was seen as an "expression of *hostile* rebellious youth."52 In recent years, rock music has come to be viewed as politically dissident and morally subversive. This is in keeping with Mannheim's suggestion that rapidity of social change leads to differential perception and ideological interpretation. As we have seen, musical styles in the last two decades changed with a rapidity not previously experienced. It appears that as musical changes occur, greater concern is expressed by those wedded to genres of the past.53

During the folk revival this "youth rebellion" came to be seen as subversive by conservative groups such as the John Birch Society and particularly, David Noebel of the Christian Crusade.54 More recently, adults have objected to rock music as an advocate of drugs and anti-establishment attitudes. The older generation's view of music has several fundamental historical roots. The first root of the older generation's view of popular music is the austere religious notion that non-religious art is sinful.55 Early American clergy, as well as American fundamentalists today, saw "secular music" as the tool of the Devil. As such, the enjoyment of "secular music," especially by the young, was viewed as Devil's work.

This demonic tenet of frontier Christianity leads to a second underlying cause for the "music is deviant" view: conspiracy. The Devil was perceived as engaging in a conspiratorial war for men's souls. He, of course, relied upon the tools of trickery and other machinations to achieve his goals. This is particularly true in the case of the youth, who, what with the image of the Pied Piper of Hamelin, has been seen as susceptible to corruption due to his un-awareness of evil. Most recent discussions of rock music, by its opponents, have exhibited these two trends:

> Throw your Beatle and rock and roll records in the city dump. We have been unashamed of being labeled a Christian nation . . . let's make sure four mop-headed anti-Christ beatniks don't destroy our children's emotional and mental stability and ultimately destroy our nation as Plato warned in his Republic.56

A president of a large independent chain of radio stations stated:

> We've had all we can stand of the record industry's glorify-
> ing marijuana, LSD, and sexual activity. The newest
> Beatles record has a line of 40,000 purple hearts in one
> arm. Is that what you want your children to listen to?[57]

Art Linkletter, appearing before a Congressional committee, argued
that rock and roll was little more than an inducement to take
drugs:

> In the Top 40 half the songs are secret messages to the
> teen world to drop out, turn on, and groove with chemicals
> and light shows at discotheques. Most of the jackets of
> record albums are merely signboards of psychedelia.[58]

One fundamental interpretation of these divergent views of rock
music is provided in Mannheim's notion of relationism and generational units. That is, generational units perceive the ideology of the
music in totally different ways: the following excerpt from an interview with the First Edition, a pop rock group, is illustrative of
Mannheim's relationism:

> They [adolescents] . . . realize the average person outside
> of their age category does not put that depth into it and
> it's a way of saying, 'I know more than you do' because I
> read something into that . . . you don't even see.
>
> Records say things very plainly and in very plain words, but
> adults don't understand them either. . . .[59]

Belz and others appear sympathetic to this position, suggesting that
"adults" have generally seen Rock 'n' Roll as lyrically "senseless
and incoherent" and could not understand how their children
could enjoy this type of music. As such, rock music is believed to
be a significant area of generational contention.

Rock and Roll, as well as Rock music, appealed to young
people. Neither appealed particularly to the adult generation, although rock music, given its more ideational or intellectual quality,
does appeal to a wider age range than its forerunner. The generational conflict over music in the 1950's, we have argued, revolved
around the representative and symbolic aspects of the music as
well as its shady origins. The generational conflict of the present
era no longer touches upon issues of symbolism or musical structure or the appearance of performers, rather the debate focuses

more on the lyrical content of the material.

In sum, we are suggesting that political indices of generational conflict, the socialization hypothesis presented by Blacks and others, have not been conclusive in regard to Mannheim's thesis of generational units and social protest. Instead, we have suggested that the Counter Culture may be a more fruitful area of investigation vis-a-vis "generational units." Moreover, it was indicated that rock music was an important factor in the life style of the counter culture and indeed the entire generational unit.

Generational Units: Music and Political Attitudes

The preceding discussion suggests a number of hypotheses, of which two are paramount: 1) differentiations between generational units will be greater than in intra-generational units; 2) differentiations, if the counter-culture thesis is correct, will be greater between generational units in the sphere of rock music than in political attitudes. The first hypothesis is addressed to establishing or falsifying Mannheim's notion of generational units as being similar rather than diversified internally, and externally in opposition to the older or previous generational unit. The second hypothesis involves testing for greatest area of generational conflict, if any, in the areas of politics and music. If generational conflict is greater between two generational units, and music is the main area of dissension, we may then suggest that Mannheim's approach to generations may be the most useful, and that the counter culture thesis may be more descriptive of the current generation than the political socialization studies.

In 1968 a random sample of 444 secondary school students and dropouts was drawn from a city in the metropolitan area of Vancouver, British Columbia.[60] The ages of individuals in this group ranged from 13 to 19. According to some observers this age range is central to generational conflict, and support for the counter culture.

To facilitate a comparison of generations, 121 parents of those students and dropouts already selected were questioned. Along with the parents, 36 teachers and administrators from the schools covered in the sample were queried, bringing the total adult sample to 157.

As Tables I through IV indicate intra-generational conflict does not appear significant in either political or musical areas.

Students do not tend to favor any particular political party more than their "dropout" counterparts.

Table I: Student-Dropouts Intra-Generational Unit Political Preferences

	Communist	Socialist	Liberal	Conservative	Total
Students	10 (3.3)	50 (16.4)	216 (70.5)	30 (9.8)	306
Dropouts	0	7 (17.9)	29 (74.7)	3 (7.4)	39
Total	10	57	245	33	345

$x^2 = 1.63$ not significant

In musical tastes the differences between students and dropouts also were not significant with a majority favoring rock music.

Table II: Student-Dropout Intra-Generational Unit Musical Preferences

	Rock Music	Show and Classic	Total
Students	280 (87.2)	41 (12.8)	321 (100.0)
Dropouts	34 (94.4)	2 (5.6)	36
Total	314	43	357

$x^2 = 1.24$ not significant

In sampling the parents and teachers of the forementioned students and dropouts no significant difference was found in their political preferences as a generational unit. The adults tended to prefer the Liberal Party of Canada, as had their children and charges.

Table III: Parent-Teacher Intra-Generational Political Preferences

	Socialist*	Liberal	Conservative	Total
Student's Parents	22 (25)	55 (62.5)	11 (12.5)	88
Dropout's Parents	3 (12)	19 (76)	3 (12)	25
Teachers	6 (21.4)	22 (78.6)	0	28
Total	31	96	14	141

$x^2 = 6.32$ not significant
*None of the respondents support the Communist Party.

In the sphere of musical tastes the parent-teacher sample nearly always favored the musical offerings of the Broadway stage and the "classics."

Table IV: Parent-Teacher Intra-Generational Unit Musical Preferences

	Rock Music	Show and Classical	Total
Student's Parents	4 (4.2)	91 (95.8)	95
Dropout's Parents	1 (5.5)	18 (94.5)	19
Teachers	1 (2.8)	36 (97.2)	37
Total	6	145	151

x^2 = .5 not significant

The findings presented in Tables I, II, III, and IV support Mannheim's hypothesis on the *entelechy* of a generational unit. Parents and teachers by-and-large did not like rock music, while their offspring overwhelmingly supported this musical genre. Respondents were also questioned with the aim of testing our second hypothesis dealing with Counter Culture, namely, that differences between generations will be substantially greater in the area of music than in politics. As the data in Tables V and VI show generational differences are exceedingly prevalent in terms of the musical tastes of those sampled, while such is not the case with reference to political preferences, thereby supporting Roszak's Counter Culture hypothesis. Among the adults, 96 percent of those sampled selected Broadway shows, movie themes, classical, or religious music as their first or second choice in an open-ended question of, "which types of music do you like best," while among the younger generational unit, these four types of music were selected in only one stance out of every eight.

In the younger generational unit, 87.9 percent chose rock and roll music as their first or second favorite choice of musical genres. In the adult sample, only 4 percent expressed such a choice. As Table V illustrates, there is a significant difference (x^2 is 319) at any level, between the older generational unit and the younger in musical preferences.

Table V: Generational Unit Differences in Musical Preferences

	Rock Music	Show and Classical	Total
Students and Dropouts	314 (87.9)	43 (12.1)	357
Adults	6 (4.0)	145 (96.0)	151
Total	320	188	508

x^2 = 319 significant at any level

The differences between parents-teachers, and students-dropouts in the political preferences is not statistically significant, $x^2 = 4.83$ at 3 degrees of freedom. This lack of significance is shown in Table VI.

Table VI: Generational Unit Differences in Political Preferences

	Communist	Socialist	Liberal	Conservative	Total
Students and Dropouts	10 (2.9)	57 (16.5)	245 (71)	33 (9,6)	345
Parents and Teachers	0 (0.0)	31 (22)	96 (68.1)	14 (9.9)	141
Total	10	88	341	47	486

$x^2 = 4.83$ not significant

These findings from a sample of secondary school students and dropouts indicate that political preferences between generational units are pretty much the same. On the other hand, significant differences in so-called "cultural areas" are observable.

Discussion

From the above findings, it would appear that Roszak's Counter Culture thesis has some empirical support, however, the authors urge caution, in extrapolating from this sample. High school students are by-and-large more experientially oriented than their more intellectual collegiate counterparts. This factor without doubt skews the data toward Roszak's anti-technology stance.

In addressing the "Political socialization" issue our data lends support to the Keniston and Flacks hypothesis of political continuity. Nevertheless, the age of the sample may be more favorable to this hypothesis as opposed to the findings of Dunlap and others. Also, the sample was of a predominantly middle and upper middle class area.

The significant finding, here, however tentative, is that generational conflict, in the Mannheimian sense, may involve more than just the political sphere generally treated by those observing "youth movements." As such, much benefit may be derived from looking at the cultural trends in youth culture such as music, films, and other experiential aspects of what may be a growing Counter Culture.

DEATH SONGS AND TEENAGE ROLES

The social location of the adolescent in American society, as most psychological and sociological observers have noted, is both contradictory and in conflict.[1] On the one hand, the adolescent role is a submissive one akin to that of the maturating child or the native colonial. He is required to learn the social skills of self government yet he is not afforded the power to do so. A further complicating factor is that the already inconsistent adolescent role and status is frequently disrupted by normal fluctuations in the dominant social order which impinge and disrupt his notion of self esteem and self government. For example, many style-of-life decisions affecting the teenager are made *for* him such as location of residence, religion, economic status, and perhaps most significantly, time allocation. All of these factors are encapsulated in adolescent love rites.

Teenage romantic love behavior has been traditionally interpreted as a major nodal or transition point in the socialization of the future adult. Here the individual makes choices and decisions encompassing many social and psychological variables, inherent in the "rating dating" system. Nowhere is adolescent role and status conflict more observable than in popular music—the genre devoted to the language of romantic love—of the "June, moon, spoon," ethos of art.[2] Nearly all of the content analyses of popular song lyrics have noted the dependence of these artifacts upon the Romeo and Juliet motif. Even themes of social dissent, until the mid-1960's, were couched in the framework of dating, "being grounded," and postponed gratification. Songs such as "Summertime Blues," "Yakety Yak," "Almost Grown," "Maybe Tomorrow," and "They Tried To Tell Us We're Too Young" negatively addressed the adolescent status and the intervention of social norms upon this position.[3] The sentiments expressed in these songs clearly objected to parental interference in marriage and dating partners. Moreover, the lyrics raged against the menial chores and jobs imposed upon teenagers. However, they concluded that adulthood would rectify all of the real or imagined hurts. Only the teenage "coffin song" offered an immediate solution to the status and role inconsistencies of youth—death.

The coffin song magnified the trials and tribulations of the usual dyadinal love match. In its earliest form the coffin song depicted the interdiction of an externally imposed element upon the participants. Donald Wood's "Death of An Angel," Thomas Wayne's "Tragedy," Mark Dinning's "Teen Angel," the Everly Brothers' "Ebony Eyes," Slim Whitman's "Twilla Lee," and Dickey Lee's "Laurie" all documented the advent of death to interrupt a teenage love affair. Originally, death in these songs takes the form of an accident or a natural disaster of an unexpected nature. Death is rarely, if ever, viewed as part of the normal life-death cycle. Remarkably, the advent of death is seen as *temporary*. The termination of physical existence is not final, but rather it is a temporary stumbling block. Jody Reynolds, in one of the first coffin songs, "Endless Sleep" repeats the following lines:

*   *   *   *   *
*   *   *   *   *

I heard a voice crying in the deep
"Come join me baby in my endless sleep."[4]

The sea, the uncontrollable factor, takes the love object away, but the singer can join his partner through death. In "Tell Laura I Love Her," a voice from the grave resounds the message that the relationship has only been momentarily suspended:

Tell Laura I love her, tell Laura I need her.
Tell Laura not to cry my love for her will never die.[5]

The closing lines of "Ebony Eyes" find the singer relating how he will be reunited with his girl friend killed in a plane wreck:

If I ever get to heaven . . . she will be my beautiful
ebony eyes.[6]

"Twilla Lee" exhibits a similar ending:

Why fate stepped in I cannot see
But Twilla died—my Twilla Lee
At heaven's gate I'll take her hand
Wait for me, my Twilla Lee[7]

In "Last Kiss" the chorus restates the same theme:

  * * * * *
  * * * * *
She's gone to heaven so I got to be good
So I can see my baby when I leave this world.[8]

Dickey Lee's "Laurie" took this motif one step further chronicling
the relationship of a teenage boy with a female *pater geist* who had
been dead for a year. This song reiterates the temporary nature of
death as well as suggesting the possibility of transmogrification of
the loved one. These coffin songs, generally ignored by most
students of popular music, when examined within the framework
of status and role inconsistency suggest several interesting hypotheses about the life expectations of the American teenager prior
to the advent of the contra-culture.[9]

  An examination of the coffin songs found on the *Billboard*
"Hot 100" indicate that they may be a metaphoric or symbolic
statement against parental interference. As in the case of the
colonial governor or the parent, death disrupts the teenager in his
daily activities within his life space. Love objects are taken away.
New situations, not of the actor's choosing, are created thus under-
mining his ability to function as an independent agent. That is, his
ability to assume the adult role is brought into question and indeed
conflict. Dickey Lee's prototype coffin song "Patches" narrates
the role of parents in isolating a teenage boy from his lower class
girl friend. Patches, the socially *declasse* romantic partner, in
response commits suicide by drowning. This action underlines
the parentally imposed ostracism. The boy, however, reasserts
his independence by vowing to follow Patches into death thus

re-establishing the forbidden relationship:

> *   *   *   *   *
> *   *   *   *   *
> It may not be right
> But I'll join you tonight
> Patches I'm coming to you[10]

In effect, the death of one partner serves to disrupt the dyadinal interaction, but in the coffin song genre, the coming of death only serves to elevate the love relationship to a status of security and permanence. In "Give Us Your Blessing" two adolescents, denied permission to wed, elope, and are killed in an automobile crash. The runaways, not the living, are the victors:

> . . . as their folks knelt beside them in the rain
> They could not help but hear . . .
> "Give us your blessing, please don't
> make us run away."[11]

This sentiment, of course, is a common one in suicide notes. Nonetheless, it was rather unique for a medium devoted to the exaltation of youth.

Coffin songs metaphorically can be defined as statements of dissent against status inconsistency as well as solutions to role dissonance since in death the broken relationship is reincarnated. This interpretation is, perhaps, best supported by looking at the time of popularity of each of these songs and comparing it to the structurally prescribed events occurring in the adolescent life space.

A preponderance of coffin songs which reached the *Billboard* chart did so during months where a maximum of status and role disequillibrium took place. May and June, which evidenced the end of spring semester and commencement ceremonies, most frequently saw death songs placing on the chart (see Table One). It was precisely during these late weeks of spring that romantic love objects were threatened by geographical dislocations—"going away for the summer"—the threat of vacation romances, and status changes such as entering the labor force, military service, or preparing for college. Songs such as "Your Graduation Means

Goodbye," "He's A Rebel" and "Don't Go Near the Indians," also abounded at these critical times reinforcing the disruption thesis.

The termination of summer vacation and the resumption of school activities marked another readjustment period. Once again, relationships were severed, summer romances ended, and a change in life chances anticipated. As with the months of spring, August and September featured a number of teenage death songs. The fall of 1964 witnessed "Last Kiss," "Death of An Angel," and "Leader of the Pack" on the best seller chart. Other periods exhibiting similar role suspensions as the winter commencement or the Christmas break correlate with the appearance of coffin songs.

TABLE ONE

The Appearance of Coffin Songs on the Billboard Hot 100*

Teen Angel	December 21, 1959
Tell Laura I Love Her	June 13, 1960
Ebony Eyes	January 30, 1960
Tragedy	April 17, 1960
Moody River	May 7, 1960
Patches	August 25, 1962
Leah	September 8, 1962
Give Us Your Blessing (Peterson version)	June 1, 1963
Last Kiss	September 5, 1964
Death of an Angel (Viceroy's version)	September 19, 1964
Leader of the Pack	October 10, 1964
Laurie	May 15, 1965
Give Us Your Blessings (Shangri-la's version)	May 27, 1965

*Sample from fall, 1959, to fall, 1965, "Endless Sleep" (May-June, 1958) and Thomas Wayne's version of "Tragedy" (April, 1959) appeared on the chart prior to the sample.

As Table One indicates a majority of 92 percent (N=13) of the coffin songs appeared on the *Billboard* listing during the most intense periods of adolescent status and role adjustment.[12] Five coffin songs appeared in the Spring and a similar number graced the charts in the Fall months. There were several exceptions. "Tragedy" by the Fleetwoods was the most deviant case appearing in April too early to qualify. The original version of the same song by Thomas Wayne, also, reached the *Billboard* chart in the month of April, 1959. Paul Antell's "Night Time" released during the Christmas season of 1962 did not place on the Hot 100. Despite these non-supportive instances coffin songs in the main do appear to correlate with readjustment periods.

Lyrically teenage coffin songs can be treated as statements of dissent and in some cases rebelliousness.[13] "Give Us Your Blessings," and the "Leader of the Pack" as well as Dickey Lee's "Patches" clearly allude to status differentiations and the interference of parents which results in or involves the loss of life. Conversely, these same songs, now considered "camp" or "perverse" may have served other purposes.

As with Christmas carols, hymns on Sunday, and Sousa at parades, coffin songs functioned to high light a given period of status and role conflict. The songs rather than proclaiming a joyous occasion as Christmas emphasized in nearly semi-operatic tones of pathos the theme of farewell, but on a very temporary basis. The transfiguration of the funeral songs heralded the transitory nature of disengagement promising the listener reunification in time. This message may be perceived as lessening anxieties produced by the structural impingements upon the individual in a manner similar to graduation ceremonies, inductions, and funerals.

Coffin songs consequently are dichotomous in that they make a statement of rebellion against structural changes while facilitating movement to other life chances. Puberty rites, marriage ceremonies, and confirmations, all with a rich array of musical artifacts, make a similar contribution. Coffin songs, then, may have functioned to explain status and role conflicts to teenagers, and perhaps, lessened the dysfunctional psychological costs of passage for the adolescent.

KENT
STATE,
MUSKOGEE,
AND
THE
GHETTO

Topical songs, although pronounced dead by a host of critics, are still very much alive. They have, however, undergone a considerable transformation since the pioneering days of the Almanac Singers, People's Songs Inc., or indeed, the songwriting boom of the early 60's. Except for a few hearty souls such as Pete Seeger, Joan Baez and Tom Paxton, the names, faces, and most importantly the musical styles have changed. The end result is a curious montage reflecting many political ideologies and appealing to a wide range of people. Consider for a moment the peculiar fact that the "best record" of 1969 as voted by the Country Music Association was Merle Haggard's *Okie From Muskogee*. In Hollywood, the Best New Vocal Group award was given to Crosby, Stills, Nash and Young (CSN&Y). Haggard's songs have been requested by the President, highlighted the July 4th pro-Vietnam Honor America Day rally in Washington, and evoked near hysteria at many concerts both North and South of the Mason-Dixon line. CSN&Y have written and recorded best selling songs commemorating the death of Robert Kennedy and urging generational understanding. In May of 1970 they recorded "Ohio" dedicated to the Kent State 4. Yet the philosophy of the group is apolitical. Steven Stills expressed it at the November 15th Moratorium Day rally as follows: "politics is bullshit, Richard Nixon is bullshit . . . our music isn't bullshit." Merle Haggard and CSN&Y are representative of both the current trend of topical songwriting as well as the increasing polarization of American society.

Haggard, an ex-resident of San Quentin Prison, is the "hottest property" in the country music field today with his collection of patriotic and "down and not out" songs. "Okie From Muskogee," condemns protest and non-conformity:

> We don't smoke marijuana in Muskogee,
> We don't take our trips on LSD.
> We don't burn our draft cards down on Main Street,
> But we like living right and being free.
>
> (chorus)
> I'm proud to be an Okie from Muskogee,
> A place where even squares can have a ball.
> We still wave Ol' Glory down at the Court House
> White lightning's still the biggest thrill of all.[1]*

"The Fightin' Side of Me," restates the "Love It, or Leave It" bumper sticker:

> If you don't love it, leave it
> Let this song that I'm singin' be a warning
> When you're runnin' down our country, hoss,
> You're walkin' on the fightin' side of me.[2]**

Haggard's compositions are in keeping with the country music tradition of Vernon Dalhart's "Trial of John Scopes," Hank Snow's "There's A Star Spangled Banner Waving Somewhere," and Ernest Tubb's "Soldier's Last Letter," however, his songs have an added sense of anger. Country singers have historically been politically conservative including Johnny Cash, Roy Acuff, Tex Ritter, and Roy Rogers, according to Paul Hemphill, author of *The Nashville Sound*. In 1968 the musicians around Nashville all came out for "Nixon, dozens for Wallace, not a soul for Humphrey."[3] Marty Robbins campaigned for George Wallace and recorded under the name of "Johnny Freedom" on the Sims label "Ain't I Right" a song advocating that the fight against Communism would be best carried out by attacking civil rights marchers, college students, and liberal United States senators. A number of country songs have both lauded and denounced welfare payments and other social services. Guy Drake's nationally controversial "Welfare Cadilac," (Drake's spelling) another Nixon favorite, relates how those on

*From the song "Okie From Muskogee," by Merle Haggard and Roy Edward Burris. Copyright © 1969 by Blue Book Music. Used by permission. All rights reserved."

**From the song "The Fightin' Side of Me," by Merle Haggard. Copyright © 1970 by Blue Book Music. Used by permission. All rights reserved.

welfare lead the good life "driving around in their Cadillac." Shortly after the release of this song, ironically, Mr. Drake was arrested for not making the payments on his Cadillac. The tendency of many northern writers to color country music as totally reactionary is somewhat misleading since it is also a mirror of the American Populist tradition. Many songs, notably those of Johnny Cash, present an anti-organizational posture stressing the injustices done by large companies at the expense of the little guy, be he convict, Indian, or farmer. Cash's version of the Pete LaFarge song "Ira Hayes," and Haggard's "Workin' Man Blues" are illustrative. Eddie Burns' "Color Me Country," on the other hand, is almost a re-creation of some of Woody Guthrie's Dustbowl ballads. The song relates the tale of a displaced farmer from Texas who "drives a wornout car pulling a homemade trailer with everything we own." Ironically, the Breckenridge, Texas, Chamber of Commerce took great offense at this *Grapes of Wrath* type song.

The populist influence in current country songs is best typified by the so-called "truck drivin" and other occupational songs which depict the role of the rugged individualist who overcomes adversity. Noteworthy is the fact that it is always some shadowy cause or fate which is responsible for the individualists' plight. Red Simpson and Roy Drusky have both made a fortune with these types of songs. Red Simpson's *Roll, Truck, Roll* and *The Man Behind The Badge* are classic evidences of a man doing his duty for family and country regardless of the costs. In "Country Sheriff" we find:

> I work in the office from eight to four
>   cruising four hours more . . .
> Country Sheriff that's what I am, . . .4
> *   *   *   *   *
> *   *   *   *   *

Johnny Cash's hit, written at the request of the evangelist, Billy Graham, "What Is Truth" puts forth a slightly different approach suggesting that social problems are caused by a misunderstanding of the rules rather than real problems. One verse, directed presumedly at the trial of the Chicago 7, is illustrative:

Young man sittin' on a witness stand
The man with the book says raise your hand,
Repeat after me, I solemnly swear.
The man looked down at his long hair
And although the young man solemnly swore
Nobody seemed to hear any more.
And it didn't matter if the truth was there:
It was the cut of his clothes and the length of
  his hair:
And the lonely voice of youth cries "What Is
  Truth."[5] *

While the song is a bit more conciliatory than Victor Lundberg's "An Open Letter to My Teenage Son," the implication is that "the true religion is better after all" in the old "No Depression in Heaven" style. Lundberg's "Open Letter" extensively aired on C&W stations, several years ago, defined "truth" and the penalties for its disavowal. A stern voice warns that the burning of a draft card should be followed by the destruction of his son's birth certificate since "from that moment I have no son."[6]

All of the songs we have discussed are not terribly unusual for the C&W genre, what is different is their widespread acceptance outside of the normal "hillbilly market." While many factors entered into this popular notion, suffice it to say that the "silent majority" has finally discovered a musical format which expresses its view of the world. An irony is that one can make a strong case that the liberally-oriented folk music revival and the pilgrimages of many politically "liberal" middle media singers helped popularize the Nashville Sound. One need only recall that Glen Campbell, a strong supporter of the Indochina War, first made the *Billboard* charts with Buffy Sainte Marie's "Universal Soldier" and "Ruby Don't Take Your Love To Town" was recorded by a packaged "new wave rock group" from Hollywood, the First Edition.

"McGuinn and McGuire keep on getting higher in LA you know where that's at . . ." recalled the Mamas and Papas. For better or worse this lyric fairly well captures the genesis of rock styled topical songs. McGuire's "The Eve of Destruction" and the Byrds' interpretations of Dylan provided the model for what was to follow. Despite the warnings of Rev. Noebel of the Christian

*From the song "What Is Truth," copyright House of Cash. Used by permission.

Crusade and Art Linkletter, topical songs on the Top Forty did not turn teenyboppers into "dope smoking Communist dupes" bent on destroying the government by force and violence, although one rock LP, "The Revolt of Emily Young" (Decca DL 75193) did present the moral degeneration of a young lady exposed to rock music and politics. Indeed, many rock reviewers including Griel Marcus, the editor of the *Rolling Stone,* discounted protest songs and singers arguing in McLuhenesque fashion that the rock genre itself was revolutionary and that was enough.[7] The Weathermen, Revolutionary 9, and Charles Manson, who built a philosophy on the Beatles' "Helter Skelter," did not seem to think so. Nor did Country Joe and the Fish, Earth Opera, the Mothers of Invention, the Fugs, Eric Burden, and MC 5. But, it is important to note that their material has not been extensively played on Top Forty stations, and only a handful of "underground" FM outlets use their material—very selectively. "Fixin To Die Rag" followed by the Fish cheer (Give me an F, give me a U . . .) is not exactly suitable for the tastes of FCC Commissioners. The Jefferson Airplane's *Volunteers,* a highly polemical LP blacklisted for obscenity, contains the following immoral statements:

> All your private property is target for
>   your enemy and your enemy is "We."
> We are forces of chaos and anarchy
>   everything they say we are, we are,
> And we are very pround of ourselves.
> Up against the wall,
> Up against the wall,
> Tear down the walls
> Tear down the walls.[8] *

Another reason given for not playing such topical lyrics on the air is length. Many pieces such as "Volunteers," the *word* not withstanding, Burden's "Sky Pilot," and Earth Opera's "American Eagle Tragedy" are purportedly too long for Top Forty airplay. In the case of "American Tragedy" this rationale does not hold since a shortened version was released by the usually inept Eleckra

*From the song "Volunteers," copyright © Icebag Music Corporation. Used by permission.

promotional department. The chorus of the song, like "Volunteers" may partially explain its absence from Big Sound programming:

> And call out the border guards the kingdom
> is crumbling
> The king is in the counting house laughing
> and stumbling
> His armies are extended way beyond the shore
> As he sends our lovely boys to die in a foreign
> jungle war.[9]

While the longer more offensive pieces were largely confined to FM outlets and concert stages, topical songs, some of which were treated in our discussion of country music, were making their way onto the Top Forty charts. The Buffalo Springfield's "For What It's Worth," generated by the Sunset Strip Rebellion of 1966, pointed to the harassment of youth by police. Janis Ian's "Society's Child" outlined the hostility encountered by an inter-racial couple, and a number of songs such as "Mr. Businessman," "2 Plus 2," "Skip A Rope," "Walk A Mile In My Shoes" chronicled the hyprocrisy of American life in economic and racial matters. These latter pieces were a hybrid between the populist indignation of country singers and the social concerns of the folkniks of the early 1960s. Johnny Cash's success in part is based on this turn in popular music: the mix of social indignation with a "new" acceptable musical structure. Perhaps, the central feature of the Top Forty topical songs, was that they did not in fact *protest*. They made a statement but offered no solutions on directions. They did not indict any specific group or individual. The Springfield's opening line "There's something happening here, what it is ain't exactly clear . . ." is a far cry from Dylan's "Masters of War" or Paxton's "We Didn't Know." Janis Ian's concluding statement of "I'm only society's child," is as full of resignation to the status quo as any Carter Family song. The public response to these popular "protest songs" was most curious. All sold well. The Ian composition became a *top* ten record in a major Southern city. Several political groups adopted names from phrases in rock songs. But, recent studies of the impact of these songs indicate that most of their listeners did not comprehend the words. On the other hand, rock music was communicating but not in any overtly measurable way.

It is difficult to specify a given historical event or series of happenings which pointed rock music toward a more topical and militant stance. The 1968 Chicago Democratic Party Convention, the intensification of the war, the murders of Martin Luther King and Robert Kennedy all contributed to this turn. The restructuring of many rock groups without question played a part. The search for new directions led some to protest songs. By 1969 some of the "name" bands were beginning to use their music to make contemporary statements of protest. The foremost example of this trend was Crosby, Stills, and Nash, later to be joined by Neil Young. David Crosby was a refugee, one of many, from the Byrds. Graham Nash was the former lead singer of the British rock group, the Hollies. Stills, the composer of "For What It's Worth," and Young were with the Springfields. As CSN&Y they were billed as a "super group." When Robert Kennedy was assassinated in a Los Angeles hotel, Dave Crosby wrote two songs "Almost Cut My Hair" and "Long Time Gone." "Long Time," the opening song to the movie *Woodstock* cautioned against "speaking out against the madness" or trying to get elected to public office, especially if one had long hair.

"Almost Cut My Hair" is a bitter rejection of working within the System, a sentiment expressed by many young people, following the deaths of Martin Luther King and Senator Kennedy, not to mention Chicago. The multiple murders prompted several songs, Dion's "Abraham, Martin, and John," and Tommy Cash's—the brother of Johnny—"Six White Horses":

> Some preach wrong and some preach right
> Some preach love and some preach fight
> It takes every kind to make the world go 'round
> It takes only one to gun you down.
> Goodbye Martin—six white horses come to take
>   you home.
> Goodbye, Reverend—took you away before
>   you sang your song.[11]

184

Both records sold well, one in the pop field, and the other climbed the country charts.

Credence Clearwater Revival has put together anti-establishment songs such as "It Came Out of the Sky," and "Fortunate Son," both featured on *Willy and The Poor Boys* (Fantasy 8997). "Out of the Sky" is the story of a farm boy named Jody who finds an object in his corn field which is believed to have come from outer space. The response to this "thing" is colored by the perspective of the interest of the beholder. The Vatican sees it as a religious symbol, Hollywood, a subject for a motion picture. Ronald Reagan (Ronnie The Popular) calls the object a "communist plot." The song transforms all things into economic terms:

> The White House said, "Put the thing in the Blue
> Room". . .
> And Jody said, "It's mine, but you can have it for
> Seventeen Million."12*

"Fortunate Son," an anti-draft song, urged:

> And when the band plays "Hail To The Chief"
> They point the cannon right at you . . .
> It ain't me, It ain't me—13**

The expansion of the Vietnam War into Cambodia, and the conflict with the Administration which led to the deaths of four students at Kent State prompted CSN&Y to record "Ohio:"

> Gotta get down to it, soldiers cutting us down;
> Should've been done long ago . . .
> What if you knew her, and found her dead on the ground;
> How can you run when you know?

Another portion of the song relates:

> Tin soldiers and Nixon's coming
> We're finally on our own
> This summer I hear the drumming
> Four dead in Ohio, four dead in Ohio14

To further muddy up the state of topical and protest songs in America, we need only consider the Canadian rock group, The Guess Who. The Guess Who, riding the crest of their most successful composition, "American Woman," a piece which rejects the United States as a domineering world power, with lines such as "I don't need your war machine, I don't need your ghetto scene," were invited to the White House to entertain visiting British royalty. After originally refusing the invitation, the band decided to do the gig regardless, much to the consternation of a number of Right-wingers, and reportedly to "the White House spokesman" who considered the lyrics in bad taste. The Guess Who did not perform their "offensive" material at the White House.

The ascendency of social commentary in the forementioned music genres was also experienced in Black "soul" music.

Rhythm and blues, as Black popular music was once called, can, if one wishes, be categorized as a form of covert protest. Rebellion in keeping with spirituals and work songs was escapist in nature. Instead of physical withdrawal from slavery or the chain gang, flights into the hereafter or the Saturday night with a good woman and a bottle were posited as remedies for seemingly unsolvable social ills. As with all escapist material the lyrics magnified reality into metaphysical feats of super endurance "let the good times roll—roll all night long." In the case of a cheap foul tasting mixture of white wine and lemon juice called WPLJ we are told "it really tastes good to me." The fantasy was delicious and good, but reality was found in Fats Domino's lament "Blue Monday, I hate blue Monday." While affirming the sensate aspect of existence r 'n' b also underlined the inflexible station of caste. The Silhouettes' version of "Get a Job" where the lead singer repeatedly points to the futility of looking for work is but one evidence of this phenomenon.

Only marginal Black singers, who appealed to predominantly political white audiences sang about discrimination and social injustice. Leadbelly, a southern blues singer, under the tutelage of a young Alan Lomax produced "Bourgeois Blues" for Marxist audiences. Josh White, in a similar vein, performed progressive ideological material as found in *Southern Exposure* (Keynote 310) for working-class intellectuals. Leon Bibb's and Harry Belafonte's original appeal was to like-minded audiences. Nina Simone, perhaps the most outspoken of the Black protest singers with "Mississippi God Damn" recalled the troublesome presence in America for collegiates and intellectuals. Only blues singer J. B. Lenior recorded protest songs such as "Eisenhower Blues" during this period. This song, due to White House opposition, was withdrawn from the record shops. It rarely was played on r 'n' b stations.

The Negro sound of protest best known to all Americans did not emanate from recorded sources but rather originated in the Southern civil rights movement. Spirituals were turned into propaganda weapons to be sung at rallies, marches, or in jails. These "freedom songs" when compared to r 'n' b were unsophisticated but highly effective. Indeed, songs played on northern black stations generally ignored the struggle in the south. Nonetheless, a racial consciousness was beginning to emerge. Barry Gordy's Mo-Town records, customarily characterized as "soul" by Black writers, utilized the artifacts of ghetto culture to sell songs and instill racial pride. Indeed, as militants were eulogizing "freedom songs" with "the time for singing is over" MoTown continued to sell millions of "soul" records.

Soul, which came from the jazz genre, stressed Afro-American culture, but not in any revolutionary sense. Its injection into popular music in the 1960's did not alter this posture. James Brown—Mr. Soul—epitomized the *machismo* of the music as well as its politics. Brown, following social critic James Baldwin, emphasized equal opportunity and self-esteem. His best selling "Don't Be a Drop Out" and "I'm Black and I'm Proud" urged self-respect and hard work as the way to reform. Brown, a millionaire in his own right, did not protest rather he urged equal opportunity and reform. He summarized his political ideology in saying:

> America is still the greatest country in the world—but we don't have to fight with each other. Otherwise, we'll blow it.[15]

In keeping with this sentiment, Mr. Soul was the first Black singer to tour Vietnam to show his support for the war policy.

Sister Soul, Aretha Franklin, also has stressed Black soli-

darity and worth in her music. Her recording of the late Otis
Redding's composition "Respect" following the Watts and Detroit
rebellions was viewed by *Ebony* magazine "as the new national
anthem."   Phyl Garland, in *The Sound of Soul*, commented:
"newspapers, periodicals, and television commentators pondered
the question of 'why' as Aretha . . . spelled it all out in one word,
R-E-S-P-E-C-T."[16]   Sam Cooke's generally forgotten "A Change
is Gonna Come" addressed gradualism and pride.   Another Mo-
Town unit, the Impressions, unlike the defeatist Silhouettes,
stressed the Protestant Ethic and social accommodation,[17] "Get
Up and Move" and "People Get Ready":

> When you've got a problem, you can't stay in bed.
> Put on your shoes and get up and move.

With the advent of the Vietnam war Black music became increasingly political.   Ernie Andrews' "Crackerbox Livin' " was anti
reconciliation:

> Crackerbox livin' ain't no kind of livin'
> What is this hole you charge for?
> What is this hole we're much too large for
> Lord of land, won't you understand.
>
> We'll trade you places just for the day,
> Maybe your kids can chase the rats away
> Maybe your kids don't need some place to play.[18]

B. B. King, in "Why I Sing the Blues," echoed desperation:

> I've slept in the ghetto flats cold and numb
> I've even heard the rats when they told the
>   roaches to give the bedbugs some
> Then everybody wanna know why I sing the blues.[19] *

Significantly, both the Andrews and King laments mirrored the
sentiments of Eddie Burns' "Color Me Country." The social conditions remain the same only the color and geography are dissimilar.   The Supremes' "Love Child" further elaborated the
ghetto status of Blacks.   The Black protest song of the 1960's

came of age with yet another MoTown property, the Temptations. The Temptations, originally were little more than a successful recording and night club act. Their only attempt at social significance "Runaway Child, Running Wild" was nearly a cover of the Supremes' "Love Child." Gillett described their material as "the sort of overstatement comparable to the easy liberalism of contemporary Sidney Poitier films. . . ."[20] The Temptations' world view, as well as their music, changed in 1970. "Ball of Confusion" placed in the coveted Billboard Top Ten. "Ball" in many respects was a restatement of the Barry McGuire song "Eve of Destruction" in that it chronicled the hypocrisy of American life such as segregation, economic exploitation, murder, suicide, hippies, and the Vietnam war. The song concludes "End the war . . . and the band played on."[21] A member of the Temptations also wrote "War," a song popularized by Edwin Starr. "War" was the first Black anti-war song in the MoTown fashion to climb the Top Forty charts.[22] The chorus posed the rhetorical question "war . . . HUH! What is it good for? Absolutely nothing." The lyric goes on to relate the costs of military involvement "Induction, destruction, who wants to die?"[23] The economic success of "Ball of Confusion," and "War" prompted in predictable fashion other soul singers to make overtly political statements such as the Voices of East Harlem's "Gotta Be a Change," and Curtis Mayfield's "If There's Hell Below, We're All Going to Go." As in country and western, and now the Black genres, social dissent is firmly entrenched in popular music.

If a pollster were to sample rock bands it is highly possible that not one percent would be found in the conservative or pro-Vietnam column, unlike the C&W field where a majority would be found supporting the Nixon policy. The so-called middle-media would fall somewhere in between the two political stances. Topical songs by rock groups have only exhibited dissent to the current youth culture in two spheres: tactics and the abuse of drugs. The Beatles' famous song "Revolution," of course, decried what the members felt were excesses by political radicals: ". . . if you go carrying pictures of Chairman Mao, you ain't going to make it with anyone anyhow, don't you know it's gonna be alright." Their "Let It Be" proclaims a similar theme of resignation. "Give Peace A Chance" is perhaps the Beatles' main contribution to the anti-war movement.

John Mayall, the father of the British blues scene, has written several anti-protest songs. The most recent is "Plan Your Revolution." The Mayall lyric is quite like the Beatles' treatment of the same subject:

> Take initial action, show them you are fair
> Show them you're constructive.[24]

In another piece, "The Laws Must Change," Mayall again presents the gradualist position:

> The laws must change one day,
>   but it's going to take some time. . . .[25]

Perhaps the most controversial position a rock band can take, at least in the eyes of many of their followers, is opposition to drugs. Donovan Leitch, John Mayall, Neil Diamond, and several other pop stars have come out condemning the smoking of marihuana and the use of addicting drugs. Mayall, in "Plan Your Revolution," included the following stanza:

> Don't become a druggie, unless you're
>   too weak to face responsibility.[26]

Neil Diamond, in the "Pot Smoker's Song," provides the bouncy chorus of:

> Pot, pot give us some pot, forget what you are,
> you can be what you're not.
> High, high, I want to get high
> Never give it up if you give it a try.[27]

Interspersed with this chorus are excerpts from interviews with ex-junkies and teenagers who have experienced bad trips. *The Revolt of Emily Young* in Ann Landers fashion describes the death of a teenybopper from an overdose in Greenwich Village. Most rock bands are not nearly as anti-dope as the above selections might suggest. Instead, one can find a number of songs ranging from "Eight Miles High" to Arlo Guthrie's "Flying Into Los Angeles" which have obvious drug references, although the quantity is not as great as Art Linkletter and other self-appointed guardians of the public morality would have it. For example, there is little reason to disbelieve Paul McCartney when he states that "Lucy in the Sky with Diamonds" is not about LSD. Most rock musicians either use some type of drug or are at least tolerant of its absorption by others. However, this tolerance is highly selective and usually confined to pills or grass. The "hard stuff" is discouraged both privately and in song. Steppenwolf's "The Pusher Man," and Canned Heat's "Amphetamine Annie" both condemn methadrine with the latter song providing the chorus of "I don't mind you getting high, but about those little pills there's one thing you ought to know: *speed kills*." This commentary, unlike the wholesale putdowns of Mayall and Diamond, finds a good deal of support, it appears, within the counter culture.

The topical song has found new life in Nashville, Detroit, Hollywood. The country, "soul" and rock genre abound with examples, some well known, others familiar to only specific social groupings. But the trend is growing into even the middle media presentations of Lee Hazelwood ("Jackson" with Nancy Sinatra) who recently took a page from Woody Guthrie and recorded "The Trouble Maker" describing a bearded long haired political agitator named Jesus Christ. Two albums were released, exhibiting the best of Ray Coniff style, opposing the pollution of the environment, *Ecology* and *Earth Rot*. The MoTown representatives in the middle media continue to make social commentaries although they are still a far cry from the political days of Leadbelly or today Elaine Browne or Nina Simone.

The topical song is alive, but its health is questionable. Consider for a moment the following description of one of the worst rock bands around:

> They are three who belong to the New Culture
> setting forth on its final voyage through a dying world . . .
> searching to find a way to bring us all closer to home.

SONGS OF PERSUASION AND THEIR ENTREPRENEURS

[1]Cf. John Greenway, *American Folksongs of Protest*, Philadelphia: University of Pennsylvania Press, 1953.

[2]For other views and functions see Archie Green, "A Discography (LP) of American Labor Union Songs," *New York Folklore Quarterly*, I (Autumn, 1961), pp. 1-8.

[3]See Edith Fowke and Joe Glazer, *Songs of Work and Freedom*, Chicago: Roosevelt University Press, 1960, pp. 9-11; Josh Dunson, *Freedom In the Air*, New York: International Publishers, 1965, pp. 13-30; and Greenway, *op. cit.*, pp. 2-4.

[4]Roland L. Warren, "German *Parteileider* and Christian Hymns as Instruments of Social Control," *Journal of Abnormal and Social Psychology*, 28 (January, 1943), pp. 96-100.

[5]Terence H. Qualter, *Propaganda and Psychological Warfare*, New York: Random House, 1963, p. 99.

[6]Sidney Hillman, quoted in Oscar Brand, *The Ballad Mongers*, New York: Funk and Wagnalls, 1963, p. 125.

[7]Barrie Stavis, *The Man Who Never Died*, New York: Haven Press, 1951, p. 20.

[8]R. Serge Denisoff, *Great Day Coming: Folk Music and The American Left*, Urbana, Illinois: University of Illinois Press, 1971.

[9]"Roll the Union On," *Fortune*, (November, 1946), p. 184.

[10]Green, *op. cit.*, p. 3.

[11]Robert K. Merton and Paul F. Lazarsfeld, "Mass Communication, Popular Taste, and Organized Social Action," in Lyman Bryson, ed., *The Communication of Ideas*, New York: Harper Bros., 1948, pp. 95-118.

[12]Cf. Irving Howe and Lewis Coser, *The American Communist Party: A Critical History*, Boston: Beacon Press, 1957, p. 392; and "OWI Plows Under the Almanac Singers," *New York Times*, January 5, 1941, p. 9.

[13]See the chapter "Class Consciousness and the Propaganda Song," in his volume.

[14]*Sing Out!*, I (August, 1950), p. 16.

[15]Ralph Chaplin, "Solidarity Forever," *Little Red Song Book*, 30th ed., Chicago: Industrial Workers of the World, 1962.

[16]*Ibid.*, p. 8.

[17]Collected from Peter Krug, San Francisco, 1964.

[18]Howe and Coser, *op. cit.*, p. 326.

[19]R. Serge Denisoff, "Protest Songs: Those On the Top Forty and Those of the Streets," *American Quarterly*, 22 (Winter, 1970), pp. 807-823.

[20]Cf. "June Records," *Time*, (June 16, 1941), pp. 50-51; "September Records," *Time*, (September 15, 1941), p. 51; and "Talking Union," *New York Times*, April 19, 1941.

[21]Charles Seeger, record reviews in *Journal of American Folklore*, 61 (April, 1948), pp. 215-218; and 62 (January, 1949), pp. 68-70.

[22]Greenway, *op. cit.*, p. 185.

[23]Sam Hinton, "The Singer of Folk Songs and His Conscience," *Western Folklore Quarterly*, 19 (July, 1955), p. 171.

[24]Ewan MacColl, "The Singer and the Audience," *Sing Out!*, 14 (September, 1964), pp. 18-19.

[25]Brand, *op. cit.*, pp. 216-232.

[26]Ellen Stekert, "Cents and Nonsense In the Urban Folksong Movement: 1930-1966," in Bruce Jackson, ed., *Folklore and Society*, Hatsboro: Folklore Associates, 1966, pp. 153-168.

[27]*Ibid.*, pp. 157-160.

[28]Robert S. Whitman and Sheldon S. Kagan, "The Performance of Folksongs on Recordings," in DeTurk and Poulin, eds., *The American Folk Scene*, New York: Dell Publishing Co., 1967, pp. 72-79.

[29]"Folk Singing," *Time*, (November 23, 1962), pp. 59-60.

[30]Dean Wallace, "A New Batch of Folk Music LP's." *This World* section of *San Francisco Chronicle*, June 30, 1963, p. 22.

[31]*Ibid.*, p. 22.

[32]Juanita Brooks, "Memories of a Mormon Girlhood," *Journal of American Folklore*, 77 (July-September, 1964), p. 196. A myriad of other definitions are also available. See *Folklore and Society, op. cit.*

[33]*Ibid.*, p. 22.

[34]Cf. Robert K. Merton, *Social Theory and Social Structure*, Glencoe: Free Press, 1957, pp. 131-144; Seymour Martin Lipset, *The First New Nation*, New York: Basic Books, 1963, pp. 101-122; and Paul Goodman, *Growing Up Absurd*, New York: Vintage Books, 1961.

[35]"An Interview With Tom Paxton," *Broadside*, 67 (February, 1966), pp. 8-11.

[36]See "Folk Music and the American Left," in this volume.

[37]See "Kent State, Muskogee, and the Ghetto," in this volume.

THE SONG OF PERSUASION REVISITED

*The author wishes to thank Shelley Levine Nye and Mark H. Levine for their assistance in the preparation of this paper.

1Quoted in Jerome Rodnitzky, "The New Revivalism: American Protest Songs, 1945-1968," paper read at American Studies Assn. meetings, October, 1969, p. 3. Other translations, such as Cornford's, express a similar thrust but not as strongly, e.g., "The introduction of novel fashions in music is a thing to beware of as endangering the whole fabric of society, whose most important conventions are unsettled by any revolution in that quarter." Plato, *The Republic*, (Trans. Francis MacDonald Cornford), New York: Oxford University Press, 1945 (Book IV, 424), p. 115.

2Gilbert Chase, *America's Music*, New York: McGraw-Hill, 1955, pp. 5-6.

3Jeremy Collier quoted in Rodnitzky, *op. cit.*, p. 3.

4*Familiar Quotations by John Bartlett*, 13th edition, 1955, p. 2906.

5Herbert Hoover quoted in Arthur M. Schlesinger, Jr., *The Crisis of the Old Order*, Boston: Houghton Mifflin Company, 1957, p. 242.

6Quoted in R. Serge Denisoff, "The Religious Roots of the American Protest Song," this volume.

7Alfred G. Aronowitz and Marshall Blonsky, "Three's Company: Peter, Paul, and Mary," *Saturday Evening Post*, (May 30, 1964), p. 32.

8R. Serge Denisoff, "Seeger Concert Shows Singers Growth, Change," *Los Angeles College Times*, May 23, 1969, p. 4.

9R. Serge Denisoff, "Folk Music and the Radical Right," California State College, Los Angeles (mimeographed paper), 1969.

10John P. Robinson and Paul M. Hirsch, "Teenage Response to Rock and Roll Protest Songs," paper read at American Sociological Assn. meetings, San Francisco, September, 1969.

11See James Downey, "Revivalism, The Gospel Songs and Social Reform," *Ethnomusicology*, 9 (May, 1965), pp. 115-125.

12John Greenway, *American Folksongs of Protest*, Philadelphia: University of Pennsylvania Press, 1953; Josh Dunson, *Freedom In the Air*, New York: International Publishers, 1965.

13Dunson, *op. cit.*, p. 47.

14Denisoff, "Songs," this volume.

15Industrial Workers of the World, *Songs of the Workers: To Fan the Flames of Discontent*, Chicago: I.W.W. Publishing Co., 31st edition, 1962, p. 9.

16Joe Glazer and Edith Fowke, *Songs of Work and Freedom*, Chicago: University of Roosevelt Press, 1960, p. 36.

17Ashleigh Brilliant, *Haight Ashbury Song Book*, San Francisco: H-B Publications, 1967, pp. 3, 8.

18Woody Guthrie quoted in Alan Lomax, *The Folk Songs of North America*, New York: Doubleday and Co., 1960, p. 434.

19Cf. Happy Traum, "The Art of the Talking Blues," *Sing Out*, 15 (January, 1966), pp. 53-60.

[20]Lewis Coser, *The Functions of Social Conflict*, Glencoe: Free Press Inc., 1956, p. 37.

[21]Coser, *op. cit.*, p. 38; also see Harry Alpert, "Durkheim's Functional Theory of Ritual," in Robert A. Nisbet, ed., *Emile Durkheim*, Engelwood Cliffs: Prentice Hall, Inc., 1965, pp. 137-141.

[22]Paul Lazarsfeld and Robert K. Merton, "Mass Communication, Popular Taste and Organized Social Action," in Bernard Rosenberg and David M. White, eds., *Mass Culture: Popular Arts in America*, Glencoe: The Free Press, 1957, pp. 457-473.

[23]Harvey Matusow, *False Witness*, New York: Cameron and Kahn, 1955, p. 24.

[24]This definition is contingent upon the social situation in which it is performed. Songs which only point to societal problems without offering solutions may be interpreted as protest songs to the already converted.

[25]Anthony Bernhard, "For What It's Worth: Today's Rock Scene," paper read at American Sociological Assn. meetings, San Francisco, August, 1967, pp. 1-2.

[26]Gary Allen, "That Music: There's More To It Than Meets the Ear," *American Opinion*, 12 (February, 1969), p. 49.

[27]Cf. Mike Gershman, "The Blues, Once Black, Now A Shade Whiter," *Los Angeles Times Calender*, January 12, 1969, pp. 1, 37; Kurt von Meier, "The Background and Beginnings of Rock and Roll," University of California, Los Angeles, (unpublished paper), n.d.; Frank Zappa, "Psyched Out," *Life*, (June 28, 1968), pp. 82-91; Charles Gillett, "Just Let Me Hear Some of That Rock and Roll Music," *Urban Review*, 1 (December, 1966), pp. 11-14; and Charles Keil, *Urban Blues*, Chicago: University of Chicago Press, 1966, pp. 44-48.

[28]von Meier, *op. cit.*, p. 16.

[29]Paul Oliver, *The Meaning of the Blues*, New York: Collier Books, 1963, pp. 321-322.

[30]For a discussion of the change in American musical tastes see James T. Carey, "Changing Courtship Patterns in the Popular Song," *American Journal of Sociology*, 74 (May, 1969), pp. 720-731; and H. F. Mooney, "Popular Music Since the 1920's: The Significance of Shifting Taste," in Jonathan Eisen, ed., *The Age of Rock*, New York: Vintage Books, 1969, pp. 9-29.

[31]Jeremy Lerner, "What Do They Get From Rock 'n' Roll?" in Ira Peck, ed., *New Sound/Yes*, New York: Four Winds Press, 1966, pp. 110-111.

[32]David Riesman, "What the Beatles Prove About Teenagers," *U. S. News and World Report*, (February 24, 1964), p. 88.

[33]Donald Horton, "The Dialogue of Courtship in Popular Songs," *American Journal of Sociology*, 62 (May, 1962), pp. 569-578.

[34]Jay Johnstone and Eli Katz, "Youth and Popular Music: A Study in the Sociology of Taste," *American Journal of Sociology*, 62 (May, 1962) pp. 563-568.

[35]James S. Coleman, *The Adolescent Society*, Glencoe: Free Press, 1961, p. 23.

[36]Cf., Horton, *op. cit.*

[37]The deviant aspect *vis-a-vis* adults and popular music is generally ignored in the literature dealing with protest songs and other content analyses of the lyrics of songs placed on the Top Forty. In recent years the tonal and musical structure of songs, it would appear, especially with the advent of acid rock, plays an increasingly important role in the communication and moods of intended messages. R. Serge Denisoff and Mark H. Levine, "The One-Dimensional Approach to Popular Songs: A Research Note," *Journal of Popular Culture,* IV:4.

[38]For a typology of folksingers see Ellen Stekert, "Cents and Nonsense in the Urban Folksong Movement: 1930-1966," in Bruce Jackson, ed., *Folklore and Society*, Hatsboro: Folklore Associates, 1966, pp. 153-168.

[39]For a discussion of the so-called protest revival see Dunson, *op. cit.*

[40]Keil, *op. cit.*, pp. 47-48.

[41]Paul Hirsch, "The Structure of the Popular Music Industry," Ann Arbor: University of Michigan, (mimeographed), 1969.

[42]Cf., Rosenberg and White, *op. cit.*

[43]Carl Belz, *The Story of Rock*, New York: Oxford University Press, 1969, p. 27.

[44]Another category of song frequently labelled as deviant on the Top Forty is the so-called "double meaning" song which attempts to have an esoteric meaning legible only to the "in" people. The author has not included this type of song, such as "Eight Miles High," etc., since there is a great deal of confusion as to what precisely these songs mean. Cf., Robinson and Hirsch, *op. cit.*; and "Songs That Have A Double Meaning," *San Francisco Chronicle*, September 25, 1966, p. 13.

[45]Belz, *op. cit.*, p. 169; and Roland L. Warren, "German Parteilieder and Christian Hymns as Instruments of Social Control," *Journal of Abnormal and Social Psychology*, 38 (January, 1943), pp. 96-100.

[46]Denisoff and Levine, "Popular Protest Song," *Popular Opinion Quarterly*, 35 (Spring, 1971), pp. 117-122.

[47]Underground stations usually concentrate upon playing selections from LP's and choosing a wider range of genres than Top Forty Stations. In recent years many FM outlets have drifted toward the "Big Sound" format. Cf., Tom Nolan, "Underground Radio," pp. 337-351 and Harry Shearer, "Captain Pimple Cream's Fiendish Plot," pp. 357-384, in Eisen, *op. cit.*

[48]Cf., Greenway, *op. cit.*

[49]Hirsch, *op. cit.*

URBAN FOLK MUSIC 'MOVEMENT' RESEACH: VALUE FREE?

[1]See R. Serge Denisoff, "The Proletarian Renascence: The Folkness of the Ideological Folk," *Journal of American Folklore*, 82 (January-March, 1969), pp. 51-65.

[2]John Greenway, *American Folksongs of Protest*, Philadelphia: University of Pennsylvania Press, 1953.

[3]Thelma McCormick, "Social Theory and Mass Media," *Canadian Journal of Economics and Political Science*, 27 (November, 1961), p. 482.

[4]See Mike Gold, "Change the World," *Daily Worker*, April 21, 1934, p. 7 and Woody Guthrie, "My Constitution and Me," *Daily Worker*, June 19, 1949, p. 12.

[5]Greenway, *op. cit.*, pp. 134, 250; Fred E. Beal, *Proletarian Journey: New England, Gastonia, Moscow*, New York: 1937.

[6]Greenway, *ibid.*, p. 262.

[7]Charles Seeger, "The Folkness of the Non-Folk," in Bruce Jackson, ed., *Folklore and Society*, Hatsboro: Folklore Associates, 1966, p. 4.

[8]See Woody Guthrie, *American Folksong*, Moses Asch, ed., New York: Oak Publications, 1961, pp. 1-14; Gordon Friesen, "Woody Guthrie: Hard Travelin," *Mainstream*, 16 (August, 1963), pp. 4-11; and Pete Seeger, "Remembering Woody," *ibid.*, pp. 27-33.

[9]See Gordon Friesen, "The Almanac Singers: End of the Road," *Broadside* 16 (November, 1962) n.p.; Seeger, "Remembering," *op. cit.*, p. 29; Guthrie, *American Folksong, op. cit.*, p. 4; and "People's Songs," *The Sunday Worker*, March 13, 1946, p. 7.

[10]Cf. Greenway *vis-a-vis* Ellen Stekert, "Cents and Nonsense in the Urban Folksong Movement: 1930-1966," in *Folklore and Society, op. cit.*, pp. 153-168.

[11]Letter, August 20, 1966.

[12]Seeger, "Remembering," *op. cit.*, p. 31.

[13]Denisoff, "Songs of Persuasion," in this volume.

[14]Stekert, *op. cit.*, p. 161.

[15]Oscar Brand, *The Ballad Mongers*, New York: Funk and Wagnalls, 1962, p. 124.

[16]Josh Dunson, *Freedom in the Air*, New York: International Publishers, 1965, p. 17.

[17]*Ibid.*

[18]"Pete Seeger-Profile," Seattle: KING-TV, November 3, 1968.

[19]Ray M. Lawless, *Folksingers and Folksongs in America*, New York: Duell and Sloane, 1960.

[20]See Thelma James, "Folklore and Propaganda," *Journal of American Folklore*, 61 (October-December, 1948), p. 311; and D. K. Wilgus, *Anglo-*

American Folksong Scholarship Since 1898, New Brunswick: Rutgers University Press, 1959, pp. 220-228.

[21]Willard Rhodes, "Folk Music, Old and New," in *Folklore and Society, op. cit.,* p. 11.

[22]Stekert, *op. cit.,* pp. 154-155.

[23]*Ibid.,* p. 162.

[24]*Ibid.,* p. 163.

[25]Jere Real, "Folk Music and Red Tubthumpers," *American Opinion,* 7 (December, 1964), pp. 19-24; and Fire and Police Research Association, "When Is Folk Music Not Folk Music?" Los Angeles, 1963; and David A. Noebel, *Rhythm, Riots, and Revolution,* Tulsa: Christian Crusade Publications, 1966.

[26]"Be Careful," *New Republic,* 23 (January, 1964), p. 8.

[27]Noebel, *op. cit.,* pp. 121-137.

[28]Irwin Silber, "An Open Letter to Bob Dylan," *Sing Out!,* 14 (November, 1964), pp. 22-23; Sy and Barbara Ribakove, *Folk Rock: The Bob Dylan Story,* New York: Dell Publishing Co., 1966, pp. 66-73; and R. Serge Denisoff, "Dylan: Hero or Villain," *Broadside,* 58 (May 15, 1965), p. 10.

[29]David Noebel, *op. cit.,* p. 128; and Harvey Matusow, *False Witness,* New York: Cameron and Kahn, 1955, p. 51.

[30]Josh White, "I Was a Sucker for the Communists," *Negro Digest,* (December, 1950), pp. 26-31; Brand, *op. cit.,* p. 136; and "Testimony of Burl Ives," *Subversive Infiltration of Radio, Television, and the Entertainment Industry,* U.S. Senate—82 Congress, 1952, pp. 205-228.

[31]Brand, *op. cit.,* p. 136.

[32]"Oscar Brand Joins Witch Hunt Hysteria," *Sing Out!,* 2 (November, 1951), p. 16.

[33]Irwin Silber, "Fan the Flames," *Sing Out!,* 17 (December-January, 1967-1968), p. 55.

[34]Archie Green, "American Labor Lore: It's Meanings and Uses," *Industrial Relations,* 4 (February, 1965), pp. 66-67.

RELIGIOUS ROOTS OF THE SONG OF PERSUASION

[1]Gilbert Chase, *America's Music*, New York: McGraw Hill, 1955, pp. 5-6.

[2]*Ibid.*, p. 15.

[3]William Sargent, *Battle For the Mind*, Baltimore: Penguin Books, 1961, pp. 21-22.

[4]Chase, *op. cit.*, p. 48.

[5]Louis F. Benson, *The English Hymn: Its Development and Use in Worship*, New York: George Doran Co., 1915, p. 239.

[6]See Josh Dunson, *Freedom in the Air*, New York: International Publishers, 1965; and R. Serge Denisoff, *Great Day Coming: Folk Music and the American Left*, Urbana: University of Illinois Press, 1971.

[7]James C. Downey, "Revivalism, the Gospel Songs and Social Reform," *Ethnomusicology*, 9 (May, 1965), pp. 115-125.

[8]Chase, *op. cit.*, p. 223.

[9]Daniel Bell, "The Background of Marxian Socialism in the United States," in Donald Egbert and Stow Persons, eds., *Socialism in American Life*, v. I, Princeton: Princeton University Press, 1952, p. 306. Also David A. Shannon, *The Socialist Party of America*, New York: MacMillan Co., 1955, pp. 26-27.

[10]Tom Tippett, *When Southern Labor Stirs*, New York: Jonathan Cape and Harrison Smith, 1931, pp. 120-121, 124.

[11]John Greenway, *American Folksongs of Protest*, Philadelphia: University of Pennsylvania Press, 1953, p. 174.

[12]*Ibid.*, p. 177.

[13]Archie Green, "John Neuhaus: Wobbly Folklorist," *Journal of American Folklore*, 73 (July-September, 1960), p. 200.

[14]F. Brown quoted in George Charney, *A Long Journey*, Chicago: Quadrangle Press, 1969, p. 51.

[15]Howard W. Odum and Guy B. Johnson, *The Negro and His Songs*, Chapel Hill: University of North Carolina Press, 1925.

[16]See J. W. Schulte Nordholt, *The People That Walk in Darkness*, New York: Ballentine Books, 1960, p. 266. In recent studies it has been noted that protest in black music was generally covert and not perceptible by whites. See Charles Keil, *Urban Blues*, Chicago: University of Chicago Press, 1966; and Paul Oliver, *The Meaning of the Blues*, New York: Collier Books, 1963.

[17]Joe Glazer and Edith Fowke, *Songs of Work and Freedom*, Chicago: Roosevelt University Press, 1960, p. 169.

[18]Greenway, *op. cit.*, p. 74.

[19]*Ibid.*, p. 89.

[20]Hyder E. Rollins, ed., *Old English Ballads 1553-1625*, London:

1920, pp. xxiii-xvii.

[21]Quoted in Edmund David Cronon, *Black Moses*, Madison: University of Wisconsin Press, 1964, p. 68.

[22]C. Wilson Record, *The Negro and the Communist Party*, Chapel Hill: University of North Carolina Press, 1947.

[23]Richard Frank, "Negro Revolutionary Music," *New Masses*, (May 15, 1934), pp. 23-29.

[24]*Ibid.*

[25]Mike Gold, "Negro Reds of Chicago," *Daily Worker*, September 30, 1932, p. 4.

[26]Charles Gaines, "The Negro Masses Speak," *Daily Worker*, November 2, 1932, p. 4.

[27]"New Defense Song Gains Wide Popularity in South," *Daily Worker*, November 7, 1933, p. 5.

[28]"Songs of Protest," *Time*, (June 15, 1936), p. 51.

[29]See Lawrence Gellert, "Negro Songs of Protest," *New Masses*, (November, 1930), pp. 10-11.

[30]Elie Seigmeister, *Music and Society*, New York: Critics Group Press, 1938, p. 9.

[31]Lee Collier, "Portrait of a New Southerner," *Daily Worker*, May 11, 1938, p. 5.

[32]Lee Hays "Let the Will Be Done," *New Masses*, (August 1, 1939), p. 15.

[33]*Ibid.*

[34]See Alan Lomax *et. al., Hard Hitting Songs for Hard Hit People*, New York: Oak Publications, 1967.

[35]H. L. Mitchell, "Oral History of the Southern Tenant Farmers Union," mimeographed, Oral History Project, Columbia University, 1956-1957, p. 71.

[36]Guy and Candie Carawan, *We Shall Overcome*, New York: Oak Publications, 1963.

[37]Robert Sherman, "Sing a Song of Freedom," in DeTurk and Poulin, eds., *The American Folk Scene*, New York: Dell Publishing Co., pp. 173-174.

[38]Denisoff "Class Consciousness" this volume.

[39]*Ibid.*

[40]Sherman, *op. cit.*, p. 173.

[41]*Ibid.*

[42]Seymour Martin Lipset, *Political Man: The Social Bases of Politics*, Garden City: Anchor Books, 1963, p. 99.

CLASS CONSCIOUSNESS AND THE SONG OF PERSUASION

I am indebted to Andrew P. Phillips, Thomas J. Duggan and especially Delfo Giglio for their evaluations of the original version of this paper.

[1]V. I. Lenin, "What Is To Be Done?" in *Collected Works,* Vol. IV, New York: International Publishers, 1929, pp. 113-154.

[2]C. Wright Mills, *White Collar,* New York: Oxford Press, 1956, p. 325.

[3]Lenin, *op. cit.,* p. 139.

[4]See "Urban Folk Movement Research" in this volume.

[5]See "Songs of Persuasion" in this volume.

[6]*Ibid.*

[7]Frederick C. Stern has objected to this terminology on the grounds that "entrepreneur" connotes the economic function of selling a product. See Frederick C. Stern "The 'New Folk' and Its Singers," unpublished paper, 1970.

[8]Robert K. Merton and Paul F. Lazarsfeld, "Communication, Taste, and Social Action," in Lyman Bryson, ed., *Communication of Ideas,* New York: Harpers, 1948, p. 115.

[9]In 1941 the Almanac Singers recorded "The Ballad of October 16th," critical of President Roosevelt. The song indicated FDR would not be happy until "everybody's dead." "June Records," *Time,* (June 16, 1941), p. 51. Several years after the song's appearance the Almanacs were publically sanctioned and discharged from the Office of War Information in part due to this song. "OWI Plows Under the Almanac Singers," *New York Times,* January 5, 1943, p. 9.

[10]Irving Howe and Lewis Coser, *The American Communist Party: A Critical History,* Boston: Beacon Press, 1957, p. 371.

[11]*Ibid.,* pp. 372-373.

[12]Peter Seeger, "People's Songs and Singers," *New Masses,* (July 16, 1946), p. 9. Also, Woody Guthrie, "People's Songs," *The Sunday Worker,* (March 13, 1946), p. 7.

[13]Expressive movements have been characterized as "marked by goaless behavior or by pursuit of goals which are unrelated to the discontents from which the movement had its source." Joseph R. Gusfield, *The Symbolic Crusade,* Urbana: University of Illinois Press, 1963, p. 23.

[14]By "relative" it is meant that the political climate of a given period may change the status of an entity from a non-legitimate movement to a legitimate institution as was the case with the trade union movement.

[15]John Greenway, *American Folksongs of Protest,* Philadelphia: University of Pennsylvania Press, 1953, p. 174.

[16]The pocket songbook employed by the IWW was modeled after the hymnal used at revival meetings. This propaganda technique was later emulated by the CPUSA, CIO, and the AFL-CIO. One factor accounting for this transference of artifacts and techniques has been the mobility of members from one movement to another. See John S. Gambs, *The Decline of the IWW,* New York: Columbia University Press, 1932, pp. 82-91.

[17]Harold D. Lasswell and Dorthy Blumenstock, *World Revolutionary Propaganda,* New York: Alfred Knopf, 1939, pp. 93-94.

[18]The tables include only those songs used in a propagandistic manner by the PSI in their songbooks. Many songs contained introductions placing them into a proletarian context, however, the songs themselves were not intrinsically propaganda songs in the framework of the definition provided.

[19]One observer indicated that "Union Maid" is far better known on college campuses than it is in the average trade union hall. See Peter Seeger, "Whatever Happened To Singing in the Unions," *Sing Out!,* 15 (May, 1965), p. 31. A similar phenomenon took place in the civil rights movement. See Anne Braden, "Highlander Folk School—The End and the Beginning," *Sing Out!,* 12 (February-March, 1962), pp. 30-31; and Josh Dunson, *Freedom In the Air,* New York: International Publishers, 1965, pp. 33-43.

[20]James O'Brien, "A History of the New Left, 1960-1968," (mimeographed) Boston: New England Free Press, 1969, is one of the better short histories of this phenomenon.

[21]R. Serge Denisoff and William F. Segan, "The Haight-Ashbury Sub-Culture: A Descriptive Analysis of a Contemporary Bohemia," San Francisco State College, (mimeographed) 1966, pp. 63-68.

[22]Dunson, *op. cit.,* p. 29.

[23]*Ibid.,* p. 29.

[24]Peter Seeger, "You Can't Write Down Freedom Songs," *Sing Out!,* 15 (July, 1965), p. 11; and Sam Clark, "Freedom Songs and the Folk Process," *Sing Out!,* 14 (February-March, 1964), pp. 13-14.

[25]Seeger, *ibid.,* p. 11.

[26]Guy and Candie Carawan, *We Shall Overcome,* New York: Oak Publications, 1963.

[27]Josh Dunson, "Freedom Singing Gathering in the Heart of Dixie," *Sing Out!,* 14 (September, 1964), pp. 34-35.

[28]National Educational Network, "Freedom Songs," 1964.

[29]See Gunnar Mydal's discussion of race and class consciousness in *An American Dilemma,* New York: Harper and Bros., 1944, pp. 676-683.

PROTEST SONGS AND SKITS OF AMERICAN TROTSKYISTS

The writers wish to thank Archie Green, D. K. Wilgus, Joe Glazer, and especially William H. Friedland, for their comments, suggestions, and relevant material they placed at our disposal. In particular, we have relied heavily upon the collected songs and skits in Professor Friedland's library.

[1]For the emergence of the Communist League and the ensuing polemic see James P. Cannon, *The History of American Trotskyism*, New York: Pioneer Publishers, 1944; Theodore Draper, *American Communism and Soviet Russia*, Viking Press, 1960; and also Daniel Bell, *The Background and Development of Marxian Socialism in the United States*, Princeton: Princeton University Press, 1967.

[2]Robert J. Alexander, "Splinter Groups in American Radical Politics," *Social Research*, 20 (October, 1953), p. 298.

[3]Draper, *op. cit.*, pp. 362-376; and Bell, *op. cit.*

[4]Max Shachtman, "Footnote for Historians," *New International*, 4 (December, 1938), pp. 377-379.

[5]Irving Howe, *Steady Work: Essays in the Politics of Democratic Radicalism*, New York: Harcourt Brace, and World, 1965, pp. 349-364.

[6]Paul Jacobs, *Is Curley Jewish: A Political Self Portrait*, New York: Atheneum Press, 1965, p. 34.

[7]*Ibid.*, p. 34.

[8]Seymour Martin Lipset, "The Left, the Jews and Israel," *Encounter*, 33 (December, 1969), pp. 24-35; and also Nathan Glazer, *The Social Basis of American Communism*, New York: Harcourt, Brace, and World, 1961.

[9]Richard A. Reuss, "The Roots of American Left Wing's Interest in Folksong," *Labor History*, 12 (Spring, 1971).

[10]Notes to *Ballads For Sectarians*, Labor Arts Recording. This song first appeared in the pages of the *Socialist Call*, an organ of the militant left-wing of the Socialist Party which subsequently merged with the Socialist Workers (Trotskyist) Party. It is set to the tune and is a partial parody of the old spiritual "Dem Bones Gonna Rise Again."

[11]R. Serge Denisoff, "The Proletarian Renascence: The Folkness of the Ideological Folk," *Journal of American Folklore*, 82 (January-March, 1969), pp. 51-65.

[12]D. K. Wilgus interview, July 18, 1967. Wilgus, now one of the leading folksong scholars in the country, formerly was a Trotskyist organizer in Ohio during his student days. The Trotskyist antipathy to folk culture outlined here also was the position sometimes taken by the Industrial Workers of the World on the same subject. Cf. Reuss, "Roots," *op. cit.*

[13]Wilgus interview. For the Communist Party's policy with regard to Negroes in the United States, see C. Wilson Record, *The Negro and the Communist Party*, Chapel Hill: University of North Carolina Press, 1947.

[14]From a skit by Gene Brooks, untitled, mimeographed from the Friedland collection.

[15]*Sing!*, mimeographed (September, 1945), p. 16. For discussion of the

work of Woody Guthrie and the Almanac Singers, see Richard A. Reuss, "Woody Guthrie and His Folk Tradition," *Journal of American Folklore,* 83 (1970), in press; and R. Serge Denisoff, " 'Take It Easy But Take It': The Almanac Singers," *Journal of American Folklore,* 83 (January-March, 1970), pp. 21-32.

[16]Morris Himelstein, *Drama As A Weapon,* New Jersey: Rutgers University Press, 1963, pp. 76-84.

[17]Cf. Alexander, *op. cit.,* pp. 282-310; and James Cannon, *The History of American Trotskyism,* New York: Pioneer Publishers, 1944.

[18]Cf. "Topics of the Times," *New York Times,* May 15, 1940, p. 24.

[19]"Walter Cliff" (Pseudonym) "Reunion in Berlin," mimeographed skit 1940-41, from Friedland collection.

[20]*Ballads For Sectarians. op. cit.*

[21]Kuppy Scott, "On To City Hall," mimeographed, no page number given (p. 4).

[22]*Ibid.* (p. 4).

[23]Friedland collection.

[24]Kuppy Scott, "Sam Spade," mimeograph, 1946, p. 4.

[25]Collected from Bill Friedland, who also recorded this song on the album *The Unfortunate Rake,* Folkways Record FA 2305. The notes by Kenneth S. Goldstein state that Miss Kuppy Scott was a member of Dodge Local 3 of the United Auto Workers, and that the song was written during the Dodge Pension Strike of 1949.

[26]William H. Friedland, letter to Denisoff, September 15, 1967.

[27]Alexander, *op. cit.,* p. 303.

[28]Cf. Chiam Waxman, ed., *The End of Ideology Debate,* New York: Funk and Wagnalls, 1969.

[29]Labor Arts Recording, 2065 Collingwood, Detroit, Michigan. The exact date of issue is uncertain, but 1952 has been suggested by several observers.

[30]Gabriel Almond, *Appeals of Communism,* Princeton: Princeton University Press, 1954, pp. 62-96.

[31]Jacobs, *op. cit.,* p. 52.

[32]Anonymous letter to Denisoff, January 29, 1969.

[33]Cannon was the head of the Socialist Workers Party, while Shachtman was the leader of the Workers Party later the Independent Socialist League. Norman Thomas led the Socialist Party, and Lee led a splinter group from the SP. Lovestone was expelled from the Communist Party and formed the Communist Party Opposition. For further elaboration see Max Shachtman "Footnote for Historians," *New International,* 4 (December, 1938), pp. 377-379. Also Daniel Bell, *The Background and Development of Marxian Socialism in the United States,* Princeton; Princeton University Press, 1967.

[1]Cf. John Greenway, *American Folksongs of Protest*, Philadelphia: University of Pennsylvania Press, 1953, and R. Serge Denisoff, "Songs of Persuasion," this volume.

[2]Edith Fowke and Joe Glazer, *Songs of Work and Freedom*, Chicago: Roosevelt University Press, 1960, pp. 12-13.

[3]Michael Quin, "Seeing Red," *Western Worker*, May 14, 1936, p. 7.

[4]"Songs of Persuasion," *op. cit.*

[5]Fowke and Glazer, *op. cit.*, p. 39.

[6]H. L. Mitchell, *Oral History of the Southern Tenant Farmers Union*, (transcribed and mimeographed) Oral History Project, Columbia University, 1956-1957, p. 71.

[7]Arlene E. Kaplan, "A Study of Folksinging in a Mass Society," *Sociologus*, 5 (Spring, 1955) pp. 14-28.

[8]*Ibid.*

[9]Cf. Oscar Brand, *The Ballad Mongers*, New York: Funk and Wagnalls, 1962.

[10]David E. Apter, ed., *Ideology and Discontent*, New York: Free Press, 1964, p. 20.

[11]Egon Bittner, "Radicalism and the Organization of Radical Movements," *American Sociological Review*, 28 (December 1963) pp. 928-940.

[12]Erik H. Erikson, *Young Man Luther*, New York: Norton, 1958 pp. 38-39.

[13]David A. Shannon, *The Decline of American Communism*, New York: Harcourt, Brace, and World, 1959, p. 38.

[14]Margaret Larkin, "Ella May's Songs," *Nation*, 129 (October 9, 1929) p. 383.

[15]Woody Guthrie, quoted in *op. cit.*, Greenway, p. 281.

[16]Cf. Sidney Finklestein, *How Music Expressed Ideas*, New York: International Publishers, 1952; and Louis Harap, *Social Roots of the Arts*, New York: International Publishers, 1949.

[17]Almanac Singers, "Songs of Work, Trouble, Hope," *People's World*, October 28, 1941, p. 5.

[18]*Ibid.*

[19]A sample essay is Charles Seeger, "On Proletarian Music," *Modern Music*, 11 (March-April, 1934) pp. 121-127.

[20]*Ibid.*, p. 122.

[21]*Ibid.*, p. 125.

[22]Richard Frank, "Negro Revolutionary Music," *New Masses*, May 15, 1934, p. 28.

[23]*Ibid.*

[24]Woody Guthrie, "Woody, Dustbowl Troubador, Sings Songs of Migrant Trails," *People's World*, April 19, 1940, p. 5.

[25]Harry Alan Potmakin and Gertrude Rady, *Songs For Workers and Farmers Children*, New York: New Pioneer PUblishing Co., 1933.

[26]Harold Lasswell and Dorothy Blumenstock, *World Revolutionary Propaganda*, New York: A. Knopf., 1939, p. 89.

[27]*Ibid.*

[28]"Woody's Folk's to Make Music For Sharecropper Blowout," *People's World*, April 4, 1941, p. 5.

[29]Brand, *op. cit.*, p. 77.

[30]Lawrence Lipton, *The Holy Barbarians*, New York: Messner, 1959, p. 290.

[31]Marjorie Crane, "The People Sing," *People's World*, September 12, 1941, p. 5.

[32]The *Daily Worker* and the *New Masses.*

[33]Mike Quin, "Double Check," *People's World*, April 25, 1940, p. 5.

[34]William Wolff, "Songs That Express the Soul of a People," *People's World*, November 24, 1939, p. 5.

[35]"Artist of the People: That's the Title Earned By Young Lee Winters Who Sings of U. S. Workers," *People's World*, April 23, 1940, p. 5.

[36]Charles Seeger, "Folkness of the Non-Folk," in Bruce Jackson, ed., *Folklore and Society*, Hatsboro: Folklore Associates, 1966, p. 4.

[37]Neil J. Smelser, *Theory of Collective Behavior*, Glencoe, Free Press, 1963, p. 199.

[38]R. Serge Denisoff, "Mass Communication and Role Theory: A Social Psychological Analysis of the Folk Entrepreneur," San Francisco, (unpublished paper) 1966.

[39]Cf. Neil Hickey, "The Old Time Music," *American Weekly*, April 7, 1963, p. 10.

[40]"Blacklist," *Broadside*, (August, 1963) n.p.

[41]Gary B. Rush and R. Serge Denisoff, *Social and Political Movements*, New York: Appleton, Century, Crofts, 1971.

[42]*Ibid.*

[43]One example is found in Paul Jacobs and Saul Landau, *The New Radicals*, New York, Vintage Book, 1966.

[44]Eugene D. Genovese, "Genovese Looks at American Left," *National Guardian*, February 19, 1966.

[45]*Op. cit.*, New Radicals, p. 14.

[46]Mario Savio, KPFA tape, 1965.

[47]Phil Ochs, "I Ain't Marching Anymore."

[48]Phil Ochs, "Love Me, I'm A Liberal."

[49]Examples of these characteristics are found in Jack Newfield "The Student Left," *Nation*, (May 10, 1965) pp. 491-495.

[50]See "The Children of Bobby Dylan," *Life*, (November 5, 1965) pp. 43-50.

[51]Interview, July 3, 1966.

[52]"Strike Ends On Note of High," Berkeley Barb, (December 9, 1966) p. 11.

[53]Josh Dunson, "Freedom Singing Gathering in the Heart of Dixie," *Sing Out!*, (September, 1964) pp. 34-35.

[54]Letter to the writer, October 1, 1964.

[55]Cf. Phil Oschs', "Bound For Glory"; Tom Paxton, "Fare Thee Well Cisco"; Peter Krug, "The Man I Never Knew"; and Bob Dylan's, "Song to Woody."

[56]Columbia Records, CL 1779.

[57]Tape.

[58]*Bosses Song Book,* New York, 1959.

[59]*Ibid.,* p. 11.

[60]*Sing Out!,* 15 (September, 1965) p. 11.

[61]Peter Seeger, "Remembering Woody," *Mainstream,* 16 (August, 1963) pp. 29-31.

[62]R. Serge Denisoff, "Folk-Rock: Covert Protest or Commercialism," this volume

[63]Marshall McLuhan, *Understanding Media: The Extensions of May,* New York: Signet Books, 1964, p. 36.

[64]Woody Guthrie, "They Stage a Benefit for Okies," *People's World,* March 14, 1940, p. 5.

[65]Interview, June 28, 1965.

[66]"Songs of the People in New Low-Priced Anthology," *People's World,* October 22, 1941, p. 5.

[67]R. Serge Denisoff, "Class Consciousness and the Propaganda Song," this volume.

[68]"Almanac Singers: Four Young Men Wity a Lot to Sing," *People's World,* August 1, 1941, p. 5.

[69]R. Serge Denisoff, "The Definition of A Folk Song and the Underground Top Ten," *Folknik,* (January, 1965) p. 2.

[70]Karl Mannheim, *Essays On The Sociology of Knowledge,* rev. ed., London: Routledge, and Kegan Paul, 1959, p. 310.

[71]Josh Dunson, *Freedom In The Air,* New York: International Publishers, 1965, p. 47.

[72]I wish to thank T. B. Bottomore for his evaluation of an earlier version of this chapter.

FOLK ROCK: FOLK MUSIC,PROTEST OR COMMERCIALISM

[1]Tom Paxton, "Johnny Appleseed," *Sing Out!*, 15 (January, 1966), pp. 103-104.

[2]Josh Dunson, "Folk Rock: Thunder Without Rain," *Sing Out!*, 15 (January, 1966), pp. 12-17; also, Sy and Barbara Ribakove, *Folk Rock: The Bob Dylan Story*, New York: Dell Books, pp. 59-65.

[3]Dunson, *op. cit.*, p. 13.

[4]Ribakove, *op. cit.*, p. 64.

[5]See David A. DeTurk and A. Poulin, Jr., *The American Folk Scene*, New York: Dell Books, 1967.

[6]Josh Dunson, *Freedom In the Air*, New York: International Publishers, 1965.

[7]Kaplan argues that protest songs are a form of dissent free from social sanctions. Arlene E. Kaplan, *Folksinging In a Mass Society*, M. A. Thesis, Berkeley: University of California, 1952.

[8]Irwin Silber, "An Open Letter to Bob Dylan," *Sing Out!*, 14 (November, 1964), pp. 22-23.

[9]Gabriel A. Almond, *Appeals of Communism*, Princeton: Princeton University Press, 1954, pp. 62-95.

[10]R. Serge Denisoff, "The Proletarian Renascence: The Folkness of the Ideological Folk," *JAF* 82 (January-March, 1969) pp. 51-65.

[11]"Songs of Persuasion," this volume.

[12]*Freedom In the Air, op. cit.*, pp. 31-33.

[13]David Riesman, "What the Beatles Prove About Teenagers," *U. S. News and World Report*, (February 24, 1964), p. 88.

[14]"Inside Beatlemania," *San Francisco Chronicle*, February 17, 1964, p. 9.

[15]Warren Hinckle, "The Social History of the Hippies," *Ramparts*, 5 (March, 1967), p. 19.

[16]*Ibid.*

[17]Ralph J. Gleason, "Another Dancing Generation?" *This World*, (October 16, 1966). p. 33.

[18]*Ibid.*

[19]Arlene E. Kaplan, "A Study of Folksinging in a Mass Society," *Sociologus*, 5 (Spring, 1955), pp. 14-28.

[20]David L. Boxer, "Folk-Rock Music: The Sound of the New Road," (unpublished paper) San Francisco State College, 1966, p. 3.

[21]Anthony Bernhard, "For What It's Worth: Today's Rock Scene," paper presented at American Sociological Association meetings in San Francisco, August, 1967, p. 7.

[22]"Inside Pop: The Rock Revolution," CBS News Special, (transcript) April 25, 1967.

[23]See Charles Kiel, *Urban Blues*, Chicago: University of Chicago Press, 1966.

24R. Serge Denisoff, "Definitions of the Folk Song and the Underground Top Ten," *folknik,* 1 (1965), p. 2.

25"Songs That Have a Double Meaning," *San Francisco Examiner,* September 25, 1966, p. 13.

26*Ibid.*

27*Ibid.*

PROTEST SONGS: ON TOP FORTY AND OF THE STREETS

[1]Herbert Hoover, quoted in Arthur M. Schlesinger, Jr., *The Crisis of the Old Order 1919-1933*, (Boston, 1957), p. 242.

[2]Alfred G. Aronowitz and Marshell Blonsky, "Three's Company: Peter, Paul, and Mary," *Saturday Evening Post*, (May 30, 1964), p. 32.

[3]"Roll the Union On," *Fortune*, (November, 1946), pp. 183-184.

[4]R. Serge Denisoff and Mark H. Levine, "Mannheim's Problem of Generations and Counter Culture," this volume.

[5]Tom Paxton, "Folk Rot," *Sing Out!*, XV (January, 1966), pp. 103-104.

[6]David A. Noebel, *Rhythm, Riots, and Revolution*, (Tulsa, 1966), p. 229.

[7]R. Serge Denisoff and Mark H. Levine, "The Popular Protest Song: The Case of "The Eve of Destruction,' " *Public Opinion Quarterly*, 35 (Spring, 1971), pp. 117-122.

[8]*Ibid.*,

[9]Julius Lester, "The Angry Children of Malcolm X," *Sing Out!*, XVI (November, 1966), p. 25.

[10]Robert Sherman, "Sing A Song of Freedom," *Saturday Review*, XLVI (September 28, 1963), pp. 65, 67.

[11]Ludlow Music Company.

[12]R. Serge Denisoff, "Protest Movements: Class Consciousness and the Propaganda Song," this volume.

[13]Cf., David Riesman, *Individualism Reconsidered*, (Glencoe, 1954); and Jacques Barzun, *Music In American Life*, (New York, 1958).

[14]"An Interview With Tom Paxton," *Broadside*, 67 (February, 1966), p. 8.

[15]Joseph R. Gusfield, *Symbolic Crusade: Status Politics and the American Temperance Movement*, (Urbana, 1963), pp. 19-23.

[16]In a study of Michigan adolescents a similar conclusion was reached. John Robinson and Paul Hirsch, "Teenage Response To Rock and Roll Protest Songs," paper read at the annual meetings of the American Sociological Association, San Francisco, 1969.

[17]A. Martynova, "Beatles as Cinderella: A Soviet Fairytale," *Rolling Stone*, 27 (February 15, 1969), pp. 1, 4.

GENERATIONS AND COUNTER CULTURE

*The authors wish to thank Stan Kanehara and Shelley Levine for their assistance in the preparation of this paper.

[1]Karl Mannheim, *Ideology and Utopia: An Introduction to the Sociology of Knowledge*, New York: Harcourt, Brace, and World, 1936, p. 79.

[2]Karl Mannheim, "The Sociological Problem of Generations," in Paul Kecskemeti, ed., *Essays on the Sociology of Knowledge*, London: Routledge and Kegan Paul, 1951, p. 292.

[3]Mannheim, *ibid.*, p. 293.   [4]Mannheim, *ibid.*, p. 309.

[5]T. B. Bottomore, *Critics of Society: Radical Thought in North America*, New York: Pantheon Books, 1968, p. 101.

[6]Daniel Bell, *End of Ideology: The Exhaustion of Political Ideas in the Fifties*, New York: Collier Books, 1963, pp. 393-407; and S. M. Lipset, *Political Man*, Garden City: Anchor Books, 1963, pp. 439-456; Daniel Boorstin decried the decline of the old ideological radical and points to the rise of the New Barbarians. Daniel Boorstin, *The Decline of Radicalism*, New York: Random House, 1969.

[7]Cf. Chiam Waxman, *The End of Ideology Debate*, New York: Funk and Wagnalls, Inc., 1968. Also, Herbert Aptheker, *The World of C. Wright Mills*, New York: Marzani and Munsell Publishers, 1960.

[8]C. Wright Mills, "The New Left," in Irving Horowitz, ed., *Power, Politics, and People: The Collected Essays of C. Wright Mills*, New York: Ballantine Books, 1963, p. 259.

[9]Mills, *ibid.*, p. 259.

[10]Albert Camus, *The Rebel: An Essay On Man in Revolt*, New York: Alfred Knopf, Inc., 1956, pp. 13-22.

[11]Interestingly, these same WASP students have turned their back on the so-called Horatio Algier ideal or the American Dream.

[12]Kenneth Keniston, "The Sources of Student Dissent," *Journal of Social Issues,* 23 (July, 1967), p. 120.

[13]Richard Flacks, "The Liberated Generation: An Exploration of the Roots of Student Protest," *Journal of Social Issues,* 23 (July, 1967), p. 68.

[14]David Jansen, et al, "Characteristics Associated with Campus Social Political Action Leadership," *Journal of Counseling Psychology,* 15 (Nov., 1968), pp. 552-562.

[15]Riley Dunlap, "Family Backgrounds of Radical and Conservative Political Activists at a Non-Elite University," Eugene: University of Oregon (mimeographed paper), 1969, pp. 21-22.

[16]While the campus remains the main staging ground for political protest, it is not directed by any one group or coalition of organizations. Campus anti-war protest is large in sentiment, however, this stance frequently has little to do with SDS and other political organizations.

[17]Theodore Roszak, *The Making of Counter Culture: Reflections on*

the Technocratic Society and Its Youthful Opposition, Garden City: Anchor Books, 1969, p. xi.

[18]Cf. Gary Rush and R. Serge Denisoff, *Social and Political Movements,* New York: Appleton Century-Crofts, 1971.

[19]Robert J. Alexander, "Splinter Groups in American Radical Politics," *Social Research*, 20 (October, 1953), pp. 282-310.

[20]Daryl Lembke and Philip Hager, "Thousands Parade Quietly in San Francisco to Show War Frustration," *Los Angeles Times*, November 16, 1969, p. B.

[21]Senior author's notes.

[22]"The Great Woodstock Rock Trip," *Life,* (Special Edition), 1969, p. 1, 3. Also see Patricia Kennedy, "Woodstock '69," *Jazz and Pop*, 8 (November, 1969), pp. 20-33.

[23]Griel Marcus "The Woodstock Festival," *Rolling Stone*, September 20, 1969, p. 24.

[24]Roszak, *op. cit.*, pp. 48-49. [25]*Ibid.*, p. xi.

[26]Cf. Jacques Ellul, *The Technological Society*, transl. John W. Wilkinson, New York: A. A. Knopf, 1964; and John Kenneth Galbraith, *The New Industrial State*, Boston: Houghton Mifflin, 1967.

[27]Lembke and Hager, *op. cit.* [28]Senior author's notes.

[29]Quote from Roszak, *op. cit.*, p. 291. Also see Timothy Leary, *Politics of Ecstasy*, New York: Putnam, 1968; J. I. Simmons and Barry Winograd, *It's Happening*, Santa Barbara: Marclaird Publications, 1966, pp. 155-165; Herbert Goldberg, "Contemporary Cultural Innovations of Youth: Popular Music," paper read at the annual meetings of the American Psychological Assn., August 31, 1968; and James T. Carey, "The Ideology of Autonomy in Popular Lyrics: A Content Analysis," *Psychiatry*, (Fall, 1969). pp. 150-163.

[30]For a discussion of the *declasse* roots of rock see Archie Green, "Hillbilly Music: Source and Symbol," *Journal of American Folklore*, 78 (July-September, 1965), pp. 204-228.

[31]Charles Gillett, "Just Let Me Hear Some of That Rock and Roll Music," *Urban Review*, 1 (December, 1966), pp. 11-14; also Mike Gershman, "The Blues Once Black, Now A Shade Whiter," *Los Angeles Times Calendar*, (Jan. 19, 1969), pp. 1, 37; and Charles Keil, *Urban Blues*, Chicago: University of Chicago Press, 1966, pp. 44-45.

[32]Robert Hilburn, "Rock Enters 70's as the Music Champ," *Los Angeles Times Calendar*, (January 4, 1970), p. 21.

[33]Kurt von Meier, "The Background and Beginnings of Rock and Roll," University of California, Los Angeles (Unpublished paper), n.d.; Charles Gillett, "Just Let Me Hear Some of That Rock and Roll Music," *Urban Review*, 1 (December, 1966), pp. 11-14; and Carl Belz, *The Story of Rock*, New York: Oxford University Press, 1969.

[34]Edgar Friedenberg, *Coming of Age in America*, New York: Vintage Books, 1963. A number of musicians originally saw rock and roll as a

transitional phenomenon which would lead listeners to a more *classe* type of music. For this argument see Nat Hentoff, "Musicians Argue Values of Rock and Roll," *Downbeat,* 23 (May 30, 1956), p. 12.

35Edith Schonberg, "You Can't Fool Public, Says Haley," *Downbeat,* 23 (May 30, 1956), p. 10.

36David Riesman, "What the Beatles Prove About Teenagers," *US News and World Report*, (February 24, 1964), p. 88.

37Cf. R. Serge Denisoff and Mark H. Levine, "The One-Dimensional Approach to Popular Music: A Research Note," *Journal of Popular Culture* IV: 4.

38Donald Horton, "The Dialogue of Courtship in Popular Songs," *American Journal of Sociology,* 62 (May, 1962), pp. 569-578.

39A handful of other songs, more in the R & B tradition, raised the same issues of parental dominance. However, unlike "Summertime Blues," the Silhouettes record "Get A Job," was a song decrying the lack for work for young Black men.

40For a discussion of the impact of "protest songs" upon its audience see John P. Robinson and Paul Hirsch "It's the Sound," *Psychology Today,* 3 (October, 1969), pp. 42-45; and R. Serge Denisoff and Mark Levine "The Popular Protest Song: The Case of the 'Eve of Destruction' " *Public Opinion Quarterly,* 35 (Spring, 1971), pp. 117-122.

41Cf. Josh Dunson, *Freedom in the Air*, New York: International Publishers, 1965; Jerome L. Rodnitzky, "The Evolution of the American Protest Song," *Journal of Popular Culture,* 3 (Summer, 1969), pp. 35-45.

42Cf. Belz, *op. cit.*, pp. 172-177. Also Josh Dunson, "Folk Rock: Thunder Without Rain," *Sing Out!,* 15 (January, 1966), pp. 12-17.

43See Jerry Hopkins, *The Rock Story,* New York: Signet Books, 1970, pp. 197-198.

44A number of so-called protest songs have sporadically made their way on to the Top Forty, particularly the Animals "We Gotta Get Out of This Place" and "Sky Pilot," Jody Miller's "Home of the Brave," Sonny Bono's "Laugh At Me," "Mr. Businessman" by Ray Stevens, "2 plus 1" by Bob Seger, "Skip A. Rope" by Hensen Cargill, "Universal Soldier" by Glen Campbell. Only the latter piece was precominantly in the rock genre. Barry Sadler's pro-administration "Ballad of the Green Berets" was put to an old Spanish Civil War March. Ironically, most "pro-Establishment" songs have been recorded either in Country and Western genre or in the middle media style of Frankie Laine and Pat Boone, neither having much to do with the Top Forty.

45Leary, *op. cit.*, p. 355.

46Burton H. Wolfe, *The Hippies*, New York: Signet Books, 1968, p. 42.

47Richard Robinson, *First Winter*, Buddah Records BSD 7515 linar notes. Also see Jerome L. Rodnitzky, "The New Revivalism: American Protest Songs, 1945-68," paper read at the annual meetings of the American Studies Assn., Toledo, Ohio, October 31, 1969.

[48]Carey, *op. cit.*, p. 162.

[49]Rodnitzky, "New Revivalism," *op. cit.*

[50]Quoted in William Glass, "The History of Rock and Protest," California State College, Los Angeles (unpublished paper), 1969, p. 1.

[51]John Cohen, "Interview with Roger McGuinn of the Byrds," *Sing Out!*, 18 (December, 1968 / January, 1969), p. 11.

[52]Belz, *op. cit.*, p. 44.

[53]There is nothing particularly new in this proposition, as Plato once suggested, "The introduction of novel fashions in music is a thing to beware of as endangering the whole fabric of society. . . ." Plato, *The Republic*, (trans. by Francis MacDonal Cornford) New York: Oxford University Press, 1945, p. 115.

[54]Cf. R. Serge Denisoff, "The Ideology of the Extreme Right and Folk Music," California State College, Los Angeles (mimeographed) 1969.

[55]R. Serge Denisoff, "The Religious Roots of the Song of Persuasion," this volume.

[56]David A. Noebel, *Communism, Hypnotism, and the Beatles,* Tulsa: Christian Crusade Publications, 1965, p. 15.

[57]Gordon McClendon quoted in John P. Robinson and Paul Hirsch, "Teenage Response to Rock and Roll Protest Songs," paper read at American Sociological Association meetings at San Francisco, September, 1969, p. 1.

[58]Ben Fong-Torres, "Feds' Dope Circus: 'How Much LSD Do You Take To Be Addicted?' " *Rolling Stone,* November 29, 1969, p. 20.

[59]Interview with senior author, Vancouver, July 27, 1968.

[60]Cf. G. B. Rush, F. B. Collinge, and R. W. Wyllie, "North Vancouver Adolescent Study," Burnaby: Simon Fraser University, 1969.

[1]Karen Horney, *The Neurotic Personality of Our Time*, New York: W. W. Norton and Co., 1937; Erich Fromm, *The Sane Society*, New York: Holt, Rinehart, and Winston, 1955; and Edgar Z. Friedenberg, *Coming of Age in America: Growth and Acquiescence*, New York: Random House, 1963.

[2]Cf. James T. Carey, "Changing Courtship Patterns in Popular Songs," *American Journal of Sociology*, 74 (May, 1969), pp. 720-731; John Johnstone and Elihu Katz, "Youth and Popular Music: A Study in the Sociology of Taste," *American Journal of Sociology*, 62 (May, 1957), pp. 563-568; Herbert Goldberg, "Feeling Rock Music: The Message in the Medium," *Voices*, 5 (Summer-Fall, 1969), pp. 42-48; and Robert A. Rosenstone, " 'The Times They Are A-Changin' The Music of Protest," *Annals*, 381 (March, 1969), pp. 131-144.

[3]See R. Serge Denisoff, " 'Teen Angel' Resistance, Rebellion, and Death on the Top Forty," paper presented at the Popular Culture Association meetings at East Lansing, Michigan, April 1971.

[4]"Endless Sleep" copyrighted by Johnstone-Montei Inc. Elizabeth Music BMI all rights reserved.

[5]"Tell Laura I Love Her," copyright by Edward B. Marks Music Corp. BMI all rights reserved.

[6]"Ebony Eyes" copyright Acuff-Rose Music Publishing Co. all rights reserved.

[7]"Twilla Lee" Travis Music Inc. BMI all rights reserved.

[8]"Last Kiss" Macon Music Co. BMI all rights reserved.

[9]The advent of the contra-culture expanded the alternatives for the teenager who was offered yet another solution for situational inconsistency, that of dropping out.

[10]"Patches" copyright Aldon Music Inc. BMI all rights reserved.

[11]"Give Us Your Blessings" Trio Music Inc. BMI all rights reserved.

[12]One note of caution here is necessary since record companies release a significant portion of their yearly output during the fall months. As a result, statistically this may influence the availability of songs.

[13]Cf. Denisoff, "Teen Angel" *op. cit.*

[1]From the song "Okie From Muskogee" by Merle Haggard & Roy E. Burris. Copyright © 1969 by Blue Book Music. Rights reserved; used by permission.

[2]From the song "The Fightin' Side of Me" by Merle Haggard. Copyright © 1970 by Blue Book Music. Rights reserved; used by permission.

[3]Paul Hemphill, *The Nashville Sound: Bright Lights and Country Music*, New York: Simon and Schuster, 1970, p. 90; also see John D. McCarthy, Richard A. Peterson, and William L. Yancey, "Singing Along with the Silent Majority" in R. Serge Denisoff and Richard A. Peterson, eds., *The Sounds of Social Change*, Chicago: Rand-McNally (forthcoming).

[4]Copyright BMI all rights reserved.

[5]Copyright, The House of Cash, all rights reserved.

[6]Copyright, ASA Music Inc.: ASCAP, all rights reserved.

[7]Griel Marcus, "A Singer and a Rock and Roll Band," in Griel Marcus, ed., *Rock and Roll Will Stand*, Boston, Beacon Press, 1969, pp. 90-104; and Tom Smucker, "The Politics of Rock: Movement vs. Groovement," in Jonathan Eisen, *The Age of Rock 2*, New York: Vintage Books, 1970, pp. 83-91.

[8]Copyright, Iceberg Music, BMI all rights reserved.

[9]Copyright, Nina Music Inc., all rights reserved.

[10]Copyright, Guerilla Music Inc., BMI all rights reserved.

[11]Copyrighted Peer International BMI all rights reserved.

[12]Copyright, Jondora Music, BMI all rights reserved.

[13]Copyright, Jondora Music, BMI all rights reserved.

[14]Copyright, Broken-Arrow-Cotillion all rights reserved.

[15]James Brown quoted in Arnold Shaw, *The World of Soul: Black America's Contribution to Pop Music Scene*, New York: Cowles Book Company, 1970, p. 254.

[16]Phyl Garland, *The Sound of Soul*, Chicago: Henry Regnery Company, 1969, pp. 193-194.

[17]Cf. Charlie Gillett, *The Sound of the City: The Rise of Rock and Roll*, New York: Outerbridge and Dienstfrey, 1970, pp. 234-5, 252, 254.

[18]Copyright, HIlkert Music Inc. all rights reserved.

[19]Copyright © 1969 by Pamoc Music, Inc., 8255 Beverly Blvd., Los Angeles, California 90048. Rights reserved; used by permission.

[20]Gillett, *op. cit.*, p. 254.

[21]Copyright, Jobete Music Inc. all rights reserved. Also see Ben Fong-Torres "There's a Place for the Tempts" *Rolling Stone* September 3, 1970, p. 22.

[22]Fong-Torres, *ibid.*, p. 22. For a further discussion see Sharan Chiasson, "Protest in Black Popular Music," unpublished paper, Bowling Green State University, 1970.

[23]Copyright, Jobete Music Inc. all rights reserved.

[24]Copyright, St. George Music Ltd. all rights reserved.

216

A BIBLIOGRAPHICAL NOTE

Since the formal investigation of protest songs in the United States has been at best a capricious enterprise there are few if any definitive works in this area. Consequently those wishing to further pursue this subject are generally left to their own resources. There are, however, several useful points of departure such as *Sing Out!* and *Broadside (NYC)* magazines and the *Journal of Popular Culture*. Also, Archie Green has compiled several excellent discographies of American labor songs published in *Labor History* (Winter, 1961) and the *New York Folklore Quarterly* (Autumn, 1961). Richard A. Reuss has produced a highly impressive bibliography on the subject of Woody Guthrie which is available from the Guthrie Children's Trust Fund, 200 W. 57th St., New York, New York 10019. The author has put together a list of songs and records addressed to the issues of war and peace with a stress on Left-wing material which is available from The Center For the Study of Armament and Disarmament at the California State College at Los Angeles, California 90032. Those interested in rock music, of course, are directed to the pages of *Rolling Stone, Creem* and *Rock*.

"A Change is Gonna Come," 187
"A Day in the Life," 132
"A Dollar Ain't a Dollar Anymore," 10
Abern, Martin, 80
"Abraham, Martin, and John," 183
"Acid Tests," 126
Acuff, Roy, 178
Adolescent roles, 171-176
 as expressed in music, 171-172
Andrews, Ernie, 187
AFL-CIO, 25
Agnew, Spiro, IX, 19
"Ain't Gonna Let Nobody Turn Me Round," 147
"Ain't I Right," 178
"All I Want," 69
"All Together," 25
Almanac Singers, 3, 85
 Detroit branch, 3, 85
 "October 16th," 6
 John Doe, 11
 press review, 12
 and Left, 43
 Talking Union, 69-71
 philosophy of, 101, 114
Almond, Gabriel, 94, 120
"Almost Cut My Hair," 183
"Almost Grown," 32
America First Committee, 7
"American Eagle Tragedy," 39, 181-182
"American Woman," 185
"Amphetamine Annie," 190
"An Open Letter to My Teenage Son," 180
"Annie Had a Baby," 28
Antell, Paul, 176, 177
anti-war marches, 155
"Art As a Weapon," 81-82
Avalon Ballroom, 163
Baez, Joan, 110
Balin, Marty, 128
"Ball of Confusion," 188

"Ballad of a Party Folk-Singer," 93
"Ballad of Harry Bridges," 69
"Ballad of October 16th," 6, 70
"Ballad of the Green Berets," 38
"Bankers and Bosses," 82
Barzun, Jacques, 161
"Bass Strings," 131
"Battle Hymn of the Republic," 97
Beal, Fred, 41
Beatles, 120
 popularity of, 124-125
 rise of, 162
Belafonte, Harry, 185
Bell, Daniel, 153
Belz, Carl, 166
"The Benson Campaign Song," 86
Bernard, Anthony, 128
Berry, Chuck, 31-32, 123, 160
 Songs, 160-161
Bibb, Leon, 185
"Billy Boy," 9
Black Panther Party, 155
Blackboard Jungle, 29
blacklist, 46
"Blowin In the Wind," 34
"Blue Monday," 185
Blumenstock, Dorthy, 102
Boone, Pat, 29, 38, 159
Bosses Songbook, 92, 112
Botkin, B. A., 15
Bottomore, T. B. 152
Boxer, David, 128
"brainwashing," IX
Brand, Oscar, 14
 on Left-Wing, 43
 on Spanish Civil War, 103
Broadside (NYC), 74
Brookins, A. B., 55
Brooks, Gene, 84
Brookwood Labor College, 50
Browder, Earl, 82
Brown, James, 186
Browne, Elaine, 190
Buffalo Springfield, 130, 182

A Note About the Author

R. Serge Denisoff is associate professor of sociology at Bowling Green State University. He received his B. A. and M. A. at San Francisco State College and his Ph.D. in 1969 from Simon Fraser University, Burnaby, British Columbia. He has contributed a number of articles to sociology, American Studies, and folklore journals. He has published three other books: *Social and Political Movements*, with Gary B. Rush (1971), *Great Day Coming: Folk Music and the American Left* (1971) and *The Controversies and Polemics of Sociology*, a reader (1972). He is also a contributor to *Creem, Rolling Stone,* and other music journals.